SHAKESPEARE'S DEFENSE OF POETRY

A Midsummer Night's Dream and The Tempest

Diana Akers Rhoads

UNIVERSITY
PRESS OF
AMERICA

LANHAM • NEW

Copyright © 1985 by

University Press of America,® Inc.

4720 Boston Way
Lanham, MD 20706

3 Henrietta Street
London WC2E 8LU England

Library of Congress Cataloging in Publication Data

Rhoads, Diana Akers, 1944-
    Shakespeare's defense of poetry.

    Thesis (Ph.D.)—University of Virginia, 1979.
    Bibliography: p.
    Includes index.
    1. Shakespeare, William, 1564-1616—Political and
social views.   2. Shakespeare, William, 1564-1616—
Aesthetics.   3. Shakespeare, William, 1564-1616.
Midsummer night's dream.   4. Shakespeare, William,
1564-1616.   Tempest.   5. Politics and literature.
I. Title.
PR3017.R48   1985   822.3'3   85-91270
ISBN 0-8191-4979-9 (alk. paper)
ISBN 0-8191-4980-2 (pbk. : alk. paper)

All University Press of America books are produced on acid-free
paper which exceeds the minimum standards set by the National
Historical Publications and Records Commission.

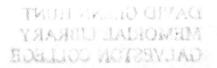

To Steven who is by no means
interchangeable with
Demetrius, Lysander or
anyone else

ACKNOWLEDGMENTS

For an accomplishment so small my debts are great. This work began as a dissertation completed at the University of Virginia in 1979 under the direction of Arthur Kirsch and Paul Cantor. Throughout my graduate career my first reader Arthur Kirsch mixed sound and intelligent guidance with human kindness. My second Paul Cantor made me rethink some of my ideas concerning The Tempest. Diane Rennell examined the original dissertation with the care which only a friend would take, and she made a number of useful changes. Cary Lord read the entire manuscript and helped me with bibliographic work on the Italian Rennaisance. His questions led to some small but significant changes. An annonymous University Press of America reader made careful, detailed and astute suggestions for improvement of the manuscript. My husband Steven read the manuscript over many years at every stage of the development, and he deserves credit for his perseverance in loving encouragement and support. Virginia Bossong made this work possible by providing the kind of child care which made me feel that I was doing my children a service to take them to her. She created a kind and loving family which I felt could serve as a model for my children. Finally, I owe thanks to Roxanne White for writing the index and proofreading, to Nicholas and John Rhoads for helping with xeroxing, and to Susan Ferrell and Kathleen Collier for typing the manuscript.

TABLE OF CONTENTS

CHAPTER I

THE POET'S RELATION TO CIVIL SOCIETY

Neglect of the poet's relation to politics and to civil society more generally has prevented critics from treating fully the consideration of poetry in Shakespeare's comedies. Although criticism has recently recognized serious themes in comedies formerly taken as frivolities, it has largely ignored the political element in these plays. Critics, for example, have corrected the attitude that _A Midsummer Night's Dream_ is simply an interlude, a dance, a pattern rather than a serious comment on life. R. W. Dent argues that _A Midsummer Night's Dream_ offers a "defense of poetry," and David P. Young presents the play as Shakespeare's "ars poetica."[1] Neither, however, treats the relation of the poet to the politician and the problems that one poses for the other.

For some time critics have seen _The Tempest_ as a serious comment on the nature of art. They generally accept Prospero as Shakespeare or as a poet of some sort. They have, however, neglected the poet's position as founder of an ideal commonwealth. Critics such as Northrop Frye have recognized allusions to Virgil's _Aeneid_, but have not related them to Prospero's position as founder.[2] Although references have been made to Prospero as an inept philosopher king,[3] the implications of this identification have been examined only superficially. Critics have found Platonic or Neoplatonic elements in the play. They often point out that Shakespeare's identification of love of beauty with love of the good derives ultimately from Plato, and Theodore Spencer and James E. Phillips[4] have written of Renaissance, and ultimately Platonic, divisions of the soul in _The Tempest_. Jackson Cope has referred briefly to the discussion in _The Republic_ of the philosopher king's unwillingness to rule.[5] Still, no one has ever explored the play as a Renaissance examination of the Platonic criticism of poetry as a danger to the city.[6]

I would argue that Shakespeare was deeply concerned with poetry's role in civil society. _A Midsummer Night's Dream_ and _The Tempest_ reveal the complexity of his understanding of this problem. They examine the poet's relation to politics, to moral philosophy, and to political philosophy. Each play considers such issues as the threat of the poet[7] to civil society, the poet's ability to balance the real and the ideal, and the poet's ability to support virtue.

These two plays are not alone in the exploration of the role of the poet in civil society. There is hardly a play of Shakespeare's which does not contain a reference to the poet or to poetry in some form, and if Shakespeare took the problem seriously, he would have to reconcile his writing of his plays with his views on the poet's role. My concluding chapter will argue that Shakespeare was concerned with the poet's proper role from the outset of his dramatic career in Love's Labor's Lost. In a sense, then, the selection of A Midsummer Night's Dream and The Tempest for discussion is arbitrary. Still, along with their traditionally recognized common inclusion of fairies, of magic, and of a dreamlike atmosphere, these two plays offer a fuller treatment of the question than any of Shakespeare's other plays. A Midsummer Night's Dream is a logical beginning for the examination of Shakespeare's consideration of the question, since this play outlines the alternative claims of poetry and of civil society. Theseus the politician represents the claims of civil society along with its judgment of poetry, while the play as a whole submits a poetic solution to a political problem along with a defense of poetry. The Tempest answers the problem of A Midsummer Night's Dream by making the poet a model politician. By combining the poet with the politician and the philosopher, The Tempest presents the fullest possible defense of poetry and in this way explores the absolute limits of what poetry can accomplish in civil society. This play incorporates political wisdom in its poetry and uses poetry to produce the best possible political situation.

Modern neglect of the relation of the poet to civil society is remarkable in view of Renaissance concern with the issue. The nature and function of poetry was a major subject of discussion in the Elizabethan age and especially during Shakespeare's life. Early in the century the subject supplied matter for learned discussion. Books like Juan Luis Vives' instructions for educating Princess Mary (1531) contain discussions of the advisability of including poets in the curriculum.[8] Sir Thomas

Elyot's influential <u>The</u> <u>Boke</u> <u>Named</u> <u>the</u> <u>Governour</u>, first published in 1531 and printed eight times by 1580, defends the poets as appropriate educators for the ruling class.[9] And poetry was a matter of general discussion at the schools. Roger Ascham in <u>The</u> <u>Scholemaster</u> (1570) mentions "many pleasant talks" which he, Watson, and Cheke had at Cambridge "comparing the precepts of <u>Aristotle</u> and <u>Horace</u> <u>de</u> <u>Arte</u> <u>Poetica</u> with examples of <u>Euripedes</u>, <u>Sophocles</u>, and <u>Seneca</u>."[10] And orations such as John Rainolds' <u>Oratio</u> <u>in</u> <u>laudem</u> <u>artis</u> <u>poeticae</u> or Richard Wills' <u>Disputio</u> <u>de</u> <u>re</u> <u>poetica</u>[11] were delivered on the subject.

The discussion of the position of poetry reached its height in the last three decades of the sixteenth century partly because of the controversy over the theatre. According to Dover Wilson, the first book in English defending the secular drama was a translation by William Bavand of a Latin treatise from Italy, <u>A</u> <u>Woorke</u> <u>of</u> <u>Joannes</u> <u>Ferrarius</u> <u>Montanus</u> <u>touchynge</u> <u>the</u> <u>good</u> <u>orderynge</u> <u>of</u> <u>a</u> <u>commonweale</u> (1559).[12] Indications of opposition appear earlier in the century, but there is general agreement that the true battle over the stage originates in written form with John Northbrooke's treatise of 1577 attacking the stage along with other abuses of the Sabbath.[13] Gosson, Stubbes, Whetstone, Denham, and Rankins joined Northbrooke in the attack, with Lodge, Sidney, and Nash speaking for the defense.[14] The interest in the function of poetry, however, was not due simply to partisanship in a local controversy over the stage. The concern about poetry's position in society was general and widespread. Sidney's <u>Apology</u>, for instance, was more than a reply to Stephen Gosson. As Shepherd points out, the <u>Apology</u> does not reply to what Gosson attacks, the social inconveniences and dangers of the new popular theatre.[15] If the <u>Apology</u> was evoked by Gosson, it nonetheless became a general consideration of the grounds for poetry's defense. That the controversy over the theatre was to some extent removed from the interest in poetry in general is evidenced by the position of a man like William Vaughan who could attack the theatre while defending poetry.[16] Furthermore, there was a series of sympathetic discussions of literature--those of Webbe, Puttenham, and Harington,[17] for example--which did not address the controversy over the theatre. And the period's general concern with the appropriate development of

English literature was based on the assumption that literature was valuable to society.

The political was a basic concern of the Renaissance discussion of poetry. Bernard Weinberg argues that the defense of poetry in the Cinquecento was largely a reply to Plato, who had banished the poets from his ideal commonwealth.[18] In England both the defenders and adversaries of poetry took seriously Plato's expulsion of the poets. Both recognized the strength of a critique of poetry which argued that it led to vice.[19] Sidney eloquently presented the position of the defenders when he admitted that he would

> not deny but that man's wit may make Poesy, which should be _eikastike_, which some learned have defined, "figuring forth good things," to be _phantastike_, which doth contrariwise infect the fancy with unworthy objects; as the painter, that should give to the eye either some excellent perspective, or some fine picture, fit for building or fortification, or containing in it some notable example, as Abraham sacrificing his son Isaac, Judith killing Holofernes, David fighting with Goliath, may leave those, and please an ill-pleased eye with wanton shows of better hidden matters. But what, shall the abuse of a thing make the right use odious? Nay truly, though I yield that Poesy may not only be abused, but that being abused, by reason of his sweet charming force, it can do more hurt than any other army of words, yet shall it be so far from concluding that the abuse should give reproach to the abused, that contrariwise it is a good reason, that whatsoever, being abused, doth most harm, being rightly used (and upon the right use each thing conceiveth his title), doth most good.[20]

4

The defenders generally argued that Plato was the enemy only of the abuse of poetry, namely, poetry which supported wrong opinions of the gods.[21] The true poetry, on the other hand, would lead man to virtue.[22] Even those who attacked poetry made concessions for its appropriate use while emphasizing the scurrility of most poetry.[23]

Poetry was generally defended by transferring to it politics' and political philosophy's classical claims that they were the master disciplines. For Aristotle politics is the architechtonic activity because its end is the highest of all goods achievable by action--the good life or that life directed to virtue. Man is by nature a political animal because he can live the good life only within the city. When Sidney defends poetry, he makes it the architechtonic activity. As for Aristotle, the end of politics is the perfection of man's nature or the production of virtuous men. For Sidney there is a

> highest end of the mistress-knowledge, by the Greeks called <u>architectonike</u>, which stands (as I think) in the knowledge of a man's self, in the ethic and politic consideration, with the end of well-doing and not of well knowing only. . . . So that, the ending end of all earthly learning being virtuous action, those skills, that most serve to bring forth that, have a most just title to be princes over the rest.[24]

This end is best fulfilled by a science which can both present universal ideas of virtues and vices and make those ideas understandable and appealing. History is deficient in the former; and philosophy, in the latter. Poetry, however, "doth not only show the way, but giveth so sweet a prospect into the way, as will entice any man to enter into it." As such it deserves to be called "the monarch" of "all the sciences."[25] Other defenders did not make their arguments as thoroughly as Sidney, but the poet was constantly praised as the first philosopher, the first legislator, and the first civilizing force.[26] That poetry had received the approbation of the princes of the greatest nations was a further well-worn argument of poetry's supporters.[27]

These discussions of poetry were accessible to Shakespeare. As Virgil K. Whitaker argues, Shakespeare must have been on intimate terms with a group of young nobles and their literary friends. That Shakespeare's poems circulated in manuscript suggests that he had access to the works and ideas circulated in the tight literary circles of London.[28] Furthermore, critics like Sidney, Webbe, and Puttenham must have debated the problems they discussed at the Mermaid and at other meeting places of poets.

Given the obvious Renaissance focus on the relation of the poet to civil society, modern neglect of Shakespeare's interest in the issue is difficult to explain. In general, however, that neglect can be attributed to changed attitudes towards both art and civil society. From the romantics through the 1960's the tendency of modern criticism to view literature as sui generis predisposed it against consideration of such questions. Some recent structuralist and post-structuralist theory does not distinguish literature from other forms of writing. But it rests on deterministic assumptions--linguistic, ethno-logical, or historical--which lead it away from the political or prevent it from considering what Shakespeare thought in his own terms. If modern attitudes towards art preclude serious consideration of the poet's role in political society, they are supplemented by a new attitude towards the political and the moral. Finding both these less central to individual happiness than the Renaissance did, moderns tend to discount their significance for previous ages.

In contradistinction to the earlier Renaissance view of art, most modern criticism has been dominated by the view that literature constitutes a class of its own. Isolation of poetry from matters outside the human mind was the first step towards this view. Change in the natural sciences was a principal factor in the general shift of attitude toward art. The rejection of final causes led to the view that truth and meaning originated in man rather than in nature. The existence of final causes was called into doubt by developments in the sciences which study the heavens. The Copernican view of the earth as a celestial body obliterated the old Ptolemaic distinction between corruptible earth and the incorruptible heavens where perfection was held to reside. Galileo's observation of changes in celestial bodies cast further doubts on the heavens' perfection. For the scholastics the movement of celestial bodies had implied the presence of a continually impelling force as its ultimate cause, Aristotle's Unmoved Mover, but Galileo's explanation of the heavens' motions in terms of inertia and Newton's explanation of why celestial bodies move in circles left no need for the continued action of an Unmoved Mover.[29]

These developments in astronomy were reinforced by Baconian experimentalism and by British empirical psychology. Both argued against finding general ideas the causes of things. Bacon placed universals within man rather than in nature as objective standards. He argued that man should study particulars, not the abstractions derived from the principles of a few received authors:

> For the wit and mind of man, if it work upon matter, which is the contemplation of the creatures of God, worketh according to the stuff and is limited thereby; but if it work upon itself, as the spider worketh his web, then it is endless, and brings forth indeed cobwebs of learning, admirable for the fineness of thread and work, but of no substance or profit.[30]

British empirical psychology also eliminated universals as objects of knowledge. Hobbes and Locke held that knowledge came wholly from sensation or from reflection upon sensation. Insofar as man used his reason, he reasoned "about particulars." The only insight into the objectively general came from "generalization" from particulars with its reliance on the individual, subjective mind.[31]

The rejection of final causes and the discrediting of universals left no ordering force in the universe outside of man. It also removed fortune as a limiting force for man. The possibility arose that man could conquer nature. He could make of it what he wished. Poetry's reference to any objective order outside the mind of the poet was destroyed. Poetry was no longer understood as reproduction or as inspired imitation but as creativity.

7

The Renaissance had been able to find the artist's relation to civil society important because it had thought of art as imitation of nature. Sidney had given two definitions of poetry, both making it imitation of some sort. The definition of poetry as a "speaking picture" came from Horace who usually thought of imitation as copying what was already created, but Sidney also thought of art as an imitation of man's essential characteristics, a "feigning notable images of virtues, vices, or what else, with that delightful teaching, which must be the right describing note to know a poet by." For Aristotle all natural beings are directed towards an end or a perfection for which they long. Things are most accurately represented in the full actualization of their potentiality. Thus the truest representation of man depicts him in terms of his end: "We in our way should follow the example of good portrait painters, who reproduce the distinctive features of a man, and at the same time, without losing the likeness, make him handsomer than he is."[32] Sidney makes the same comparison. The right poets are like those painters who "bestow that in colours upon you which is fittest for the eye to see: as the constant lamenting look of Lucretia, when she punished in herself another's fault; wherein he painteth not Lucretia whom he never saw, but painteth the outward beauty of such a virtue."[33] For Sidney, then, the nature which art imitates is man's nature or the end for which man longs. This end is virtue. Once the existence of universals was discredited, this particular view of art as imitation of objective virtues was also destroyed.

The idea that art is autonomous is usually dated from Kant's _Critique of Judgment_ (1790). Although this view is reinforced by and derived from a complex of other ideas, it is first stated in its radical form by Kant. Kant's argument shows how distant this view is from the Renaissance opinions that art should be useful and moral.[34] Kant specifically differentiates art from the morally good, what is good "in itself," and from the useful, what is good "for something." He argues that a judgment that something is beautiful is disinterested. Interest for Kant derives from pleasure in the idea of the existence of an object. But when we ask if something is beautiful, we are not interested in the existence of the thing. One "wants to know how we judge it in mere contemplation." Questions about the utility or morality of the object are irrelevant. If someone asks if a palace is beautiful, it is beside the point to say either that one does not care for the sort of thing that is made only to be gaped at (for an object of no utility) or to inveigh against the vanity of the great who waste the sweat of the people on such superfluous things (on matters of no intrinsic or moral worth). When we find a particular act or thing useful or moral, we relate it to some idea of what something should be used for or of what is moral. We have some idea of what the act or thing is supposed to be. But to find an object beautiful we do not need an idea of what is beautiful. "Flowers, abstract designs, line aimlessly intertwined (so-called foliage) serve no end, depend on no determinate concept, and yet please."[35]

The assumption that art is sui generis is behind the most prevalent kinds of modern criticism of Shakespeare's comedies. At the turn of the century biographical criticism dominated. Once art was considered an imaginative construct rather than an imitation of nature, interest turned from art's reference to the external world to the creating mind of the poet. Interest became mainly psychological rather than political and social. Shakespeare's plays were studied for clues to the artist's personality. Typical of the criticism were Morton Luce's comment that style was "a revelation of soul" and Lytton Strachey's assumption of "the generally accepted view that the character of the one [the artist] can be inferred from that of the other [art]."[36] What interested the late Victorians was the progress of Shakespeare's mind or mood from one play to the next. For Furnivall, for example, A Midsummer Night's Dream belonged to Shakespeare's first period when he thought of men and women as "toys for fairies' whims to play with," while The Tempest belonged to a final period of reunion, reconciliation and forgiveness.[37] Dowden treated A Midsummer Night's Dream as the product of Shakespeare's "adolescence" and discussed it in a chapter on the "Growth of Shakespeare's Mind and Art." Prospero was identified with Shakespeare at the end of his service as an artist because of his "harmonious and fully developed will."[38]

In the first half of the twentieth century the most common way to study Shakespeare's comedies was through a study of his characters.[39] It is often

9

noted that the interest in character derived from A.
C. Bradley and ultimately from Coleridge. For
Coleridge the study of character was another way of
studying the mind of the poet:

> Shakespeare's mode of conceiving
> characters out of his own
> intellectual and moral faculties, by
> conceiving any one intellectual or
> moral faculty in morbid excess and
> then placing himself, thus mutilated
> and diseased, under given
> circumstances. This we shall have
> repeated occasion to re-state and
> enforce.[40]

Once again the interest was psychological rather than
political and social. Emphasis on analysis of
character meant that little attention was given to
plays which did not lend themselves to such
analysis. A _Midsummer Night's Dream_ was either
neglected or viewed as a frivolous play.[41] It was
not until Paul Olson's respected article relating the
play to Renaissance views of love that critics
considered attending to the play's ideas,[42] yet
since then the opinion persists that the play is
"best seen as a lyric divertissement, or a suite of
dances."[43]

The largest and most influential type of
twentieth century criticism of the romances sees the
plays as myth, ritual, symbol, or allegory.[44] This
sort of criticism also derives from the view that art
is a creation of the imagination. Literary theorists
used modern developments in comparative religion and
psychology to describe a kind of truth which could
issue from the poet's imagination. These
developments presented a means of attaching an
objectivity and permanence to the working of the
individual poet's imagination. Carl Jung, for
example, postulated a "collective unconscious" to
explain the common patterns found in mythologies.
The "collective unconscious" was the inheritance in
the brain consisting of "countless typical
experiences of our ancestors." Archetypes were the
unconscious memories of the experiences of the race,
and myths were expressions of archetypes.

Criticism which views literature as symbol, myth,
ritual, or archetype is predisposed against

consideration of the problems of civil society. According to this view, modern man insofar as he is an artist reflects primitive or presocietal forces. What the artist embodies in his work is not considered to derive from an understanding of man as a political animal. Furthermore, because the emphasis of this approach is on what works of art have in common with one another, differences of opinion among different periods about the relevance of the political are likely to be overlooked.

The general interpretation of <u>The</u> <u>Tempest</u> current for the last fifty years or so originated with G. Wilson Knight. Knight's theory of criticism depends on the romantic notion that art is unique and on more modern explanations of the truth of the imagination. Knight sees art as an imaginative construct rather than as a mirroring of nature. In setting down the "Principles of Shakespeare Interpretation," he maintains that a proper interpretation will attempt to uncover something in the poet's mind or soul: "a true philosophic and imaginative interpretation will aim at cutting below the surface to reveal that burning core of mental and spiritual reality from which each play derives its nature and meaning."[45] Knight gives the artist's imaginative construct a validity by relating it to religion. In "Myth and Miracle" he finds that art is an "extroverted expression of the creative imagination which, when introverted, becomes religion." Shakespeare's last plays become "myths of immortality." These myths are in a sense at odds with nature. In the last plays the poet's "intuition of immortality and conquest" occurs "within apparent death and failure."[46] And yet all of the plays express a sort of irrational truth: Shakespeare's optimism is "no doubt, irrational: but it is potent." It is "in the finest sense of the words, philosophic and mystic." The poet expresses the "darkest and deepest truth of the mind or soul."[47]

Critics have viewed Knight's work as Christian in nature, but Knight sees Christianity as another mythology. For Knight "tragedy and our religion are inter-significant," and the "Christian cross is only the symbol of the greatest of the tragedies."[48] By this Knight means that tragedy's ability to acknowledge the evil in humanity parallels Christ's ability to accept evil and forgive it: "Jesus' God is a God of the living, not of the dead. The old order of revenge, an 'eye for an eye, a tooth for a tooth,' must give way to the new order of acceptance: 'resist not evil.'"[49]

Although Knight refers to elements the plays have in common with religion, he maintains that art has a unique status which requires that it be understood in terms of aesthetics rather than ethics. In "On Imaginative Interpretation" he argues that "in the theatre we are surely concerned rather with imaginative effects than ethical problems." Although "often the imaginative will roughly correspond to the ethical 'good,'" we must sometimes "be prepared to modify our ethical response till it is in tune with our imaginative vision."[50]

As Edwards points out, the symbolic or mythic approach has become so generally accepted that it has influenced the work of others whose basic approach is not symbolic. E. M. W. Tillyard, for example, tries to define a general pattern of tragedy in Shakespeare's Last Plays (1938): prosperity, destruction, regeneration. He argues that the tragedies only hint at regeneration, but that the romances complete the pattern. And he finds that tragedy is symbolic of the destruction and re-creation found in all growth, material and spiritual.[51]

Some recent genre critics of The Tempest distinguish themselves from G. W. Knight in the significance which they attach to romance, for Knight argues that one must ignore the romance "trappings" and focus on the universal myths available in the romance form.[52] And yet much of modern genre criticism differs little from Knight's myth criticism. Renewed interest in genre probably began with Northrop Frye[53] whose archetypes are little more than myths recurring universally as different genres. Myth, or what Knight sees as spirit, Frye sees as form. More recent critics such as Thomas McFarland also tend to describe the romance in terms reminiscent of myth criticism. Thus, the romance form becomes the "structure of hope," "a human universal" akin to myth; and just as myth critics equated myth with religion, McFarland sees romance as it occurs in The Tempest as joining the pastoral and religion.[54] In any case, insofar as recent genre criticism is concerned to describe formal aspects of the plays it is unconcerned with political questions.

12

During most of the twentieth century the
influence of the assumption that art constitutes a
class of its own has been pervasive. Critics have
been continually at pains to separate art from the
philosophic or didactic. J. Dover Wilson, for
example, argues that The Tempest is important because
of its mood: "Shakespeare was not a philosopher and
his plays do not stand for intellectual statements of
any kind. But he brooded, in the service of his art,
upon life in general and human character in
particular, more continuously and more intensely than
any other poet has ever done."[55] Critics often
make a distinction between Shakespeare's "romantic"
comedy and Jonsonian or corrective comedy.[56] They
consider Shakespeare's plays to be creations of the
imagination as opposed to works representing ideas
strictly available outside of art. Charlton, for
example, argues that Shakespeare is "creative," not
"conservative," that Shakespeare's way is the "way of
imagination rather than that of pure reason." What
is important for Shakespeare and the reader is the
"way of apprehending existence." Shakespeare does
more than preserve "the good which was; he has
refined, varied, and widely extended it."[57] Even
those who find Renaissance ideas useful in the
analysis of the plays are influenced by the view that
Shakespeare's art transcends the philosophical and
ethical. E. C. Pettet, for example, relates
Renaissance conceptions of poetry to Shakespeare's
view of poetry, but he argues that Shakespeare
"ignores the moral and didactic emphasis of
contemporary theory."[58]

Although in the last twenty years or so some
critical theory has countered the view that
literature is unique, that view remains strong.
Shakespeare critics continue to try to distinguish
art from the didactic. Thomas McFarland, for
example, argues that The Tempest is not "propaganda
for Christianity." And Howard Felperin tells us that
we need not think of the last plays as Christian
since "the Christian story is a romance, but not all
romances are Christian."[59]

Challenging this continuing commitment to
literature's autonomy, a few theorists of this
generation seem to offer a chance to reassert the
significance of politics to literature. The work of
these theorists, however, has not led to the
reexamination of Shakespeare's view of the political

13

and its relation to poetry. E. D. Hirsch in <u>Validity in Interpretation</u> (1967) argues that the literary text has no special ontological status which distinguishes it from any other linguistic text.[60] Hirsch's attempt to recover the author's intention as determinant of the meaning of the text could have led to a reconsideration of Shakespeare's work along the lines attempted here, but Hirsch stands almost alone in his view and has had little impact on the theory and practice of criticism.

Although some recent structuralist and post-structuralist theory has found literature no different from other forms of writing, this theory also has added little to the consideration of Shakespeare's view of the poet's role. For one thing, structuralism and post-structuralism, for all their copiousness, have not been productive of much practical criticism. In fact, a certain aspect of the theory--the attack on the study of major figures--predisposes it against consideration of Shakespeare. Critics such as Foucault and Barthes deny Shakespeare any special status, for they argue that instead of assuming the uniqueness of a major writer's discourse the critic should try to consider a collective literary mentality or language.[61]

Most importantly, however, structuralism and post-structuralism have been governed by the assumption of ethnological, linguistic and/or historical determinism which makes them ignore the political or induces them to discuss politics in terms alien to Shakespeare. The origin of these critical theories in the linguistic theory of Ferdinand de Saussure helps to explain why their emphasis is not political, for the ends of literary structuralists become similar to those of the linguist. In his <u>Cours de Linguistique Générale</u> (1916) Saussure argues that language consists of rules and patterns underlying actual utterances and that these are the primary objectives of linguistic study. Structuralists look to these underlying structures as the source of meaning in a text. Rather than focusing on an author's views, structuralists focus on the text as a construct whose mode of functioning must be described.[62]

Claude Lévi-Strauss serves as the best example of structuralist thinking since he both pushed Saussurean ideas to the center of European thought in

the 1950's and brought Saussure to America in
Structural Anthropology (1963).[63] Lévi-Strauss
makes an analogy between ethnology and linguistics
which leads him to treat South American myths as
unchanging and universal structures. These myths can
be treated independently of the consciousness and the
attitudes of their author,[64] and thus they are not
necessarily actively determined by the poet's
imagination.

Lévi-Strauss' work, thus, becomes another version
of the old myth criticism, and the results for
consideration of the political are the same. To the
extent that the myths and laws of primitive societies
operate in modern civilization, structuralists such
as Lévi-Strauss can be said to consider society, and
yet such myths and laws constitute only the
unconscious aspects of culture, not the traditional
subjects of politics--law, education, the role of the
philosopher, how to deal with citizens of different
natures, etc.

Jacques Derrida, generally considered the pivotal
figure in the shift from structuralism to
post-structuralism, continues the emphasis on
language in determining the meaning of a text.
According to Derrida, one cannot determine a text's
meaning by reference to any reality outside the words
of the text themselves.[65] As Derrida's American
disciple J. Hillis Miller explains it, "If meaning in
language rises not from the reference of signs to
something outside words but from differential
relations among words themselves, . . . then the
notion of a literary text which is validated by its
one-to-one correspondence to some social, historical,
or psychological reality can no longer be taken for
granted."[66] Thus, a critic cannot determine a
political meaning of a work, and if he does, that
meaning is a mere invention of the critic.

In some recent post-structuralist theory there is
a political element. This theory consists of an
application of the historicist perspective to
structuralism. According to historicists, the
imagination is determined by one's horizon or moment
in history. In this sense, post-structuralism is no
different from the earlier Marxist perspective except
that the inexorable pattern of history usually
becomes linguistic as well as economic. Thus, in his
post-structuralist works Roland Barthes argues that

15

myth arises from history, not from nature. The true mythologist is a revolutionary who abolishes myth, in Barthes' case the bourgeois myth of formalist thought.[67] In a similar manner, Michel Foucault transfers Marx's discussion of class struggle from economics to literature: "[D]iscourse is at once the object of the struggle for domination and the means by which the struggle is waged."[68] Although arguing that he is not a Marxist, Edward Said applies Marxist thought when he approves of demystifying all "values, institutions, and definitions" by considering them under the aspect of power, and his recent book's deconstruction of modern criticism is certainly derivative from Marxist thought. Said argues that the State under Reagan, needing to silence its culture in order to pursue its "imperial wars and colonial settlements," has induced critics to sever the link between the "text" and the "world."[69]

Clearly criticism deriving from such theory would not be concerned with considering what Shakespeare thought in his own terms. Thoroughgoing Marxists argue that one cannot escape one's own archive, or historical climate, and thus Shakespeare's work is depicted as a record of the class struggles of his times. Political questions become uninteresting because all are assumed to be determined by identification with a class.

Although recent structuralist and post-structuralist theory has led to little criticism of Shakespeare's plays, it has reinforced some old approaches and has introduced at least one new one to the criticism of A Midsummer Night's Dream and The Tempest. Whether reinforcing a previous approach or introducing a new one, criticism based on structuralism and post-structuralism embodies the determinism which leads away from Shakespeare'e view of the political. Réné Girard's new analysis of A Midsummer Night's Dream applies ethnology to literature. He sees relations between men as governed by mimetic rivalry--in A Midsummer Night's Dream the desire to imitate another's desire and to appropriate the object of that desire. This leads to a mimetic crisis which involves the protagonist's becoming more and more undifferentiated and which signals the collapse of social forms. Girard attacks structuralism and post-structuralism for ignoring the undifferentiating in determining meaning. And yet

16

Girard's views actually derive from both structuralism and post-structuralism. Like some structuralists, he applies ethnology to literature to derive a theory of meaning. Like the deconstructionists, he advocates demythification, for his description of the un-differentiating makes it a kind of decoding of myths.[70]

In _Tempest_ criticism structuralist and post-structuralist theory has reinforced both the old myth criticism and the old Marxist approach, though often with a new terminology. As argued above, much new genre criticism simply translates myth as structure.[71] Marxist critics use the linguistic element in structuralism and post-structuralism to support their historical determinism. Thus, the emphasis on Shakespeare as an exponent of colonialism remains, but elements of the new theory are used to reinforce the old view. Bruce Ehrlich, for example, notes that the literary text is "less a mirror than a sign system" in order to defend his view that _The Tempest_ actively formed the "historical direction of Jacobean society."[72] Lorie Leininger provides a "semiology" of what she sees as _The Tempest_'s defense of colonialism. She argues that Shakespeare seduces his audience into approving of colonialism through strategies of indirection, through imaginative collusion with domination, and through supplying contradictory information about Caliban.[73]

In summation, then, those recent developments in theory which challenge the unique status of literature have not corrected neglect of Shakespeare's view of the political. A further factor contributing to modern criticism's inattention to the artist's role in civil society has been the change in attitude towards politics and morality. Moderns find politics and ethics less important to individual happiness than the Renaissance did. For most people of the Renaissance happiness derived from virtue and was realized within civil society. Following Aristotle, they believed that a human's nature or end is indicated by his reason.[74] Humans are composite, having an irrational element in common with plants or animals, and a rational faculty peculiar to them. Happiness is living in accordance with nature, which for people means developing the distinctively human faculty and allowing it to rule them. Exercise of the virtues depends upon a person's subordination of his passions to reason.

17

For most people the life of virtue or happiness can be realized only within civil society. Because speech as well as reason distinguishes humans from other animals and because speech is communication, people are naturally social animals. Association with other people does not derive from mere calculation of one's pleasures. Love, friendship and sympathy are as natural as selfish concern with one's own good. These are realized partly as a person's perfection rather than as his current state; their full exercise depends on reason's rule. People thus need laws and education in the laws to attain happiness. Nature has given people speech so that they can communicate to other people what is advantageous and what is not, or what is just and what is not. Only through politics can they use this innate capacity to develop a complete and common system of justice which can direct them and their fellows toward the good life.

All of these ideas are assumed in Sir Thomas Elyot's discussion of justice in his popular The Boke Named the Gouvernour:

> Verely the knowledge of Justyce is nat so difficile or harde to be attayned unto by man as it is communely supposed, if he wolde nat willingly abandone the excellencie of his propre nature, and folisshely applicate him selfe to the nature of creatures unreasonable, in the stede of reason embrasynge sensualitie and for societie and beneuolence folowinge wilfulnesse and malice, and for knowledge, blynde ignoraunce and forgetfulnesse.[75]

For moderns, on the other hand, happiness is not necessarily equated with virtue or thought to derive from society and politics. We have tended to accept Hobbes' view that happiness is continued success at getting what we desire. Hobbes assumes that all desires are equal, that there is nothing in humans which implies that reason is higher than passion or that some pleasures are better than others. There are as many goods as there are desires. In other words, Hobbes argues that we get no guidance from nature about what we should be; we are, thus, in a way our own makers. Unlike the men and women of the

18

Renaissance, for the most part we think of government as a necessary evil rather than as a means to help educate and form virtuous, happy men and women. For us the aim of the state is the protection of life, liberty and property, and beyond that it should leave the individual alone.

Powerful modern attitudes have worked against a full consideration of Shakespeare's comedies and romances. Despite Renaissance concern with the relation of poetry to civil society, modern critics have neglected this dimension of <u>A Midsummer Night's Dream</u> and <u>The Tempest</u>. The principal critical approaches to these plays have been based on the assumption that literature is distinct from politics, ethics, and philosophy. Even those critics interested in Renaissance ideas have been influenced by the view that literature constitutes a class of its own. Moreover, that recent critical theory which does not see literature as different from other forms of discourse has been based on a determinism which leads away from the political or which represents a view of the political alien to Shakespeare. In addition, the modern tendency to reject virtue and the political as sources of happiness reinforces the literary-critical predisposition to neglect moral and political questions in the plays.

If the twentieth century has neglected Shakespeare's view of the political, its reasons for doing so constitute an argument against my attempt to reverse the trend. If literature is distinct from politics, it makes no sense to discuss the political as such. If one's own views are determined entirely by the history, language, or culture of one's own time, then it is futile to try to recover another's views. If today the political is less important to happiness than in the Renaissance, then considering poetry's role in politics becomes less important.

This is not the place to develop a full response to these assaults. Rather I refer the reader to E. D. Hirsch's <u>Validity in Interpretation</u> (1967) and <u>Aims of Interpretation</u> (1976) for a complete defense against the first two attacks.[76] In response to the view that literature is <u>sui generis</u> Hirsch argues that there is no way to distinguish literature from other forms of discourse, because no characteristics can be found which universally distinguish texts considered literary from other texts. Texts studied

19

as literature include what is also thought of as philosophy, psychology, theology, etc. Literary works cannot be said to be predominantly aesthetic because many works considered literature were conceived with other ends in mind (_Aims_, pp. 124-25; _Validity_, pp. 111-26).

Hirsch's defense against historical, linguistic or cultural relativism consists of developing a theory of meaning which allows for knowledge in interpretation and of pointing out logical and empirical difficulties with relativism. To develop his theory of meaning Hirsch takes from Piaget the idea that understanding is based on corrigible schemata. According to Piaget, we learn to live in the world by overcoming an infantile confusion of content and context. We learn to recognize the stable self-identity of physical objects despite great variations in our perceptual experience of those objects. Hirsch extends this insight to understanding a text's meaning apart from one's individual perspective (_Aims_, pp. 3, 29-31). Although _Aims_ introduces this theory, a similar idea is found in _Validity_'s description of a genre conception as an hypothesis subject to modification and amendment (_Validity_, pp. 72-77, 90-99, Chapter V).

The concept of corrigible schemata suggests that one might simultaneously entertain the perspective of one's self and that of the author of a work even if that author comes from another era or culture or speaks a different mother language. Hirsch argues that every act of interpretation involves at least these two perspectives of self and author. He points out that doubling of personality is the ground of all human intercourse, a universal fact of speech (_Aims_, p. 49).

The idea of corrigible schemata assumes the existence of a domain of experience outside that area which is historically, culturally, or linguistically determined. As Hirsch points out, one's spiritual world consists of a limited domain of shared cultural experience along with an unlimited domain of unshared experience. The development of a hypothesis about meaning could arise from this larger domain rather than from the domain which defines one's historicity or ethnocentricity (_Aims_, pp. 83-84).

In addition to developing a theory of meaning,

Hirsch lists logical and empirical difficulties with relativism which I will not reproduce in full here. Most telling perhaps is the argument that by its own principles any sort of relativism is incapable of logical or empirical verification. For example, the statement "All thought is relative to the culture which produced it" is itself relative if it is true, but if it is relative, it cannot be assumed universally true.

Defending the possibility of knowledge in interpretation has little point if one does not find that knowledge valuable. Most of us would agree that what is productive of human happiness must be thought of value. And yet if the modern view of government as a necessary evil is true, one does not expect government to be a source of happiness in any positive sense. Why, then, should one examine poetry's relation to politics?

The political is vital to human happiness because it tells us where to seek happiness and provides the conditions which make it possible to seek happiness there. Paradoxically, the very idea that government is a necesary evil which should limit us as little as possible constitutes a controlling element in our lives. We are able to consider the political unimportant in our lives only because of a prior political act, namely, the founding fathers' establishment of a limited government. In the founders' view, people should be left free to find their own happiness in the private sphere, and government's role should be limited to facilitating the process by preventing domestic and foreign strife and by carrying out some other minimal caretaker functions. Only because politicans, the founding fathers, decided that it was inappropriate for government to concern itself with most of what happens in society can spontaneous individual and societal forces play such an independent and self-determining role in our country today. To see that in principle it can be otherwise one need do no more than look to Mao's China or Khomeini's Iran.

The following examination of A Midsummer Night's Dream and The Tempest, then, is based on three views which have been questioned by modern literary theory: First, literature is not necessarily distinct from politics or morality. Second, at least a portion of one's own views can be independent of

history, language, or culture.   Third, the political
is important to human happiness.

Notes

[1]R. W. Dent, "Imagination in *A Midsummer Night's Dream*," *SQ*, 15, (1969), p. 129; David P. Young, *Something of Great Constancy* (New Haven and London, 1966), pp. 178-80.

[2]Northrop Frye, "Introduction," *The Tempest* (Baltimore, 1959), pp. 15-26; rpt. in *Twentieth Century Interpretations of The Tempest*, ed. Hallett Smith (Englewood Cliffs, New Jersey, 1969), p. 65.

[3]E.g., Bonamy Dobrée, "*The Tempest*," *Essays and Studies*, n. s. 5 (1959), 25. Since this writing Paul Cantor has published two articles requiring amendment of this statement. The first--"Shakespeare's *The Tempest*: The Wise Man as Hero," *SQ*, 31 (1980), 64-75--refers to Prospero as a philosopher hero without making reference to Plato. The second--"Prospero's Republic: The Politics of Shakespeare's *The Tempest*," in *Shakespeare as a Political Thinker*, ed. John Alvis and Thomas G. West (Durham, 1981), pp. 239-55--begins with a quotation from Plato's *Republic* on philosopher-kings. This article uses insights from *The Republic* to elucidate *The Tempest*'s illustration of the relationship between wisdom and power. Cantor does not deal with *The Tempest* as a defense of poetry.

[4]Theodore Spencer, *Shakespeare and the Nature of Man* (New York), 1942), pp. 195-99; James E. Phillips, "*The Tempest* and the Renaissance Idea of Man," *SQ*, 15 (1964), 147-59.

[5]Jackson Cope, *The Theatre and the Dream* (Baltimore, 1973), p. 239.

[6]Although Marxist criticism is concerned with the relation of the poet to civil society, it does not deal with Shakespeare's treatment of the issue. Rather Shakespeare is viewed from a perspective assumed broader than his own because it is historically posterior. As Bruce Ehrlich argues in his article on "Shakespeare's Colonial Metaphor," even the greatest minds cannot transcend the limitations of their time [*Science and Society*, 41 (1977), 63]. Shakespeare is thus seen as an exponent of colonialism who participates in history either actively or as its passive by-product [See, for example, Ehrlich, pp. 43-65; Lorie Leininger,

"Cracking the Code of The Tempest," in Shakespeare: Contemporary Critical Approaches, ed. Harry R. Garvin (Lewisburg, 1980), pp. 121-31; O. Mannoni, Prospero and Caliban: The Psychology of Colonization, trans. Pamela Powesland (New York, 1956); Philip Mason, Prospero's Magic: Some Thoughts on Class and Race (London, 1962)]. This is not the place to attack in detail the Marxist approach. It must suffice to restate the argument of modern radical historicists--that once one accepts the principle of historical determination, one cannot privilege one's own view as ahistorical.

[7]I use "poet" to refer to all conceptions of the poet deriving from the plays. "Poet," thus, can refer both to poet as character and poet as playwright. In addition, the poet may be defined by discussions of poetry by characters or by examples of plays within the plays. In A Midsummer Night's Dream and The Tempest Shakespeare gives the reader a conception of his view of the poet through his own play as a whole as an example of poetry as well as through characters who act as poets. In A Midsummer Night's Dream, for example, Puck and Bottom act as poets at times, and Oberon often performs the tasks of stage manager. But Shakespeare also points to his own work as playwright in solving the conflicts which Theseus could not resolve. In The Tempest Prospero operates as a poet, but the play as a whole illustrates the operation of Shakespeare as playright --especially in exemplifying the descriptions of poetry in Ariel's songs.

[8]Juan Luis Vives, Vives on Education, trans. Foster Watson (Cambridge, 1931), pp. 125-38.

[9]Sir Thomas Elyot, The Boke Named the Governour, ed. H. H. S. Croft, I (London, 1880), Book I, XIII.

[10]Roger Ascham, The Scholemaster (1570), in Elizabethan Critical Essays, ed. G. Gregory Smith, I (London, 1937), 23-24.

[11]John Rainolds, Oratio in laudem artis poeticae (1572), ed. William Ringer, trans. W. Allen (Princeton, 1940); Richard Wills, De Re Poetica, ed. A. D. S. Fowler (Oxford, 1958).

[12]J. Dover Wilson, "The Puritan Attack Upon the Stage," _Cambridge History of English Drama_, VI (New York and Cambridge, 1933), 426.

[13]Wilson, pp. 42-27, 437; Smith, I, 61; Russell Fraser, _The War Against Poetry_ (Princeton, 1970), p. 13.

[14]See Smith, I, 61-63, for a list of contributions to the anti-state controversy.

[15]Geoffrey Shepherd, "Introduction," _An Apology for Poetry_ (New York and Manchester, 1973), p. 3.

[16]William Vaughan, _The Golden-Grove, moralized in three books: a work very necessary for all such as would know how to gouerne themselues, their houses, or their country_ (1600), in Smith, II, 325-26.

[17]William Webbe, _A Discourse of English Poetry_ (1586), in Smith, I, 226-302; Puttenham, _The Arte of English Poesie_ (1589), in Smith, II, 1-193; Sir John Harington, _A Preface, or rather a Briefe Apologie of Poetrie_ (1591), in Smith, II, 194-222.

[18]Bernard Weinberg, _A History of Literary Criticism in the Italian Renaissance_, I (Chicago, 1961), 251.

[19]Russell Fraser argues that, although poetry was condemned on moral grounds, the critical objection was to its lack of utility (Fraser, p. 4). To say, as Fraser does, that the critical objection to poetry is lack of utility simply because a moralist discusses moral utility and a businessman economic utility seems fallacious. In one case the critical objection is moral, and in the other it is economic. What is useful for virtue is distinct from what is useful for moneymaking. Fraser's argument that the moral critique masks a "more thorough-going animus" whose source is "delight in Naked Truth" (p. 28) also is problematic. Fraser doubts the validity of the moral critique on the grounds that the pagan theatre no longer existed as a legitimate target (p. 22) and on the basis of John Selden's opinion that the prohibition of _Deuteronomy_ against a man's wearing a woman's attire is founded on its connection with pagan worship (p. 26). But I see no reason to believe that Renaissance attacks on license in contemporary theatre are insincere. Surely the

pagan theatre is not the only possible source of license. Besides, John Selden's opinion was a response to Ben Jonson's request to examine that passage. Jonson's request must have been motivated by some doubt concerning the issue.

[20]Sir Philip Sidney, An Apology for Poetry, ed. Geoffrey Shepherd (New York and Manchester, 1973), pp. 125-26.

[21]Sidney, pp. 129-30; Harington, in Smith, II, 204; Thomas Nash, "From The Anatomie of Absurditie," in Smith, I, 328; E. Hoby's translation of Coignet's Politique Discourses (1586)," in Smith, I, 341. Poetry's proponents sometimes settle for an attack on Plato's authority in addition to or as a substitute for this argument. See, for example, Lodge's attack on Plato's definition of the soul and on Plato's view that the Idea was the principal cause of things (Thomas Lodge, A Defence of Poetry, in Smith, I, 67). Sidney (pp. 128-29) and Lodge (in Smith, I, 67) condemn Plato for objecting to filth in poetry while admitting it in his own writing.

[22]Harington, in Smith, I, 197; Sidney, p. 104; Lodge, in Smith, I, 76. Nash is an exception. He finds that a mature man can find "profitable knowledge" in some of "the filthiest Fables" (in Smith, I, 332).

[23]See, for example, Stephen Gosson, The School of Abuse (1579), in Shakespeare Society Publications, XV (Nendelin, Liechtenstein, 1966), 15. John Northbrooke's exceptions are fewer [A Treatise Against Dicing, Dancing, Plays and Interludes (1577), in Shakespeare Society Publications, XV (Nendelin, Liechtenstein, 1966), 52, 103].

[24]Sidney, p. 104.

[25]Sidney, p. 113.

[26]See, for example, Puttenham, in Smith, II, 6-10; Webbe, in Smith, I, 231; Nash, in Smith, I, 328-29; Harington, in Smith, II, 198-99; Elyot, Book I, XIII.

[27]See, for example, Puttenham, in Smith, 16-24; Lodge, in Smith, I, 64, 69-72; Sidney, pp. 127-28, 131; Harington, in Smith, II, 195; Webbe, in Smith,

I, 232-33; Francis Meres, "From _Palladis Tamia_" (1958), in Smith, II, 321-22; George Chapman, "Dedication of _Achilles Shield_" (1598), in Smith, II, 302.

[28]Virgil K. Whitaker, _Shakespeare's Use of Learning_ (San Marino, California, 1953), pp. 6-7.

[29]See Basil Willey, _The Seventeenth Century Background_ (Garden City, New York, 1953), pp. 21-30.

[30]Francis Bacon, _The Advancement of Learning_, in _Selected Writings of Francis Bacon_, ed. Hugh G. Dick (New York, 1955), pp. 183-84.

[31]See Walter Jackson Bate, _From Classic to Romantic_ (New York, 1946), pp. 93-112.

[32]_Aristotle on the Art of Poetry_, trans. Ingram Bywater (Oxford, 1909); rpt. in _Rhetoric and Poetics_ (New York, 1954), 1454b. All further references to this work appear in the text.

[33]Sidney, p. 102. See also George Puttenham, _The Arte of English Poesy_ (1589), in Smith, II, 19-20.

[34]As indicated above, poetry's defenders usually argue that the true poetry would demonstrate moral utility. Poetry was also useful in comforting man (e.g., Puttenham, in Smith, II, 25), and in helping him to gain knowledge (e.g., Nash, in Smith, I, 328-29; Webbe, in Smith, I, 250).

[35]Immanuel Kant, _Analytic of the Beautiful from the Critique of Judgment_, trans. Walter Cerf (New York, 1963), pp. 5-6 (§4). See also pp. 25-26 (§11), 26-27 (§12), 32-35 (§15). Later in the _Critique of Judgment_ Kant draws analogies between the aesthetic and the moral, but he consistently maintains the disinterestedness of judgments of taste.

[36]Morton Luce, ed., _The Tempest_ (Indianapolis, 1899), p. li; Lytton Strachey, "Shakespeare's Final Period," _Independent Review_, 3 (1904); rpt. in _Literary Essays_ (New York, 1949), p. 2.

[37]Frederick James Furnivall, _Leopold Shakespeare Introduction_ (1877), p. lxxxviii, as quoted in _The Tempest_, ed. Horace Howard Furness (New York, 1964), pp. 365-66.

[38]Edward Dowden, Shakespeare: A Critical Study of His Mind and Art (New York, 1902), pp. 37, 59-63, 371-80.

[39]John Russell Brown, "The Interpretation of Shakespeare's Comedies: 1900-1953," Shakespeare Survey, 8 (1955), 7.

[40]Samuel Taylor Coleridge, Shakespearean Criticism, ed. T. M. Rayso (New York and London, 1960); rpt. in English Romantic Writers, ed. David Perkins (New York, 1967), p. 496.

[41]Brown, p. 7; Enid Welsford, The Court Masque (Cambridge and New York, 1927), pp. 324-36.

[42]Paul Olson, "A Midsummer Night's Dream and the Meaning of Court Marriage," ELH, 24 (1957), 95-119.

[43]G. K. Hunter, Shakespeare: The Late Comedies (London, 1962), p. 8.

[44]Philip Edwards, "Shakespeare's Romances: 1900-1957," Shakespeare Survey, 11 (1958), 6.

[45]G. Wilson Knight, The Wheel of Fire (London, 1930), p. 15.

[46]The Crown of Life (New York, 1966), pp. 13, 23.

[47]Knight, Wheel of Fire, pp. 270, 268.

[48]Knight, Crown of Life, p. 12.

[49]G. Wilson Knight, The Imperial Theme (London, 1931), p. 124.

[50]Knight, Imperial Theme, pp. 21-23.

[51]Edwards, pp. 12-13.

[52]Knight, Crown, p. 31; Robert Merrill, "The Generic Approach in Recent Criticism of Shakespeare's Comedies and Romances: A Review Essay," Texas Studies in Language and Literature, 20 (1978), 481, 484; Howard Felperin, Shakespearean Romance (Princeton, 1972), p. 313.

[53]Merrill, p. 474.

[54]Thomas McFarland, Shakespeare's Pastoral Comedy (Chapel Hill, 1972), pp. 37, 39.

[55]J. Dover Wilson, The Meaning of The Tempest (Newcastle Upon Tyne, 1936), pp. 2-3.

[56]Brown, p. 1; Milton Crane, "Shakespeare's Comedies and the Critics," SQ, 15 (1964), 69-70; and see, for example, Ashley H. Thorndike, English Comedy (New York, 1929), pp. 136-37; George Gordon, Shakespearian Comedy (London, 1944), pp. 14-34, esp. 34; Nevill Coghill, "The Basis of Shakespearian Comedy," in Essays and Studies, n.s. 3 (1950), 2-28. I do not deny that the distinction holds, but I would argue that the emphasis on it helps to perpetrate the idea that Shakespeare was not deeply concerned with moral and political questions.

[57]H. B. Charlton, Shakespearian Comedy (New York, 1940), pp. 277-78.

[58]E. C. Pettet, "Shakespeare's Conception of Poetry," Essays and Studies, n.s. 3 (1950), 45.

[59]McFarland, p. 38; Felperin, p. 169.

[60]E. D. Hirsch, Validity in Interpretation (New Haven and London, 1967). All further references to this work appear within the text.

[61]Roland Barthes, On Racine, trans. Richard Howard (New York, 1964), pp. 158-62; Michel Foucault, "Nietzsche, Genealogy, History," in Language, Counter-Memory, Practice: Selected Essays and Interviews, trans. Donald F. Bouchard and Sherry Simon (Ithaca, 1977), p. 145.

[62]Josué V. Harari makes this last point in "Critical Factions / Critical Fictions," in Textual Strategies: Perspectives in Post-Structuralist Criticism, ed. Josué V. Harari (Ithaca, 1979), p. 23.

[63]Frank Lentricchia, After the New Criticism (Chicago, 1980), pp. 124-25.

[64]Eugenio Donato, "On Structuralism and Literature," MLN, 82 (1967), 555.

[65]The key essay in establishing this position is Derrida's "Structure, Sign and Play in the Discourse of the Human Sciences," in _Writing and Difference_, trans. Alan Bass (Chicago, 1978), pp. 278-93. See especially pp. 292-93.

[66]J. Hillis Miller, _Charles Dickens and George Cruikshank_ (Los Angeles, 1971), pp. 1-2.

[67]Roland Barthes, _Mythologies_, trans. Annette Lavers (New York, 1972), pp. 110, 129-30.

[68]Harari, p. 42. Foucault, _La Volonté de Savoir_ (Paris, 1976), p. 123. Although Foucault has reservations about Marx, his views derive from Marx's thought.

[69]Edward Said, _The World, the Text and the Critic_ (Cambridge, Massachusetts, 1983), pp.

[70]René Girard, "Myth and Ritual in Shakespeare: _A Midsummer Night's Dream_," in _Textual Strategies_, ed. Josué V. Harari (Ithaca, 1979), pp. 189-212.

[71]McFarland, pp. 37; see p. 12 above.

[72]Ehrlich, pp. 43-65, esp. 43 and 65.

[73]Leininger, pp. 121-31.

[74]See _Troilus and Cressida_, II.ii.163-67, for a direct reference by Shakespeare to the _Nicomachean Ethics_.

[75]Elyot, II, 201.

[76]E. D. Hirsch, Jr. _Aims of Interpretation_ (Chicago and London, 1976). All further references to this work are in the text.

CHAPTER II

A MIDSUMMER NIGHT'S DREAM: POLITICS VERSUS POETRY

I. The Politician's View of Art

The view of drama presented in A Midsummer Night's Dream becomes clear only if one understands the political aspects of the play. The claims of the political, including its right to judge art, are embodied in Theseus. Theseus exemplifies the best that politics has to offer.[1]

Although the Renaissance view of Theseus was divided, it seems safe to assume that Shakespeare chose the side of the tradition which saw Theseus as a wise and model ruler. It is widely accepted that A Midsummer Night's Dream was written for the nuptial ceremony of a noble house,[2] and the parallel between the marriage of Theseus and Hippolyta and that of the noble couple must have been intended as a compliment. Shakespeare would hardly have made an invidious comparison. The play continually suggests the relationship of its events to those of the manor house in which it is presented. Just as Theseus and Hippolyta and the rest of his court are the audience at Bottom's play, the groom and bride and the wedding guests are the audience at Shakespeare's play. The mechanicals' apology for their play might be seen as Shakespeare's indirect apology for his. Just as Theseus comments on the story told by the Athenian lovers, the wedding guests might comment on Shakespeare's play containing the lovers. It is likely that the parallels between the play and the solemn nuptials of the manor house were extended from the verbal level to the physical. As Siegel suggests, the play may have been presented in the three hours between "after-supper and bedtime" (V.i.34) as a final part of the wedding revels and at the time approaching the consummation of the actual marriage.[3] The fairies' blessing of the marriage bed in the masque may have become an actual blessing of the manor house. And the dance called for by Oberon (V.i.403) may have involved taking members of the audience as partners in the traditional masque manner.[4]

Shakespeare does take note of the passionate side of Theseus' nature, but he turns this to compliment by making it clear that Theseus now has the desires under control. Formerly, Titania may have led him "through the glimmering night / From Perigenia, whom he ravished." She may have made "him with fair Aegles break his faith, / With Ariadne and Antiopa" (II.i.77-80).[5] But now Theseus plays the eager bridegroom who, despite his desires, will await the wedding day:

> Now, fair Hippolyta, our nuptial hour
> Draws on apace. Four happy days bring in
> Another moon; but, O, methinks, how slow
> This old moon wanes! She lingers my desires,
> Like to a stepdame, or a dowager,
> Long withering out a young man's revenue.
>
> (I.i.1-6)

The play concludes with the lawful fulfillment of Theseus' desire. It is also concerned in a more general way with bringing order to the desires. Although aided by Oberon and the fairies, Theseus participates in the play's happy harmonious solution by acquiescing in the lovers' choices, by overruling Egeus, and by setting a marriage date.

Theseus represents the statesman preoccupied with practical government: he must uphold the laws of Athens which are based on ancestral custom and must support the aged, because age provides validity for the law. Age is a practical substitute for wisdom which, unlike wisdom, is politically recognizable and easily defined. Furthermore, obedience to the law is secured through habit, and habit can be created only through the passage of time. As the play begins, Theseus upholds the "ancient privilege of Athens" which gives Egeus the right to decide upon his daughter's mate, and Theseus supports the father as one who to his daughter "should be as a god" (I.i.120). At the same time that Theseus defends Egeus' rights as a father, he tempers Egeus' demands by adding life in a nunnery as an alternative to death as punishment for disobedience.

Later the possibility of absolute adherence to the law is questioned by Theseus' overriding Egeus' objection to the marriage of Hermia and Lysander (IV.i.182-184). Initially Theseus indicates that he is ready to uphold the law. As the court party comes upon the sleeping lovers, he asks Egeus, "Is not this the day / That Hermia should give answer of her choice?" (IV.i.138-139). Lysander then proves that law's ineffectiveness by admitting his and Hermia's intent to escape the Athenian law by running away. Theseus recognizes that in this case harmony in the state is best produced by acquiescing in the desires of the pairs of lovers.

In general, though, the statesmen must uphold the laws by punishing all those who break them. If he is to maintain a stable, orderly government, he may not publicly look to standards beyond those of the city. The artist is acceptable to the city only insofar as he supports its government, and Theseus judges art according to its indication of love to the ruler of Athens. Trying to persuade Hippolyta that his choice of the mechanicals' play makes sense, Theseus argues:

> Where I have come, great clerks have purposèd
> To greet me with premeditated welcomes;
> Where I have seen them shiver and look pale,
> Make periods in the midst of sentences,
> Throttle their practiced accents in their fears,
> And, in conclusion, dumbly have broke off,
> Not paying me a welcome. Trust me, sweet,
> Out of this silence yet I picked a welcome;
> And in the modesty of fearful duty
> I read as much as from the rattling tongue
> Of saucy and audacious eloquence.
> Love, therefore, and tongue-tied simplicity
> In least speak most, to my capacity.
>   (V.i.92-105)

Theseus' standard for art is compatible with his view of the artist's capabilities. At one point he argues that "The best of this kind [plays] are but shadows; and the worst are no worse, if imagination amend them" (V.i.212-213). He allows the artist no more than Socrates seems to allow him in his representation of the poet as a man who holds up a mirror to reflect what surrounds him (Republic, 596c-e). Poetry is dependent on the world around it. It does not make its objects. It merely imitates them. Socrates compares the poet's knowledge with the knowledge of artisans who make the things imitated. Because the poet is not a knower of all the diverse arts, his representation is only a shadow of the competent opinions of the artisans.[6] Earlier Theseus had given the poet's creation even less credibility by denying its truth altogether: "I never may believe / These antique fables, nor these fairy toys" (V.i.2-3).

This well-worn charge that poets are liars is disputed in the Renaissance. Many fifteenth and sixteenth century humanists deny the charge. Boccaccio, for example, devotes a major section of The Genealogy of the Gentile Gods (XIV.ix-xiv) to responding to the view that poets are "tale-mongers" who produce "idle nonsense." In England Sidney makes poetry's falsehood the second of the three major charges to which he responds, and Lodge and Harrington both find it necessary to defend the poets against the charge of mendacity.[7] Shakespeare himself allows Touchstone (As You Like It, III.iii.16-21) and Apemantes (Timon of Athens, I.i.223-25) the liberty of calling poets liars.

Given the limited credibility of the poet's creations to Theseus' mind, works of art are best viewed as recreation for man when he is not involved in more important matters. For Theseus plays are simply entertainment to "beguile / The lazy time" (V.i.40-41). Even an opponent of the Renaissance stage like John Northbrooke was willing to concede this much to drama. He cites Cicero's book of Offices to the effect that "honest games and pastimes are allowable, but we ought to use them as we doe sleepe and other eases of the body, and to be taken after such time, as we have laboured inough in weightie matters and serious affaires."[8]

Someone, however, must judge which plays deserve to be called "honest pastimes" and which might be dangerous to the state and to public morality. As argued in Chapter I, both the Renaissance proponents and opponents of the stage support morality as the standard by which poetry is to be judged.[9] In line with this view some Renaissance humanists give the statesman the right to choose which poetry is salutary. Mazzoni, for example, argues that "the civil faculty is that which not merely found out the use of poetry, but afterwards should consider the norm and rule of the poetic image."[10] Tasso finds it "the statesman's duty to consider what poetry and what delight should be prohibited."[11] In A Midsummer Night's Dream Theseus is in the position of the statesman judging the moral worth of poetry. It is unlikely that his judgement would accord with that of the artist, for according to Theseus the mechanicals' play deserves as much attention as the story of the young lovers, "For never anything can be

amiss / When simpleness and duty tender it"
(V.i.82-83).

II. The Dangers of Poetry to Politics

Shakespeare, of course, is unwilling to let the case rest with Theseus' representation of the poet. Both recognizing the dangers of the poet's vision and suggesting its superiority, he attempts a reconciliation of poetry and politics which gives the poet a function compatible with the orderly government of Athens.

Shakespeare's exploration of the issue is complex. One aspect is his examination of tragedy's threat to the city. Shakespeare's play, of course, is a comedy, but by drawing extensive parallels between the Pyramus and Thisbe story and the story of the young Athenian lovers he calls attention to his turning a potentially tragic situation into a comedy.

In the two stories both sets of lovers are obstructed by parental observation. Both sets meet by moonlight. The violence of the Pyramus and Thisbe story suggests actualization of the potential violence in the Athenian lover's story: Demetrius leaves Helena alone in the wood, and Lysander deserts Hermia. Then Lysander and Demetrius try to duel over Helena. Furthermore, the parallels between the two stories are emphasized by their juxtaposition in A Midsummer Night's Dream. The first rehearsal of the mechanicals' play occurs just after Hermia and Lysander outline the paradoxes of true love and decide to run away. The second rehearsal, which culminates in the translation of Bottom into an ass, follows the transformation of the lovers in which Lysander is made to shift his love from Hermia to Helena.

These points of similarity between the two stories suggest that Shakespeare is illustrating what he is preventing his play from being. By writing a comedy Shakespeare has saved his audience from the offenses of tragedy. At the same time he has pointed out that tragic drama endangers the city because it makes apparent the conflict of the natural with the city. First, love can conflict with the laws of the city. For both Pyramus and Thisbe and Hermia and Lysander, love contradicts parental choice which, for Hermia and Lysander, is supported by the law of

Athens. In <u>A</u> <u>Midsummer</u> <u>Night's</u> <u>Dream</u>, desire has
been strong enough to overcome the force of the law
as Hermia and Lysander are moved to defy Theseus by
escaping from Athens to the wood.

Second, desire conflicts with the virtues
supported by the law of Athens. Married love is
threatened by Lysander's desire to sleep near Hermia
(II.ii.41-42, 45-52) and by the desire represented in
Hermia's dream:

> Help me, Lysander, help me! Do thy best
> To pluck this crawling serpent from my breast!
> Ay me, for pity! What a dream was here!
> Lysander, look how I do quake with fear.
> Methought a serpent eat my heart away,
> And you sat smiling at his cruel prey.
> (II.ii.145-50)

Moreover, as Demetrius' and Lysander's alterations
indicate, there is no guarantee of lovers' fidelity
to one another. As Denis de Rougemont points out,
fidelity is one of the least natural virtues. He
argues that "it is to be distinguished from passion
by its persistent refusal to submit to its own dream,
by its persistent need of acting in behalf of the
beloved. . . ." One is faithful simply because one
has pledged oneself to be so--not for any rational
reason.[12] One remains faithful by denying oneself
the pleasure that submitting to one's desires could
entail.

The tension between desire and both law and the
virtues implies the conventional nature of the city.
The legislator must represent virtue and the law as
harmonious with man's nature. He must argue that
virtue and obedience to the law produce happiness.
The poet, on the other hand, represents powerfully a
portion of man's soul, desire, whose suppression
virtue sometimes requires.

Since <u>A</u> <u>Midsummer</u> <u>Night's</u> <u>Dream</u> is a comedy, the
representative of the law, Theseus, eventually is
reconciled to those whose desires threaten the law,
the young lovers. Ultimately the play directs the
lovers towards obedience to the city and towards
marriage. At the same time, however, it makes clear
the dangers of desire to the city. In addition to
pointing towards the threat of desire to both law and
virtue, the story of the Athenian lovers shows that

desire is the source of potential discord within the city. Men and women do not readily share the object of their desire, and there is no guarantee that this object will be a different woman for each man or a different man for each woman. The result in the case of Lysander and Demetrius is an attempted duel over one woman between two citizens. Hermia also attempts physical combat with Helena over Lysander.

Although within the city, Athens, love is certainly problematic, Shakespeare turns to the forest, to nature, to express in extreme form those aspects of man which are known to the poet, but which cannot be acknowledged by the city. In the city Demetrius has been unfaithful, but in the wood the love potion produces infidelity to the point of absurdity. Lysander is unfaithful to Hermia and then to Helena, and Demetrius also becomes doubly unfaithful, formerly to Helena, and now to Hermia. This infidelity is repeated in Oberon and Titania and in Theseus' former exploits in love.

The interchangeability of the lovers suggests the irrationality of love and marriage. In the context of Athens Lysander has pointed out that he and Demetrius are equally worthy. As Lysander argues, he is "as well derived as" Demetrius, "as well possessed," his "fortunes every way as fairly ranked" (I.i.99-101). Helena has also made herself and Hermia equivalents: "Through Athens I am thought as fair as she" (I.i.227). That Helena is taller and Hermia more shrewish seems contrived for the sake of argument, so that the lovers can convince themselves that their love makes sense. Ironically, the lovers believe that the alterations of their hearts are rational:

Not Hermia but Helena I love:
Who will not change a raven for a dove?
The will of man is by his reason swayed
And reason says you are the worthier maid.
Things growing are not ripe until their season:
So I, being young till now not ripe to reason.
And touching now the point of human skill,
Reason becomes the marshal to my will,
And leads me to your eyes, where I o'erlook
Love's stories, written in love's richest book.
(II.ii.113-22)

37

The incidents in the wood, however, illustrate
aptly Helena's charge that

> Things base and vile, holding no quantity,
> Love can transpose to form and dignity.
> (I.i.232-33)

Titania's love for Bottom turns to ridicule any claim
that the object of love possesses what the lover
finds in him or her. In a sense, then, Bottom's
vision is truer than that of Lysander. At least
Bottom recognizes that Titania's love for him is
absurd: "And yet, to say the truth, reason and love
keep little company together nowadays; the more the
pity, that some honest neighbors will not make
them friends" (III.i.144-47). In addition to
representing in radical form love's tendency towards
infideltiy and the irrationality of love, the wood
serves to reveal love's potential contribution to
violence and its possible refusal to be bound by
marriage. The wood is the setting of the duel of
Lysander and Demetrius, of the attempted combat of
Hermia and Helena, and of the revelation of
Lysander's and Hermia's sexual impulses.

At the same time that Shakespeare examines the
disruptive power of natural desire he protects the
city from his poetic vision by suggesting the
unreality of the wood--making it an area of
artificiality, dream, moonlight and madness.
Artificiality occurs in the patterning of the pairs
of lovers. Hermia and Lysander are lovers.
Demetrius pursues Helena. And Hermia looks for
Lysander. Finally, the lovers return to their
original state--Hermia matched with Lysander and
Helena with Demetrius. All of the Athenian lovers
come under the control of another set of lovers,
Titania and Oberon, which parallels the control of
still more lovers, Theseus and Hippolyta, in Athens.

The insistence on the playlike character of what
the audience sees in the wood also emphasizes the
artificiality of the poet's work. Oberon and Puck
are like stage managers of the wood scenes with the
Athenian lovers. Puck's association with the poet
writing A Midsummer Night's Dream is suggested by his
ability to make serious story into a comedy, as both
Shakespeare and the mechanicals do:

The wisest aunt, telling the saddest tale,
Sometime for three-foot stool mistaketh me;
Then slip I from her bum, down topples she,
And "tailor" cries, and falls into a cough;
And then the whole quire hold their hips and laugh,
And waxen in their mirth, and neeze, and swear
A merrier hour was never wasted there.
(II.i.51-57)

Because he is invisible, Oberon is able to watch the
Athenians without their noticing him, just as the
audience watches the actors without the actors'
seeming to notice them. And, of course, Puck
observes the "fond pageant" (III.ii.114) put on by
the Athenian lovers in the wood. A series of plays
also calls attention to Shakespeare's production of a
play. The play of Pyramus and Thisbe parallels that
of the Athenian lovers and is observed in rehearsal
by Puck and later by the Athenian lovers.

The dreamlike character of the pastoral is
implied by the sleeping of the lovers, who are
awakened by Theseus and his party. At first, it is
unclear where the dream has ended:

                    Are you sure
That we are awake? It seems to me
That yet we sleep, we dream. Do not you think
The Duke was here, and bid us follow him?
(IV.i.195-98)

But then Hermia, Helena, and Lysander agree that the
Duke was indeed there, and Demetrius attributes only
the time spent in the wood to dream:

Why, then, we are awake. Let's follow him,
And by the way let us recount our dreams.
(IV.i.201-02)

Yet Shakespeare protects his play more generally by
allowing the possibility that it is a dream in its
entirety. Puck leaves the stage saying,

        If we shadows have offended,
Think but this, and all is mended:
That you have but slumb'red here,
While these visions did appear.
And this weak and idle theme,
No more yielding but a dream.
(V.i.425-30)

The unreality of the wood is further suggested by associating it with moonlight and madness. In Elizabethan times "wood" meant "mad" as well as "forest," and the play itself exploits this pun:

> Thou told'st me they were stol'n unto this wood;
> And here am I, and wood within this wood,
> Because I cannot meet my Hermia.
>   (II.i.191-93)

Making the Elizabethan association of the moon with madness, Egeus accuses Lysander of bewitching Hermia by wooing her in the moonlight (I.i.27-35). The wood is a place of moonlight and "moonlight revels" (II.i.141), and Puck demonstrates the wood's association with love madness:

> Cupid is a knavish lad,
> Thus to make poor females mad.
>   (III.ii.440-41)

As Ernest Schanzer points out, the events of the play are associated both with Midsummer's Eve and May Day. The Eve of May Day or Walpurgisnight and Midsummer Night or St. John's Eve are the two chief nights of the year for witchcraft and magic. Midsummer Eve was specifically associated with flower magic like that of love-in-idleness and with madness.[13] Most importantly, of course, love itself is called a kind of madness. Helena voices this view:

> Things base and vile, holding no quantity,
> Love can transpose to form and dignity.
> Love looks not with the eyes, but with the mind,
> And therefore is winged Cupid painted blind.
> Nor hath Love's mind of any judgment taste;
> Wings, and no eyes, figure unheedy haste:
> And therefore is Love said to be a child,
> Because in choice he is so oft beguiled.
>   (I.i.232-39)

This is precisely the result which love-in-idleness produces in the woods:

> Flower of this purple dye,
> Hit with Cupid's archery,
> Sink in apple of his eye.
> When his love he doth espy,

Let her shine as gloriously
As the Venus of the sky.
(III.ii.102-07)

Shakespeare, then, reveals the nature of desire
but obscures his revelation by suggesting its
unreality and absurdity. Since his play is comedy,
desire does not endanger the city. In comedy the
heroes' and heroines' desires ultimately harmonize
with the city, but in tragedy the conflict remains,
as in the Pyramus and Thisbe story.[14]

Bottom's actions suggest a further danger of
poetry. Tragedy endangers the decent regime by
preparing the way for tyranny. As suggested above,
tragedy brings the desires out into the open and
encourages them without bringing them into harmony
with the city. The story of Pyramus and Thisbe makes
fulfillment of their love seem appealing and
desirable. At the same time in causing the audience
to lament the deaths of its hero and heroine the
tragedy gives free rein to pity, fear and terror,
passions which the city must not indulge if its
citizens are to put law above all else and to exhibit
courage in the face of threats to the city. The
ultimate result of allowing too much scope for the
passions is a turning of the regime toward tyranny.

Bottom first suggests this possibility when he
inquires of Quince whether Pyramus, the part Bottom
must play, is "A lover, or a tyrant" (I.ii.22). The
association of lover and tyrant is not accidental.
The man whose desires know no limits is the tyrant.
Tyranny provides the freedom, power and money a lover
needs, for the tyrannical man is the man who can
fulfill his desires at the expense of the city. He
is willing to break the law or to deny convention in
his quest for all good things of nature. That
Shakespeare has this in mind is supported by his
reference in other plays to the tyrant as the lover
who fulfills his sexual desire as he wishes.

The concept of desire as tyrannical plays a major
role in at least two of Shakespeare's plays. In
Measure for Measure the principal action concerns the
lover as tyrant. Angelo's attempt to fulfill his
illicit desire for Isabella constitutes the main
instance of his tyranny. And, as Paul Cantor argues,
in Antony and Cleopatra Antony's love for Cleopatra
enslaves him to her to the extent that it becomes a

tyrant which crushes all other elements in his soul.[15]

References to lover as tyrant appear in other plays. In <u>Romeo</u> <u>and</u> <u>Juliet</u>, for example, Sampson, one of Capulet's servants, makes the connection jokingly:

Sampson. I will show myself a tyrant.
When I have fought with men, I will be civil with the maids--I will cut off their heads.
Gregory. The heads of the maids?
Sampson. Ay, the heads of the maids or their maidenheads.

(I.i.23-28)

In <u>Troilus</u> <u>and</u> <u>Cressida</u> the lover as tyrant reappears in Cressida's fear that Troilus' desire will become despotic when he discovers her feelings for him: "If I confess much you will play the tyrant" (III.ii.121).

Perhaps the best commentary on Bottom's reaction to performing Pyramus and Thisbe occurs in the ultimate source of the critique of tragedy as a forerunner of tyranny. According to Socrates, Euripides claims that tyrants gain their wisdom from tragic poets. These poets, like Euripides, "extol tyranny as a condition 'equal to that of a god' and add much else, too." Furthermore, "going around to the other cities, gathering crowds, and hiring fine, big and persuasive voices, they draw the regimes towards tyrannies and democracies."[16]

In Socrates' view, tragedy is honored "most of all by tyrants" and "in the second place, by democracy" (568c) because it requires an emancipation of and appeal to desires which are suppressed by other regimes as dangerous to moral virtue. Socrates uses as an example "the tragic poets imitating one of the heroes in mourning and making quite an extended speech with lamentation." He goes on to point out that in our private life we try not to give way to such passions, but "we praise as a good poet the man who most puts us in this state." As for sex and all the desires, poetic imitation "fosters and waters them when they ought to be dried up and sets them up as rulers in us when they ought to be ruled" (<u>Republic</u> 605-606).

42

Bottom exhibits both parts of the Platonic critique of tragedy. Like the tragic poet, Bottom is eager to water the passions and displays a fascination with the tyrant. The weaver's enthusiasm for the part of Pyramus arises from a desire to move the audience to pity with just such a speech as Socrates mentions:

> That will ask some tears in the true
> performing of it: if I do it, let
> the audience look to their eyes. I
> will move storms, I will condole in
> some measure.
>
> (I.ii.26-28)

Despite the attraction of the lover, Bottom's "chief humor is for a tyrant." He reserves his highest praises for Hercules who has become godlike through military prowess which has allowed him to meet and conquer death:

> The raging rocks
> And shivering shocks
> Shall break the locks
>   Of prison gates:
> And Phibbus' car
> Shall shine from afar,
> And make and mar
>   The foolish Fates.
>
> (I.ii.33-39)

The appeal of such a life is not lost on Bottom who, like the tyrant, wants to experience everything. At the mention of each new part in the Pyramus and Thisbe play he cannot contain himself, and he reveals that he wishes to play all the parts--Thisbe, Pyramus, the lion.

The elements of the Platonic argument are not explicitly stated in A Midsummer Night's Dream. Rather they are embodied in the actions of Bottom. Elsewhere Shakespeare does make explicit reference to ideas derived from Plato. Measure for Measure contains the argument that license leads to tyranny. There Claudio explains to Lucio that the restraint which Angelo exercises arises

> From too much liberty, my Lucio, liberty.
> As surfeit is the father of much fast,
> So every scope by the immoderate use

Turns to restraint. Our natures do pursue,
Like rats that ravin down their proper bane,
A thirsty evil, and when we drink, we die.
                    (I.ii.128-33)[17]

Shakespeare's reconciliation of poetry and
politics and his defense of poetry, to be discussed
in the following chapters, represent the positions of
a man who knows his weaknesses. A Midsummer Night's
Dream illustrates the dangers of poetry to politics
while protecting its audience from that threat.
Shakespeare examines tragedy's threat to the city
through the Pyramus and Thisbe story and its
parallels to the story of the young Athenian lovers.
Tragic drama makes apparent the conflict of the
natural with the city without ever bringing the two
into harmony. It reveals that love can conflict with
the laws of the city and with virtue and that it can
lead to discord within the city. Shakespeare
protects the audience from his revelation of the
disruptive power of desire by suggesting the
unreality of the wood where his revelation occurs and
by pointing to love's absurdity. His play further
protects its audience by virtue of its comic
character, which produces ultimate harmony between
the lovers' desires and the city. Bottom's
fascination with acting a tyrant playfully suggests
the seriousness of the case against tragedy: it can
lead to tyranny.

Notes

[1]D'Orsay Pearson ["'Unkinde' Theseus: A study in Renaissance Mythography," _English Literary Renaissance_, 4 (1974), 276-98] argues that Theseus' "classical, medieval, and Renaissance image as an unnatural, perfidious, and unfaithful lover and father far outweighed his accomplishment in organizing the demes of Athens into a single political unit or his reputation as an icon for the virtue of friendship." Finding Shakespeare's Theseus "no different," Pearson faults him for "love avarice," lack of charity to other lovers, for neglect of duty, and for an irrational shift from tyranny to charity in his treatment of the lovers. The text explains my defense of Theseus as a political figure. Also, for a discussion of Renaissance views favorable to Theseus, see Paul A. Olson, "_A Midsummer Night's Dream_ and the Meaning of Court Marriage," _ELH_, 24 (1957), 101-02 and Geoffrey Bullough, _Narrative and Dramatic Sources of Shakespeare_, I (London and New York, 1957), pp 369-69.

[2]See, for example, E. K. Chambers, "The Occasion of 'A Midsummer Night's Dream,'" _A Book of Homage to Shakespeare_, ed. Israel Gollanez (Oxford, 1916), pp. 154-60; Enid Welford, _The Court Masque_ (Cambridge and New York, 1927), p. 324; Sir Arthur Quiller-Couch and J. Dover Wilson, ed., _A Midsummer Night's Dream_ (Cambridge, 1924), p. xv; Paul N. Siegel, "_A Midsummer Night's Dream_ and the Wedding Guests," _SQ_, 4 (1953), 139-44; John W. Draper, "The Queen Makes a Match and Shakespeare a Comedy," _Yearbook of English Studies_, 2 (1972), 61-67.

[3]Paul N. Siegel, "_A Midsummer Night's Dream_ and the Wedding Guests," _SQ_, 4 (1953), 142.

[4]James L. Calderwood, "_A Midsummer Night's Dream_: The Illusion of Drama," _MLQ_, 26 (1965), 509-10.

[5]All references to Shakespeare in the text are to _Complete Signet Classic Shakespeare_, ed. Sylvan Barnet (New York, 1972).

[6]As Bernard Weinberg points out, one of the primary interests of Renaissance literary criticism was Plato's discussion in the _Republic_ of the poet as imitator of mere appearances [_A History of Literary_

<u>Criticism</u> <u>in</u> <u>the</u> <u>Italian</u> <u>Renaissance</u>, I (Chicago,
1961), 251]. In addition, Ficino's Latin translation
of the <u>Republic</u>, completed in 1482, was available to
Renaissance authors [Paul Shorey, <u>Platonism</u>: <u>Ancient</u>
<u>and</u> <u>Modern</u> (Berkeley, 1938), p. 121]. In my
references to Plato here and elsewhere I do not claim
that Shakespeare used Plato as a direct source, but
only that he shared ideas of his age which are often
most clearly understood in their ultimate source in
Plato. The Shorey and Weinberg volumes cited above
describe the pervasiveness of Plato's influence in
the Renaissance. If the mechanicals in <u>MND</u> are taken
to represent artisans who know more than the poet,
their knowledge of poetry at least is sadly lacking.

[7]Sidney, <u>An</u> <u>Apology</u> <u>for</u> <u>Poetry</u>, ed. Geoffrey
Shepherd (New York and London, 1973), pp. 123-25;
Thomas Lodge, <u>A</u> <u>Defence</u> <u>of</u> <u>Poetry</u> (1579), in
<u>Elizabethan</u> <u>Critical</u> <u>Essays</u>, ed. G. Gregory Smith, I
(London, 1937), 73; Sir John Harrington, <u>A</u> <u>Brief</u>
<u>Apology</u> <u>for</u> <u>Poetry</u> (1591), in Smith, II, 199-206.

[8]John Northbrooke, <u>A</u> <u>Treatise</u> <u>Against</u> <u>Dicing</u>
<u>Dancing</u>, <u>Plays</u> <u>and</u> <u>Interludes</u> (1577), Shakespeare
Society Publications 15 (Nendelin, Liechtenstein,
1966), p. 45. See also p. 51.

[9]See pp. 4-5 above.

[10]Jacopo Mazzoni, "On the Defense of the
Comedy," <u>Literary</u> <u>Criticism</u>: <u>Plato</u> <u>to</u> <u>Dryden</u>, ed.
Allan H. Gilbert (Detroit, 1962), p. 373.

[11]Torquato Tasso, <u>Discourses</u> <u>on</u> <u>the</u> <u>Heroic</u>
<u>Poem</u>, in <u>Literary</u> <u>Criticism</u>: <u>Plato</u> <u>to</u> <u>Dryden</u>, ed.
Allan H. Gilbert (Detroit, 1962), p. 468.

[12]Denis de Rougemont, <u>Love</u> <u>in</u> <u>the</u> <u>Western</u>
<u>World</u>, trans. Montgomery Belgion (Greenwich,
Connecticut, 1966), pp. 320-25.

[13]Ernest Schanzer, "The Central Theme of <u>A</u>
<u>Midsummer</u> <u>Night's</u> <u>Dream</u>," <u>UTQ</u>, 20 (1951), 233-38.

[14]In <u>Tragedy</u>: <u>A</u> <u>View</u> <u>of</u> <u>Life</u> (Ithaca, New
York, 1956), Henry Alonzo Myers argues that <u>A</u>
<u>Midsummer</u> <u>Night's</u> <u>Dream</u> is the comic equivalent of
<u>Romeo</u> <u>and</u> <u>Juliet</u>, but the subjects of the plays are
only superficially the same. The sets of lovers are
both "star-crossed" for a time. <u>Romeo</u> <u>and</u> <u>Juliet</u> is

about the need to put love of the city above love of the family. A city cannot survive if its citizens are not at peace with one another. The quarrel of the Capulets and Montagues destroys the best of the city's offspring and in this way threatens to destroy the city itself. Love, however, has the power to rise above family feuds and ultimately to unite the city.

[15]Chapter 6, especially p. 193.

[16]The Republic of Plato, trans. Allan Bloom (New York, 1968), § 568. All further references to this work are in the text. Many Renaissance critics seek to defend poetry from this attack. See, for example, Sir Thomas Elyot, The Boke Named Governour, ed. H. H. S. Croft (London, 1880), I, 71; Sidney, pp. 112, 117; Thomas Heywood, An Apology for Actors, in Literary Criticism: Plato to Dryden, ed. Allan H. Gilbert (Detroit, 1962), pp. 554, 561.

[17]As in Plato, Coriolanus depicts democracy as another regime which attends to the body. In that play the plebians are concerned principally with obtaining corn and reveal themselves unable to face bodily harm, fearful in the face of battle. The one patrician capable of intermediating between the patricians and the plebians is Menenius, a man characterized by his fondness for eating and drinking (II.i.47-43, 83-85).

CHAPTER III

A <u>MIDSUMMER</u> <u>NIGHT'S</u> <u>DREAM</u>: SHAKESPEARE'S DRAMATIC SOLUTION TO THE PROBLEMS POETRY POSES FOR POLITICS

There are basically two critical attitudes towards Theseus. One sees him as a representative of reason and of rational love as opposed to the madness and irrational love of the other Athenian lovers. His love becomes the norm or the social ideal.[1] Critics who espouse this attitude often refer to Theseus as the ideal ruler, and they give him the attitudes of the Theseus of Chaucer's <u>Knight's</u> <u>Tale</u>.[2] Like Chaucer's Theseus, he is seen as the reasonable man imposing order on nature. In the <u>Knight's</u> <u>Tale</u> Palamon and Arcite are friends who fall in love with the same woman, Emelye. They are fighting for her like wild animals when Theseus arrives. He is on an organized hunt for wild animals. Theseus stops the fighting and orders an organized contest between Palamon and Arcite according to civil regulation. The story is taken to suggest reason's conquest of the violent and erotic. Shakespeare's Theseus is seen likewise restoring order to nature in his conquest of the Amazons, women who have rebelled against nature by fighting men. The cry of Theseus' hounds like bells in phase (IV.i.126-29) becomes symbolic of this imposition of human pattern on nature.

The second basic attitude towards Theseus focuses on the limitations of his understanding. Critics with this attitude agree that Theseus represents rational love, reason, and the model ruler, but they emphasize the limitations of reason and of the understanding of a representative of good government. They see reason as making man fit for guiding the affairs of men, but not for fully understanding other aspects of the world--romantic love or poetry or grace. G. K. Hunter, for example, argues that it is a mistake to see the whole world from the point of view of Theseus and Hippolyta. He points out that the young lovers need not be judged as substandard simply because they lack the virtues of a ruler who lives in rational daylight, and he goes on to suggest that Theseus' rejection of art in the form of the lovers' dream is not the only viable position that Shakespeare presents to us. The lovers can live in the result of their dream.[3] Other critics suggest even greater limits to Theseus' view of the world. Sidney Homan, for example, argues that Theseus is unaware of the artist's ability to use reason in conjunction with imagination to give us "both a sense of a universal nature and a specific picture of things."[4] Critics such as Frank Kermode and Stephen Fender go even further to suggest that Theseus lacks an understanding of grace which is available to the poet.[5]

There is some truth in each of the two attitudes towards Theseus. As argued in Chapter II above, Theseus is the model politician who has subordinated his own desire to order in the city. As Chapter IV will argue, there are limitations to Theseus' ability to understand art and even perhaps the nature of grace. But both of the attitudes also require substantial modification. Although Theseus represents the best that politics has to offer, he has limitations even within his own sphere. He never fully understands the nature and strength of desire and therefore its danger to the city, and he is unable to control desire in his citizens. Rather the ability to understand desire and to control it rests with the poet.

The limitations of Theseus' understanding and his power are made clear in his actions towards the young Athenian lovers. When faced with the love of Hermia and Lysander, he upholds the law and gives Hermia the alternative of submitting to her father's will or of choosing between life in a nunnery and death. The play suggests that Theseus is inattentive to matters of the heart and their possible disruption of his domain. First, he admits that, having heard of Demetrius' inconstancy to Helena, he had forgotten to speak with him about it (I.i.111-14). Later Theseus indicates his misunderstanding of matters of love when he mistakes the lovers' reasons for being asleep on the edge of the wood. He explains that

> No doubt they rose up early to observe
> The rite of May; and, hearing our intent,
> Came here in grace of our solemnity.
> (IV.i.135-38)

But Lysander and Demetrius have fallen asleep because they are exhausted from chasing one another in their attempted duel, and Helena has slept after running away from the other three with Hermia running after her. The lovers are not there to display respect for their ruler, Theseus. Rather against his wishes, to disobey the law, they have run off into the wood. Desire has been strong enough to threaten the law and to produce potential conflict among Athens' citizens. Initially at least Theseus does not recognize the power of desire. Only after Lysander explains his and Hermia's intention to escape Athenian law does Theseus realize that a harmonious solution to the lovers' conflicts now requires the overbearing of Egeus' will in direct opposition to the law. Even if one were to allow that the lines at IV.ii.135-38 could be read as a tongue-in-cheek explanation for finding the lovers asleep, there is no sign at that point that Theseus recognizes the lovers' attempt to defy the law, for the following two lines indicate that he expects Hermia to follow his decree that she choose between a nunnery and acquiescing in her father's wishes.

A careful examination of the play's action reveals that the fairies have more power than Theseus to produce order in Athens. In fact, during most of A Midsummer Night's Dream, the portion which takes place in the wood, Theseus functions as a spectator more than as a participant. His and Hippolyta's comments at V.i about the story of the Athenian lovers as a work of art give the reader a strong sense of the hand of the poet in creating the story of the young lovers' time in the wood and, by extension, in creating the whole of A Midsummer Night's Dream. This makes the fairies' power to produce order suggestive of the poet's ordering power.

The atmosphere of the wood has made critics forget that the fairies do produce order. The wood outside of Athens where the fairies preside is often associated by critics with the irrationality and inconstancy of love. Critics see the madness and darkness of the wood as a contrast to the rationality and daylight of Athens and its ruler. This view is accurate on the surface (see pp. 40-41 above), but there is also madness before the lovers get to the wood. Hermia and Lysander have loved. Demetrius has been inconstant. Helena has loved Demetrius although he has spurned her, and Demetrius has loved Hermia although she has spurned him. Even before she gets to the wood Helena recognizes the irrationality of love:

Through Athens I am thought as fair as she.
But what of that? Demetrius thinks not so;
He will not know what all but he do know.
And as he errs, doting on Hermia's eyes,
So I, admiring of his qualities.
Things base and vile, holding no quantity,
Love can transpose to form and dignity.
Love looks not with the eyes, but with the mind,
And therefore is winged Cupid painted blind.
Nor hath Love's mind of any judgment taste;
Wings, and no eyes, figure unheedy haste:
And therefore is Love said to be a child,
Because in choice he is so oft beguiled.
                    (I.i.227-41)

Further, the wood does not produce simply madness
and inconstancy. There are two juices,
love-in-idleness which will make "man or woman madly
dote" (II.i.171) and another herb which takes away
all error (III.ii.368). By applying love-in-idleness
to Demetrius' eyes the fairies have returned him to
his first love, and once Lysander's error is remedied
with the second herb the fairies have ordered the
desire of the Athenian lovers by making them into
mutually affectionate couples. When this has been
accomplished, the fairies produce constancy in the
lovers. The young Athenians will continue to love
their respective mates. Oberon promises that

        back to Athens shall the lovers wend
With league whose date till death shall never end.
                    (III.ii.372-73)

And later he repeats that

        So shall all the couples three
        Ever true in loving be.
                    (V.i.409-10)

The fairies, then, have done what Theseus could not
do. They have sorted out the lovers so that they are
paired harmoniously, and they have produced constancy
in the three sets of lovers.

    There are other indications that the fairies
rather than Theseus control the action. The play
suggests that order has already been restored before
Theseus enters. Titania and Oberon have already
joined each other in a dance at the end of which
Oberon says, "Now thee and I are new in amity." As

Oberon has said earlier, once Oberon has the Indian boy and Titania's eye has been released from its love for Bottom, "all things shall be at peace" (III.ii.374-77). Earlier the control of Titania and Oberon over natural forces has been implied by their quarrel's effect on nature (II.i.81-117). It has generally destroyed the order of the seasons, and in so doing it has caused destruction in nature in the form of fogs and floods, rotted crops, and the death of cattle from murrain. It has also caused destruction in the human world in the form of epidemics, and its filling up the "nine men's morris" with mud and its ruining paths "for lack of tread" are symbolic of its destruction of the order which man attempts to impose on nature. Now Titania and Oberons' amity suggests a comparable concord in nature and in the human world. Oberon foreknows that Theseus will overrule Egeus and that the three pairs of lovers will marry tomorrow:

Now thou and I are new in amity,
And will tomorrow midnight solemnly
Dance in Duke Theseus' house triumphantly,
And bless it to all fair prosperity.
There shall the pairs of faithful lovers be
Wedded, with Theseus, all in jollity.
(IV.i.90-95)

The fairies have been responsible for the production of order. Order has not resulted from Theseus' control or from any independent change in the young lovers' vision. Although the lovers have been altered in the harmony and constancy of their loves, there is no indication that their characters have been transformed. As Demetrius explains it,

I wot not by what power--
But by some power it is--my love to Hermia,
Melted as the snow, seems to me now
As the remembrance of an idle gaud,
Which in my childhood I did dote upon;
And all the faith, the virtue of my heart,
The object and the pleasure of mine eye,
Is only Helena.
(IV.i.167-74)

The lovers' reactions to the Pyramus and Thisbe play also imply a lack of alteration in their understanding. The play suggests to none of them the dangers caused by their own desire and by their trip to the wood. Rather they laugh and joke at the ineptitude of the mechanicals' production.

Shakespeare makes the fairies rather than Theseus responsible for ordering desire because he wants to point out that if it were not for the poet the story of the lovers could have been a tragedy like the Pyramus and Thisbe story. A tragedy would imply that there were forces in nature or in the city hostile to the happiness of the lovers. Shakespeare produces a comedy by making the forces of nature, as represented by Titania and Oberon, harmonize both with the happiness of the lovers and the laws of the city. Titania and Oberon have made desire conform to the laws of the city by sorting out the pairs of lovers and then by defending the virtues necessary to the city--constancy and marriage. On the cosmic level they have produced this harmony through their renewed amity.

The study of Katherine M. Briggs supports the view that Shakespeare is making a point in attributing to his fairies the production of order. Briggs argues that fairies are traditionally concerned with mischief but that Shakespeare's fairies are striking for their benevolence. Titania's followers drive away owls, snakes, spiders, newts, and bats--all creatures of witchcraft. Oberon distinguishes himself from night-wandering spirits.[6] Puck mentions the "ghosts," "damned spirits all," who inhabit the night so that daylight will not shame them (III.ii.378-88), but Oberon suggests that his actions can take place in the light of day:

> But we are spirits of another sort.
> I with the Morning's love have oft made sport;
> And, like a forester, the groves may tread,
> Even till the eastern gate, all fiery-red
> Opening on Neptune with fair blessed beams,
> Turns into yellow gold his salt green streams.
> (III.ii.389-93)

Shakespeare has made his fairies acceptable to Athens by having them order desire and support the virtues necessary to the city.

The quarrel of Titania and Oberon helps to explain how one must deal with desire. It does not, as Paul Olson suggests in his influential article,

symbolize the appropriate hierarchy of heavenly love,
as represented by Oberon, over earthly love, as
represented by Titania.[7] The earthly is apparent
in both Titania and Oberon. Both are jealous, and
both accuse one another of infidelity. Titania says
that Oberon has wooed the "amorous Phillida" and his
"warrior love," Hippolyta (II.i.64-73), while Oberon
attacks Titania for her "love of Theseus" (II.i.76).
There is no reason to find Titania lustful in her
attachment to the Indian boy. She tells us that she
keeps the boy for the sake of the love she felt for
his mother, a votaress of Titania's order
(II.i.122-37), and the boy is young, still a "child"
(II.i.122). Further, the play as a whole does not
denigrate earthly love as the love between men and
women. It mocks it at times, but in the end the play
celebrates the mutual affection of the three sets of
lovers protected by a fourth set, Titania and Oberon.

A more fruitful line of criticism concerning
Titania began with C. L. Barber's discussion of the
play in Shakespeare's Festive Comedy. He takes note
of a side of Titania other than the erotic. In her
description of the fun she shared with her votaress,
Barber sees a "glimpse of women who gossip alone,
apart from men and feeling now no need of them,
rejoicing in their own special part of life's power.
At such moments the child, not the lover, is their
object." Later Titania fulfills the play's
association of love with growth by giving up the
Indian boy to the man's world of Oberon and renewing
their ritual marriage.[8]

There are three aspects of Titania which require
explanation. She is associated with childbirth, with
chastity and with the forces of erotic love. These
three aspects derive in part from Titania's
identification with Diana. It is generally thought
that the source of Titania's name is Ovid's
Metamorphoses (III, 173)[9] where "Titania" is an
epithet given Diana as a descendant of the Titans.
Titania's mention of the pregnant votaress of her
order (II.i.133-37) suggests that she is fulfilling
Diana's function as goddess of childbirth. In her
association with the moon Titania takes on other
aspects of Diana as goddess of the moon. Critics
have frequently pointed out that Titania and the
other fairies preside over the night: Lysander and
Hermia escape to the wood at midnight, and Hippolyta
calls the story told by the four Athenian lovers

about their time in the wood the "story of the night"
(V.i.23). Oberon's first words to Titania are "Ill
met by moonlight" (II.i.57). "Moonshine" recurs in
the Pyramus and Thisbe parallel to the Athenian
lovers' tale. The moon itself appears as Diana the
huntress, "a silver bow / New-bent in heaven"
(I.i.9-10), and as Diana goddess of chastity, "the
cold and fruitless and moon" (I.i.73, also II.i.162)
which laments "some enforcèd chastity" (III.i.200).
The moon also appears as the heavenly body presiding
over erotic love,[10] the moonlight by which,
according to Egeus, Lysander bewitches Hermia
(I.i.30-35).

Titania is associated, then, with the goddess of
childbirth, with the goddess of chastity, and also
with the forces of erotic love. The quarrel of
Titania and Oberon implies that these three aspects
of humankind ought to be in a particular harmonious
relation to one another. This quarrel and its effect
on nature suggest that Titania and Oberon begin in an
improper relationship to one another. The cause is
the changeling whom Titania has kept, but she has
also foresworn Oberon's bed and company. In doing
so, she has made herself one of the play's three
examples of women subsisting outside the company of
men. The other two are Hippolyta, Queen of the
Amazons, before her conquest by Theseus and the
girlhood of Hermia and Helena.

Life without men has its appeal. The innocent
childhood love before one is aware of the body and
desire involves a kind of carefree and spiritual
union which is impossible later in life--in
hererosexual love. Helena and Hermia

> Like to a double cherry, grew together seeming
> parted,
> But yet an union in partition;
> Two lovely berries molded on one stem;
> So, with two seeming bodies, but one heart;
> Two of the first, like coats in heraldry,
> Due but to one, and crownèd with one crest.
>   (III.ii.208-14)

They are like The Winter's Tale's "twinned lambs,"
the youthful Leontes and Polixenes, who

> The doctrine of ill-doing, knew not nor dreamed
> That any did; had we pursued that life,

And our weak spirits ne'er been higher reared
With stronger blood, we should have answered heaven
Boldly, "not guilty"; the imposition cleared,
Hereditary ours.
                         (I.ii.69-74)

Ultimately, however, one cannot deny the body.
Men and women must recognize that they are of
composite nature. A few may be meant for the "single
blessedness" of the nunnery, but they will find their
happiness after death. The married life, however, is
"earthlier happy" (I.i.76). The foolishness of men
who cannot understand their own mixed natures is
epitomized in the "little academe" of the King of
Navarre in Love's Labor's Lost. Navarre's court
takes an oath to devote itself to the contemplative
life and to deny the body by seeing no ladies, by
fasting, and by sleeping only three hours a night.
Berowne points out that most men are not capable of
the philosophic life which is the ideal of Navarre:

Small have continual plodders ever won
Save base authority from others books.
                         (I.i.86-87)

The men of the little academe are so ignorant of
themselves that they all fall in love and are
foresworn soon after they take their oaths. The same
representation of earthly love as a combination of
body and soul appears in As You Like It, where
Orlando complains to Ganymede that he "can live no
longer by thinking" (V.ii.50) of his love without
having her before him.

Once Hermia and Helena love men they must
recognize two bodies. Each must choose a different
lover. For most earthly lovers there is no Platonic
ladder of love moving from love of a particular
beauty to love of beauty in general. Rather there is
the opposite impulse--to assume that the ideal beauty
is available in one's own love. This is the charm
Oberon offers as he anoints Demetrius' eyes with love
in idleness:

When his love he doth espy,
Let her shine as gloriously
As the Venus of the sky.
                         (III.ii.105-07)

It matches Helena's claim that

> Things base and vile, holding no quantity
> Love can transpose to form and dignity.
> (I.i.232-33)

or Theseus' characterization of the lover as seeing "Helen's beauty in a brow of Egypt" (V.i.11).

Erotic love is necessary to the city for the simple reason that a civil society must reproduce its citizens. As Benedick argues in _Much Ado_, the "world must be peopled" (II.iii.237). In _A Midsummer Night's Dream_ Titania and Oberon preside over erotic love as well as over the limitations which constancy and the orderly pairing of men and women put on it. When Titania has foresworn Oberon's marriage bed, there is disorder both in nature and in the patterns which man attempts to impose upon it. One may assume that this disorder would extend to the city in its attempts to control human nature. Once Titania and Oberon renew their harmonious relationship, then they can perform their proper function by guaranteeing fertility to the city through blessing the marriage beds of its rulers, Theseus and Hippolyta, and of its citizens, the young Athenian couples. In making this blessing Titania retains her function as goddess of childbirth, but now she shares it with Oberon. Oberon's inclusion of constancy as part of the joint blessing allows Titania to retain her function as goddess of chastity, now applied to married love.

The escapades of the young Athenian lovers have revealed some of the ways that the erotic can get out of hand. Titania's love for Bottom reveals another.[11] If love fastens on an improper object, then it can become mere "dotage," as does Titania's love for Bottom: Once her error has been removed by "Diana's bud," Titania's love is directed toward an appropriate object, Oberon.

If the poet's abilities are superior to the politican's in understanding and bringing a solution to the problem of desire, it is important to recognize that Shakespeare's solution is spurious to some degree. It is produced by magic herbs and by fairies whose reality the audience might doubt. Only Puck and Oberon have prevented the lovers from harming one another. The story of the wood appears to the young lovers as a dream and to Theseus as simply untrue, and Shakespeare playfully refuses to vouch for the seriousness of his drama by having Puck advise the audience to consider it a dream. All of this suggests that Shakespeare recognizes an intransigent incompatibility between desire and politics. He realizes that desire is disorderly and can produce conflict and upset the law. He also sees that law is sometimes of necessity incompatible with the fulfillment of desire.

[1]See, for example, Schanzer, pp. 233-38; Siegel, pp. 139-44; Olson, pp. 95-119; Calderwood, pp. 506-22.

[2]See, for example, Olson, pp. 101-02, 107; Bullough, I, 368-69; Young, pp. 117-18. D'Orsay Pearson takes exception to the idea that the Renaissance image of Theseus was entirely favorable (see p. 45 note 1 above).

[3]Hunter, pp. 18-20.

[4]Sidney R. Homan, "The Single World of A Midsummer Night's Dream," Bucknell Review, 17 (1969), 78-79.

[5]Frank Kermode, "The Mature Comedies," in Early Shakespeare, eds. John Russell Brown and Bernard Harris (New York, 1961), pp. 218-20; Stephen Fender, Shakespeare: A Midsummer Night's Dream (London, 1968), pp. 48-58.

[6]Katherine M. Briggs, The Anatomy of Puck (London, 1959), pp. 45-46.

[7]Olson, pp. 107-11.

[8]C. L. Barber, Shakespeare's Festive Comedy (Princeton, 1959), pp. 135-38.

[9]Bullough, I, 371.

[10]Olson argues that Shakespeare develops Titania from a single one of the three aspects of Diana, from Hecate or Proserpina (pp. 109-11).

[11]John A. Allen argues that Titania's attentions to Bottom should be regarded "more as those of doting mother to child than those of lover to beloved" ["Bottom and Titania," SQ, 18 (1967), 115], but compare this with Puck's report that his "mistress with a monster is in love" (III.ii.6).

Chapter IV

A MIDSUMMER NIGHT'S DREAM:

SHAKESPEARE'S DEFENSE OF POETRY

Shakespeare may recognize the nature of desire, but the questionable reality of his solution would give credence to Theseus' claim that the young lovers' story has no more validity than a "fairy toy" or an ancient myth. And yet when Shakespeare playfully includes disclaimers of any reality in his work, he writes in the Platonic tradition of a Socrates always pleading ignorance. In the tradition the dream appears in two senses. A man who is dreaming is one who does not see clearly what is true. Or a man who is dreaming is one who has left his body behind so that the soul is free to view truth unhampered. The first sort of dreamer appears in Plato's Republic, where those who do not know how to employ dialectic can at most know only right opinion, the phantom of the good produced by dreams and sleeping through one's present life (543c, see also 520c). The second sort of dreamer occurs in the Symposium, where Socrates says that his knowledge is only a dream, but at the end of the banquet Socrates is the only one who has resisted the call of the body and is still awake.[1] The two views of dreams appear in Castiglione's Renaissance version of the ladder of love. At one point sleep is the condition in which men have their eyes closed to the highest reality: the soul, "as it were raised out of a most deepe sleepe," through "the studies of true Philosophie . . . openeth the eyes that all men have" to a vision of angelic beauty. But later sleep is the condition which frees the soul from the earthly so that it may reach a vision of the heavenly: "And otherwhile when the stirring vertues of the bodie are withdrawne alone through earnest beholding, either fast bound through sleepe, when she is not hindred by them, she feeleth a certaine privie smell of the right Angelike beautie. . . ."[2]

Macrobius in his Commentary on the Dream of Scipio also provided the Renaissance with dual possibilities for the value of dream. Macrobius classifies dreams under five main types. Two, the nightmare and apparition, are false dreams. The other three--the enigmatic, the prophetic, and the oracular--are true dreams which provide us with a means of foretelling the future.[3]

Shakespeare leaves unclear which category of dream describes his play, but in A Midsummer Night's Dream he reveals that he understands how both interpretations could apply to poetry. Poetry could represent either a dream which is untrue or a dream containing the highest truths. Theseus' speech on poetry presents the grounds for an attack on poetry as well as suggesting the possible grounds for its defense. Shakespeare treats the subject thoroughly, including in Theseus' speech references to the major clichés of Elizabethan poetic theory.

The first basis of Theseus' attack is the imagination's tendency to distort:

Lovers and madmen have such seething brains,
Such shaping fantasies, that apprehend
More than cool reason ever comprehends.
The lunatic, the lover and the poet
Are of imagination all compact.
One sees more devils than vast hell can hold,
That is the madman. The lover, all as frantic,
Sees Helen's beauty in a brow of Egypt.
                                        (V.i.4-11)

As William Rossky explains, in the Renaissance the imagination is always seen as one faculty operating within a hierarchy of faculties:

> The general course of communications runs from the perception of the outward senses to common sense, or directly to imagination, which unites the various reports of the sense that are in turn submitted to the examination of a rational power and then passed to memory which retains the impressions and reflects them back to the Imagination and Sensible Reason, should they turn to it to recall past incidents. Beyond these faculties and functions lies the seeing and judging power of the highest Understanding, which in turn informs the Will.

62

A healthy imagination reflects only accurate images of reality, but an imagination which reports falsely the objects and matters perceived misleads injured minds, like those of madmen. In this latter case, man's reason, which is dependent on imagination, is faulty. Since reason discriminates good from evil, the ultimate result of a distorting imagination is immorality:

> But if a frenzy do possess the brain;
> It so distorts and blots the forms of things,
> As Phantasy proves altogether vain,
> And to the Wit, no true relation brings.
>
> Then doth the Wit admitting all for true,
> Build fond conclusions on those idle grounds!
> Then doth it fly the Good, and ill pursue!
> Believing all that this false spy propounds.[4]

One source of distortion in the imagination is passion. Affections "In fancy make us heare, feele, see impressions, / Such as out of our sense they doe not borrow." Lovers' imaginations, then, are considered corrupt.[5]

Although the disrepute of the imagination in the Renaissance is well documented by Rossky, writing dealing specifically with poetry is more apt to attack poets on the grounds that they are liars.[6] This is the criticism at which Theseus glances when he argues that the

> imagination bodies forth
> The forms of things unknown, the poet's pen
> Turns them to shapes, and gives to airy nothing
> A local habitation and a name.
>   (V.i.14-17)

The third basis for Theseus' attack lies in his equation of the poet with the madman. As Rossky points out, madness is often equated with an improperly functioning imagination. One cure for madness is the confinement of the patient to a dark room or to a room with no pictures to stimulate the imagination.[7] The relating of poetry to madness also derives from the Renaissance notion that poetry is an irrational activity springing from possession, rapture, or frenzy. This notion is suggested by Theseus' characterization of the poet's eye as rolling "in a fine frenzy" (V.i.12). The Renaissance

view of poetry as possession is derived from Plato's
Ion, where Socrates argues that good epic poets

> have their excellence, not from art,
> but are inspired, possessed, and
> thus utter all these admirable
> poems. So it is also with the good
> lyric poets; as the worshiping
> Corybantes are not in their senses
> when they dance, so the lyric poets
> are not in their senses when they
> make these lovely lyric poems.[8]

Supporters of poetry relate poetic possession to
divine inspiration,[9] but a sceptic would be
inclined to call it simple lunacy.

In criticizing the poets for giving "to airy
nothing a local habitation and a name," Theseus
argues that poetry is simply not to be believed,
whereas later he at least allows that poetry could
present "shadows" by imitating the things of the
world around us (V.i.212-13). In this latter case,
the attack on poetry would amount to an argument that
products of art would be further removed from reality
than those things which are imitated (see pp. 33-34
above). This critique of poetry as mimetic is
embodied in the mechanicals' excessively literal
play. Wall must carry "lime and roughcast" to
indicate what he represents, and Moonshine must carry
a lantern. The Duke sees the humor in the attempted
imitation and argues that the players must carry it
one step closer to reality by having the man inside
the moon. Even without the mechanicals' ineptitude,
imitation which attempts an accurate picture of
actual things is bound to fail.

There is, however, another view of imitation
suggested by the play. Notice that although Theseus
does not "believe these antique fables or these fairy
toys" (V.i.2-3), his words suggest a theory of poetry
which does not depend on simple copying of objects in
the world around us. According to this theory,
poetry is imitation of essences (see p. 8 above),
either generalized from particulars or derived
through some superior vision or inspiration. The
"things unknown" are not necessarily untrue. They
are derived through a poet's vision, the product of
glancing "from heaven to earth, from earth to heaven"
(V.i.12-17). The poet recognizes the divine pattern

in heaven, the ideal, and tries to find a way to represent it and to fulfill it on earth. The poet also understands what is on earth. He looks for the godly in man and tries to make man as godlike as possible. To move man to virtue the poet's understanding of man's nature must be general. In addition to knowing the godlike or what must be encouraged in man, he must also know the earthly or what must be suppressed or controlled. In other words, the poet must understand desire.

What the poet represents is not strictly an idea; it is the embodiment of an ideal or a universal on earth, in the form of particular actors and of particular actions. The poet's representation, then, in a further sense partakes of the earthly, the particular, as well as the heavenly. One technique for the production of virtue is its embodiment in heroes such as Theseus. Theseus is the man of action who has performed great feats for the sake of the city. Although in A Midsummer Night's Dream Theseus' heroic actions are represented as in the past, the play is a celebration of the hero's victory over the Amazons through a celebration of his marriage. The play also represents the ruler's actions in a time of peace. He is the dignified lover and lawgiver.

The poet's glancing "from heaven to earth, from earth to heaven" has further implications concerning the poet's knowledge about the gods. One of the poet's means of bringing the pattern of virtue to earth is through his representation of the gods as supporting virtue. Socrates recognizes this function of poetry when in Books II and III of the Republic he attacks the poets for saying untrue things about the gods, i.e., things which imply that the gods themselves are not virtuous or that they do not cause good. Although Sidney believes that Christianity has eliminated the difficulty in knowing the true representation of God, he finds value in the Platonic argument which occurred when there were "many and many-fashioned gods."

> Plato found fault that the poets of his time filled the world with wrong opinions of the gods, making light tales of that unspotted essence, and therefore would not have the youth depraved with such opinions. [10]

Shakespeare seems to be fashioning supernatural beings supporting virtue in his depiction of Titania and Oberon. He may emphasize his own part in their creation by choosing the pagan atmosphere of Athens for his play and by making its gods pagan. There is evidence that Shakespeare may have emphasized the classical background of the play by having Theseus and his court dressed in ancient costume, as Madeline Doran and D'Orsay Pearson suggest. Puck is to recognize Demetrius by the Athenian garments he is wearing, and Titania refers to Hippolyta as Oberon's "buskin'd mistress and . . . warrior love." Pearson notes that a mid-fifteenth century engraving of Theseus and Hippolyta depicts Theseus in Oriental-style metal armor and Hippolyta in the full-length draped gown of classical Greece.[11] In addition, relying on no specific source for his play, Shakespeare himself creates the action of the play and the gods' control over the lives of humans. As argued in Chapter III, Shakespeare fashions the action of Titania and Oberon so that they bring order to the city, virtue and fertility to the Athenians, and general cosmic harmony.

As just argued, the "things unknown" referred to by Theseus could be universals or gods known to the poet who glances "from heaven to earth, from earth to heaven." The Renaissance provides two possible sources for the poet's special knowledge, and Shakespeare considers them both. The first view, originating in the passage from the Ion mentioned above, is that poetry's substance is provided by divine inspiration. In the Ion Socrates suggests this view in conjunction with the idea that the poets have no knowledge understood through their own intelligence but that they are merely vehicles for the words of gods and can only speak well when possessed by a god:

> . . . these lovely poems are not of
> man or human workmanship, but are
> divine and from the gods, and the
> poets are nothing but interpreters
> of the gods, each one possessed by
> the divinity to whom he is in
> bondage (534e).

Sidney is cautious about attributing divine inspiration to poetry: Plato "attributeth unto Poesy more than myself do, namely, to be a very inspiring

66

of a divine force. . . ." But in his peroration he invokes the theory in support of poetry: ". . . I conjure you all . . . to believe with Landino, that they [the poets] are so beloved of the gods that whatsoever they write proceeds of a divine fury. . . ."[12] Puttenham and Chapman have no qualms about the theory. The former argues that "this science in his perfection can not grow but by some divine instinct--the Platonists call it _furor_; or by great subtiltie. . . ."[13] Chapman finds that "_Homers_ poems were writ from a free furie."[14] Shakespeare, himself, refers to "heavenbred poesy" in _Two Gentlemen of Verona_ (III.ii.72) and to the gods' ability to make Audrey "poetical" in _As You Like It_ (III.iii.24-25). He also refers to the poet's rage or fury in Sonnets XVII and C.

The difficulty with viewing poetry as divine inspiration is the impossibility of distinguishing it from madness. Shakespeare recognizes this problem in Sonnet XVII, where he says that if he wrote of his beloved's virtues, even though his writing would be inadequate to describe such excellence, people would ascribe it simply to a "poet's rage." In _A Midsummer Night's Dream_ Theseus simply equates the poet's imagination with that of the madman.

The alternative position is that the poet himself possesses some knowledge perceived through his own abilities. Renaissance support of this view is even more widespread than support of the idea that poetry proceeds from divine inspiration or possession. Sidney calls the poet the "right popular philosopher," and it is commonplace to refer to poets as the first philosophers (see p. 5 above).

Shakespeare's poetry is playful. He, like Socrates, will never be explicit about what he knows, but in his reference to dreams in _A Midsummer Night's Dream_ he allows for the possibility that the poet is truly awake while the rest of us are dreaming. Hippolyta's speech also includes inferences that the poet knows something:

> But all the story of the night told over,
> And all their minds transfigured so together,
> More witnesseth than fancy's images,
> And grows to something of great constancy;
> But, howsoever, strange and admirable.
> (V.i.23-27)

Hippolyta says that the story of the Athenian lovers seems real because it is consistent. This consistency is the clue to the nature of the poet's knowledge. Renaissance defenders of poetry argued regularly that this kind of verisimilitude has more validity than historical fact.[15] As Sidney says, a single example from history gives little basis for generalization which would allow one to accurately predict what will occur: "an example only informs a conjectured likelihood." Moreover, many things occur which man does not understand and therefore attributes to fortune rather than a divine plan which supports virtue and wisdom: "the historian in his bare <u>was</u> hath many time that which we call fortune[16] to overrule his best wisdom. Many times he must tell of events whereof he can yield no cause; or, if he do, it must be poetical." The "truth of a foolish world" often argues against the perfect pattern which a poet might present. The poet, however, is able "to frame his example to what is most reasonable." Sidney, of course, refers to poetry's ability to represent virtue in its pure form and to support it in a way in which life is not always able to do. Sidney implies that people would accept the poet's pattern as true if their understanding were not limited.[17]

Hippolyta's view of the lovers' story as "strange and admirable" suggests another Renaissance notion of poetry associating it with knowledge. From Aristotle the Renaissance derived the ideas that the end of poetry is the production of wonder and that wonder is a cause of learning. Thus poetry is also a cause of learning. In the <u>Poetics</u>, for example, Aristotle argues that a poet's impossibilities are justifiable "if they serve the end of poetry itself--if (to assume what we have said of that end) they make the effect of either that portion of the work or some other more astounding."[18] In the <u>Rhetoric</u> Aristotle associates wonder with learning:

> Learning things and wondering at things are also pleasant as a rule; wondering implies the desire of learning so that the object of wonder is an object of desire. . . . Again, since learning and wondering are pleasant, it follows that acts of imitation must be pleasant--for instance, painting, sculpture,

poetry--and every product of skillful
imitation; this latter, even if the
object imitated is not itself
pleasant; for it is not the object
which here gives delight; the
spectator draws inferences ('That is
a so-and-so') and thus learns
something fresh.[19]

As J. V. Cunningham points out, that the idea of
wonder recurs in the scholastic philosophers as well
as in Cicero and Quintilian suggests that it was
commonplace in the Renaissance. Cunningham finds the
idea in Pontanus, Fracastoro, Minturno, Sidney,
Spenser, and Shakespeare.[20] But one need not go so
far from A Midsummer Night's Dream to find support
for the view that Hippolyta's words on wonder might
call forth its association with learning. In the
play Quince tells his audience that wonder can lead
them to inquiry:

> Gentles, perchance you wonder at this show;
> But wonder on, till truth make all things plain.
>   (V.i.127-28)

Hippolyta's reference to wonder, then, has
implications for the value of poetry as a source of
learning, but is that learning of a kind worth
seeking? In the passage from the Rhetoric cited
above and in the Poetics (1448b) Aristotle describes
learning from poetry merely as recognizing what the
work of art is meant to represent. In the Poetics,
however, he allows for another case:

> . . . if one has not seen the thing
> before, one's pleasure will not be
> in the picture as an imitation of
> it, but will be due to the execution
> or coloring or some similar cause.

Aristotle does not explain in the Poetics what one
might learn when one sees represented an object which
he has not seen before. The Metaphysics suggests the
answer. Wonder implies the desire to learn about
causes. Metaphysics is a science which investigates
"the first principles and causes." Wonder led and
now leads men to seek knowledge, first of simple
difficulties and ultimately of first causes:

> For it is owing to their wonder that
> men both now begin and at first
> began to philosophize; they wondered
> originally at the obvious
> difficulties about the greater
> matters, e.g., about the phenomenon
> of the moon and those of the sun and
> of the stars, and about the genesis
> of the universe. And a man who is
> puzzled and wonders thinks himself
> ignorant (whence even the lover of
> myth is in a sense a lover of
> Wisdom, for the myth is composed of
> wonders) . . . .[21]

More specifically, one sometimes wonders about God,
for "God is thought to be among the causes of all
things and to be a first principle" (983a).

Later writers often speak of the wonder in poetry
and rhetoric as deriving from wonder about the gods.
Cicero, for example, argues that an epideictic speech
should contain a good deal of what is wonderful,
things foreshadowed by portents, prodigies, and
oracles, and what seems to be the result of divine
intervention or of fate.[22] St. Albert in his
Commentary on the Metaphysics of Aristotle argues
that wonder is caused by

> amazement at the sensible appearance
> of something so portentous, great,
> and unusual, that the heart suffers
> a systole. This effect of wonder
> then, this constriction and systole
> of the heart, springs from an
> unfulfilled but felt desire to know
> the cause of that which appears
> portentous and unusual. . . .
> Aristotle shows in that branch of
> logic which is called poetic that
> the poet fashions his story for the
> purpose of exciting wonder, and that
> the further effect of wonder is to
> excite inquiry.[23]

Minturno makes the following statement derived from
Aristotle's Poetics (IX):

> . . . the business of the tragic
> poet is to put his reader into a

70

condition of astonishment. And we
consider those accidents astonishing
that move us to compassion or
horror, and yet the more when they
come about with probability against
our hopes and opinions, since events
brought about by fortune, though of
themselves they do not appear very
worthy to cause astonishment, yet
greatly excite us to wonder when we
think they come about through the
divine will or as a result of a
plan.[24]

The examples could be multiplied,[25] but enough
has been said to suggest a possible interpretation of
Hippolyta's words. The story of the night seems
lifelike because the lovers' tales are consistent,
and it seems "strange and admirable" because it
includes events which imply the presence of some
divine force. The chase through the wood in which
Demetrius and Lysander, Helena and Hermia cannot find
one another may seem possible, though unlikely, but
the four lovers' finding themselves all sleeping
together certainly seems strange--as though it were
designed by some superior force. The degree of
fickleness of Lysander and Demetrius seems
extraordinary, but their eventual fidelity to their
original choices again seems the work of more than
chance. Hippolyta hears of no gods, but the story of
the lovers might well remind her of divine forces.

For the audience Shakespeare supplies the gods.
They are not the gods in which his audience believes,
but they carry out the functions of deities in the
play. Because Hippolyta believes in gods of some
sort, she can accept the truth of the wonderful.
Perhaps Shakespeare is giving us an example of the
ancient poets' manner of dealing with the gods. The
fable which he invents about Titania and Oberon would
be believable to an Athenian. As Tasso argues, "the
ancients who lived in the error of their vain
religion saw no improbability in the miracles that
not the poets alone but the historians as well fabled
of their gods."[26] Perhaps what Jean Seznec
describes as the conscious effort of the Renaissance
to establish harmony between the pagan world and
Christianity would have made Shakespeare's audience
all the more alert to the functioning of mythological
characters as gods.[27]

The words of Theseus' speech at the opening of
Act V, as opposed to Theseus' meaning, imply a
further Elizabethan view of poetry which gives the
poet some claim to the possession of knowledge. By
relating the lover to the poet Theseus calls to mind
the notion that love is an impulse to poetry which
can lead to understanding of the human, the
universal, and the divine. The Elizabethan view is
based on the connection of the lover and the poet in
Plato's _Phaedrus_. Both are included in four
divisions of madness--prophecy, mystery, poetry,
love--whose common source is divine inspiration (244,
245, 265). Ficino in his commentary on the _Symposium_
makes the connection even more explicit. He reverses
Plato's ordering of the forms of madness to make them
seem to lead toward worship of a Christian God--from
poetic madness to mystery to prophecy and then to
desire for divine beauty or passion for good. All
forms of madness, including the poetic, depend upon
love:

> For we achieve neither the poetic,
> the religious, nor the prophetic
> madness without a great zeal,
> flaming piety, and sedulous worship
> of the divine. But zeal, piety, and
> worship, what else do we call them
> but love? Therefore all the
> madnesses depend upon the power of
> Love. It is also most noble, since
> to it as to an end, the others are
> referred; moreover, it is this which
> joins us most closely with God.[28]

The _Phaedrus_ also joins the lover and poet by making
their souls those which have seen the most "Reality"
in heaven (248). Plato describes heaven as a place
where

> Reality lives, without shape or
> color, intangible, visible only to
> reason, the soul's pilot; and all
> true knowledge is knowledge of
> her.[29]

Further, the _Phaedrus_ suggests that Socrates is both
the true lover and the true poet. Socrates is the
lover of wisdom (278) who, like the true rhetorician,
knows how to make the truth match the soul of his
listener (277). He is forced to make a complex

speech composed of poetic figures to Phaedrus (257) whose complicated and unstable soul requires such a speech (277).

The association of lover and poet by Theseus suggests that the poet possesses the knowledge traditionally available to the true lover. Most Renaissance theorizing on love derives from Plato's Phaedrus and Symposium. The poetic and amatory madness of the Phaedrus do not contravene the possibility that the poet and the lover possess some knowledge. The Ion gives the poet's madness or divine inspiration as an alternative only after Ion has been unable to show that the poet knows anything, but the Phaedrus argues both that a man must know the truth before making speeches and that the soul which has seen the most reality enters "into a future seeker for wisdom or beauty, a follower of the Muses or a lover" (248). The human soul attains a vision of reality by yielding to its rational impulses and checking its bodily desires.

This version of poetic madness and of love could have become available to Shakespeare in the original, through Ficino, or through Castiglione. Ficino argues that poetic madness separates "reason and opinion . . . from confused fancy and sense desire." It does this by arousing the soul, calming the discords of the body, and producing harmony between body and soul.[30] Castiglione expresses the same view in Bembo's discourse on love, where the true beauty is said to be the bodiless one available to reason.[31] This is a possible response to Theseus' accusation that the poetic imagination is irrational and led by sense desire. For Theseus the lunatic, the lover, and the poet "are of imagination all compact." Such an imagination apprehends "more than cool reason ever comprehends." Desire or fear produce confused images.

> Such tricks hath strong imagination,
> That, if it would but apprehend some joy,
> It comprehends some bringer of that joy;
> Or in the night, imagining some fear,
> How easy is a bush supposed a bear!
> (V.i.18-22)

The Phaedrus provides an even greater degree of knowledge to the true poet than Ficino does. For Ficino poetic madness is the first and thus the lowest of the four madnesses leading toward God. Love as piety is the highest. In the _Phaedrus_ the "follower of the Muses" has seen the most reality. On the other hand, the soul which is sixth in the amount of reality viewed enters "a poet's life or some other devoted to imitation" (248). This soul is ranked below the law-abiding monarch or warlike ruler, the statesman or merchant, the athlete or physician, and the prophet or priest. This lower poet is one who imitates either the words of other poets or produces shadows of the real world. Such a poet is the best which Theseus envisions, for he claims that the "best" plays "are but shadows" (see pp. 33-34 above). In the _Phaedrus_ "the follower of the Muses" is a higher poet, ranked above the law-abiding monarch. The true poet is he who knows the truth before making speeches (277). He is among those who "sing the most sweetly in their preoccupation with heavenly things and with discourse mortal and divine" (259). Minturno recognizes this strain in the _Phaedrus_ when he argues that poetry is responsible for all perfections of the world:

> And the Muses, the offspring of Jove and nine in number, what other do they signify than the nine choruses of the celestial spirits, which sing the praises of God and also inspire in mortals all their knowledge of things, what other than the means by which God teaches men the sciences and arts and gives them laws? And the nine Intelligences of the nine spheres of the heavens that move and rule everything, and disseminate the seeds of all things, and, as the Platonists say, inform souls, are they not these same? Thus, the world has no excellence of things, no ornament, and no perfection that cannot be attributed to the Muses and to poetry.[32]

A vision of the universal and ultimately of the divine becomes available to poet as lover through the _Symposium's_ ladder of love. Diotima describes an ascent of a lover from love of one beautiful body to recognition of beauty in another body to love of all beautiful bodies to love of the beauties of the mind. Love of beauty of the mind produces further ascent from love of institutions and laws to love of sciences to love of the single source of beauty everywhere (210a-211e). Some version of a ladder of love is common in the Renaissance. In Castiglione it occurs as a "stayre of love" which leads from the bodily to the ability to "beholde the beautie that is seene with the eyes of the minde." With the mind one can ascend to a vision of "heavenly beautie" and finally to union with "the nature of Angels." One is able to see the "inner-most secretes of God."[33] Any reference to the ladder of love in Theseus' speech must derive from the general association of lover and poet, but the ascent will be applicable in the discussion of Bottom below.

A further Renaissance notion of love might help to define the precise nature of the poet's knowledge by presenting a possible gloss on Theseus' depiction of the poet as glancing "from heaven to earth, from earth to heaven." From the Symposium the Renaissance derived the idea that love was a bond between men and the gods. Castiglione echoes Diotima's definition by describing love as "a sweet bond of the world, a meane betwixt heavenly and earthly thinges."[34] Ficino seems to recall this definition as well when he interprets Pausanias' speech:

> This Divine Beauty creates in everything love, that is, desire for itself, because if God draws the world to Himself, and the world is drawn [from Him] there is one continuous attraction, beginning with God, going to the world, and ending at last in God, an attraction which returns to the same place whence it began as though in a kind of circle.[35]

If Ficino can be applied to Theseus' words, then the poet as lover would seek divine beauty in all things, in both heaven and earth.

Further explanation of the poet's activity as lover is suggested by the ultimate source of Ficino and Castiglione. Whether Shakespeare read the Symposium in Ficino's Latin translation cannot be determined. By Shakespeare's time Plato had been assimilated into European thought to a degree which makes uncertain any reference to borrowings from his works. Still this very assimilation makes study of the Symposium fruitful for understanding the ideas

which may have been available to Shakespeare. The
quarrel of Titania and Oberon produces results so
similar to those described by Eryximachus in the
Symposium that it suggests that its source is either
the Symposium or the work of someone who reproduced
closely parts of the Symposium.[36] In the Symposium
inordinate love influences the seasons and produces
frost, hail, blight and epidemics:

> And again, we find these two
> elements in the seasons of the year,
> for when the regulating principle of
> Love brings together those opposites
> of which I spoke--hot and cold, wet
> and dry--and compounds them in
> ordered harmony, the result is
> health and plenty for mankind, and
> for the animal and vegetable
> kingdoms, and all goes as it
> should. But when the seasons are
> under the influence of that other
> Love, all is mischief and
> destruction, for now plague and
> disease of every kind attack the
> herds and crops, and not only these,
> but frost and hail and blight--and
> all of them are due to the
> uncontrolled and the acquisitive in
> that great system of Love which the
> astronomer observes when he
> investigates the movements of the
> stars and the seasons of the
> year.[37]

In A Midsummer Night's Dream the quarrel of Titania
and Oberon causes great disorder in the seasons and
produces fogs and floods, the spoiling of crops, and
rheumatic diseases.

> Therefore the winds, piping to us in vain,
> As in revenge, have sucked up from the sea
> Contagious fogs; which, falling in the land
> Hath every pelting river made so proud,
> That they have overborne their continents.
> The ox hath therefore stretched his yoke in vain,
> The plowman lost his sweat, and the green corn
> Hath rotted ere his youth attained a beard:
> The fold stands empty in the drownèd field,
> And crows are fatted with the murrion flock;
> The nine men's morris is filled up with mud;

And the quaint mazes in the wanton green,
For lack of tread, are indistinguishable.
The human mortals want their winter here;
No night is now with hymn or carol blest.
Therefore the moon, the governess of floods,
Pale in her anger, washes all the air,
That rheumatic diseases do abound.
And through this distemperature we see
The seasons alter: hoary-headed frosts
Fall in the fresh lap of the crimson rose,
And on old Hiems' thin and icy crown
An odorous chaplet of sweet summer buds
Is, as in mockery, set. The spring, the summer
The childing autumn, angry winter, change
Their wonted liveries; and the mazed world,
By their increase, now knows not which is which.
                                    (II.i.88-114)

        Further references in Eryximachus' speech have
implications for the lover and the poet which may
apply to A Midsummer Night's Dream. Eryximachus
argues that people ought to care for earthly love as
well as heavenly. As a doctor he finds that
medicine's purpose is to allow people pleasure
without sustaining diseases. Divination allows
humans to enjoy earthly love by bringing desire in
accord with virtue and sobriety. In so doing it
establishes good will between gods and humans:

        It is the diviner's office to be the
        guide and healer of these Loves, and his
        art of divination with its power to
        distinguish those principles of human
        love that tend to decency and reverence,
        is, in fact, the source of concord
        between gods and men.
                            (188b-d)

In A Midsummer Night's Dream Shakespeare seems to be
following Eryximachus' prescription. If so, the poet
becomes something of a diviner. In Eryximachus'
speech divination is not love as such, but the art
"directed to the preservation or the repair of
Love." Diotima later gives Love the function of
divination. Spirits, she says,

        are the envoys and interpreters that
        play between heaven and earth,
        flying upward with our worship and
        our prayers, and descending with the

heavenly answers and commandments, and since they are between the two estates they weld both sides together and merge them into one great whole. They form the medium of the prophetic arts, of the priestly rites of sacrifice, imitation, and incantation, of divination and of sorcery, for the divine will not mingle with the human, and it is only through the mediation of the spirit world that man can have any intercourse, whether waking or asleep, with the gods. And the man who is versed in such matters is said to have spiritual powers, as opposed to the mechanical powers of the man who is expert in the more mundane arts. There are many spirits and many kinds of spirits, too, and Love is one of them.

(202e-203a)

As commonly noted, Socrates comes to represent love incarnate as described by Diotima. In doing so he serves in the capacity of a poet. He is a Silenus or a "latter-day Marsyas" who uses words to charm men and who can bring tears to Alcibiades' eyes like a tragedian (215-16). In his speeches he seems to follow Eryximachus' prescription for mediating between gods and men to produce virtue. Those speeches are "godlike" and "rich in images of virtue," although they are grounded in base everyday matters such as "packasses and blacksmiths and shoemakers and tanners" (221d-222a). Because a poet such as Socrates is closer than most men to the heavenly, he has no parallel among humans but must be described by reference to Silenus or satyrs (221c-221d). Is it too much to suggest that Shakespeare had all of this in mind when he depicted his poet as looking from earth to heaven, from heaven to earth? Did he really think of the true poet as a kind of Socrates? The discussion of Bottom below will suggest that he might very well have had these or similar ideas in mind.

The poet as lover must be distinguished from the young Athenians as lovers. The young lovers are far more limited in vision than the poet. John Vyvyan

argues that in the young lovers Shakespeare embodies
the widely current assumption derived from the
Symposium and Ficino that love on earth is
"recognition between companion souls, who may at last
perceive in one another, if they have true lovesight,
the beauty of their divine self-nature."
Shakespeare, indeed, makes use of this idea, but his
use suggests the self-deception of lovers as much as
their achievement of true vision. As evidence Vyvyan
cites Lysander's assertion that he sees through
Helena to her heart, but Lysander's eventual
companion is Hermia. Vyvyan also cites Helena's
depiction of herself and Hermia as having "two
seeming bodies" and "one heart," but the notion of
companion souls implies that each soul has only one
true mate.[38] Lysander thinks that reason has made
him see that Helen is "the worthier maid"
(II.ii.116), but the reader recognizes that the love
juice, not reason, has altered Lysander. In Ficino
lovers

> accept the false for the true, in
> thinking their loves are more
> beautiful, wiser, and better than
> they really are. They contradict
> themselves because of the violence
> of their love, for reason persuades
> them of one thing [true beauty,
> wisdom, and virtue], and desire
> pursues another [the actual
> beloved.][39]

As Oberon says, the love juice can make the beloved
"shine as gloriously / As the Venus of the sky"
(III.ii.106-07), the Heavenly Venus who in Plato, in
Ficino and in the tradition in general embodies all
noble love.

In Bottom's activities Shakespeare examines a
number of the ideas behind Theseus' speech on
poetry. Bottom is like a poet in many ways. First,
like a poet, he thinks that he understands the
whole. He wants to play all of the parts in the
Pyramus and Thisbe play. He presumes that he
understands all of the characters or, in other words,
all kinds of people. Second, like the author of A
Midsummer Night's Dream and poets in general, he is
concerned that the audience will take fiction for
truth. He wants to have a prologue written so that
the ladies will know that the actors do not actually

harm themselves with their swords. This prologue will go a step further than Sidney's argument that the poet "nothing affirms, and therefore never lieth" by announcing that Pyramus is really Bottom, the Weaver. The lion himself will announce that he is Snug the joiner. The prologue, of course, is unnecessary because the play is so inept that there is no chance that it will seem lifelike. Third, like Shakespeare, Bottom and the mechanicals change a tragedy into a comedy.[40] The mechanicals produce tragical mirth through ineptitude, while Shakespeare uses the fairies and Theseus' acquiescence in their solution to produce a comedy.

Bottom's dream has affinities with the poet's vision. The subject matter of his dream is appropriate to poetry, or so Bottom thinks, for he will have a ballad written about it. That a dream might supply the subject matter for a play is intimated by the lovers' dream and by the suggestion of Puck in his epilogue that the audience view the entire play as a dream. As argued earlier, a number of Renaissance ideas supported the view that the substance of a dream might be truer than actual life. This is implied by the dream's inclusion of a vision of a goddess, Titania. This higher vision, like a vision of ideas or of the divine, is available only to the appropriate faculty or is beyond sense. As Bottom says, "The eye of man hath not heard, the ear of man hath not seen, man's hand is not able to taste, his tongue to conceive, nor his heart to report, what my dream was" (IV.ii.214-17). This passage is reminiscent of two others in Castiglione, both of which imply something about the nature of Bottom's vision. Castiglione's Bembo argues that the true beauty is bodiless and thus beauty is available only to a faculty with "little bodily substance" in it--sight:

> And as a man hearest not with his mouth, nor smelleth with his eares: no more can he also in any manner wise enjoy beautie, nor satisfie the desire that she stirreth up in our minds, with feeling, but with the sense, unto whom beautie is the very butte to level at: namely, the vertue of seeing.

Eventually the courtier may climb the ladder of love to attain the "beautie that is seene with the eyes of the minde" rather than those of the senses. The soul sees the "Angelike beautie" within itself, and then it ultimately reaches sight of the "universal beautie of all bodies."[41] If Bottom has not reached a vision of beauty unadulterated by the body, he is promised by Titania a more spiritual existence: "And I will purge thy mortal grossness so, / That thou shalt like an airy spirit go" (II.i.161-62). Titania promises Bottom something precious as a result of his association with her--"jewels from the deep" (II.i.159), perhaps knowledge or perhaps true love such as Shakespeare has given the young lovers. Helena, upon awakening, thinks that she has "found Demetrius like a jewel, / Mine own, and not mine own" (IV.i.193). Bottom's knowledge, then, is like the poets', and his vision parallels that of poet as diviner who requires a vision of the gods to mediate between them and men.

The well-known echo of St. Paul in Bottom's description of his dream has implications for the poet.[42]

> I have had a most rare vision. I
> have had a dream, past the wit of
> man to say what dream it was. Man
> is but an ass, if he go about to
> expound this dream. Methought I
> was--there is no man can tell what.
> Methought I was--and methought I
> had--but man is but a patched fool
> if he will offer to say what
> methought I had. The eye of man
> hath not heard, the ear of man hath
> not seen, man's hand is not able to
> taste, his tongue to conceive, nor
> his heart to report, what my dream
> was. I will get Peter Quince to
> write a ballet of this dream. It
> shall be called "Bottom's Dream,"
> because it hath no bottom. . . .
>   (IV.ii.207-20)

1 Corinthians ii explains the vision which Bottom attains:

> That we speak of is wysdome
> amonge thē that are perfecte: not

81

the wysdom of thys worlde (which go
to nought): but we speake ȳ wysdome
of God which is in secret and lyeth
hyd: which God ordeyned before the
worde unto oure glory: which
wysdome none of the rulers of this
worlde knewe. For had they knowen
it they wolde not have crucified the
Lord of glory. But as it is
wrytten: The eye hath not sene and
the eare hath not hearde nether have
entred into the hert of mã the
things which God hath prepared for
them that love hym.

But God hath opened thē unto us
by hys sprete. For the sprete
searcheth all thynges, ye the botome
of Goddes secretes. For what man
knoweth the things of a man: save
the sprete of a man which is within
him. . . . For the naturall man
perceaveth not the things of the
sprete of God. For they are but
folysshnes vnto him.[43]

Bottom's dream coincides with Corinthians in the
following ways: First, Bottom has had a vision of
God's wisdom, not of man's. For it is "past the wit
of man to say" what dream Bottom had. It is a dream
which is infinite, with "no bottom." And, as argued
above, it is beyond apprehension by the senses.
Second, like God's wisdom, Bottom's dream would seem
foolish to the natural man if Bottom were to expound
it: "Man is but an ass, if he go about to expound
this dream." If the passage from Corinthians may be
extended further to include the entire play and the
poet's vision in general, then Bottom's dream becomes
the poet's dream. It is a dream which seems foolish
to the rulers of the world just as the lovers' story
and the mechanicals' play seemed foolish to Theseus.
And yet it contains within it more than the practical
worldly wisdom of a Theseus. It has elements of the
universal, of the divine, within it.

But Bottom does not simply appear foolish. He is
an ass. He himself is fallen, and there are limits
to his own understanding of his vision. In fact,
there are limitations to all human understanding, and
all humans have difficulty recognizing their

limitations. Theseus' view is inadequate. The young lovers do not see well enough to find themselves in the Pyramus and Thisbe play. Man's knowledge of God comes through God's grace, for man's fall makes such knowledge undeserved.

To the extent that the poet is just a man, his knowledge is also limited, and yet in A Midsummer Night's Dream the poet acts like a god. Through a kind of grace he makes things turn out well for the lovers. He is like an omniscient god who sees all that goes on, has a divine plan for the universe, and is beneficent. He sees all that goes on in earth and heaven, and he makes the heavenly relevant to man. The poet can help to bring harmony to the universe in a way which Theseus cannot. He does it by way of the very eloquence which Theseus attacks and with a vision superior to Theseus'.

Puck's epilogue serves as one last reminder of the grounds of the defense of poetry in A Midsummer Night's Dream. Puck's words can be taken either as those of an actor, one of the "shadows" who may "have offended," or as those of a poet, with whom he has an affinity as one who, like Shakespeare and Bottom, can turn a serious tale into a comedy. In either case his epilogue reasserts the possibility of a defense which takes account of the elements of the attack on poetry. By pointing to himself as a "shadow" Puck points to the accusation that as an actor he is but a poor imitation of what he represents or, more generally, that poetry is but a poor imitation of real objects taken literally. By admitting that the audience could "Puck a liar call" Puck suggests the critique of the poet as a teller of untruths.

The epilogue recognizes the audience as the ultimate judge of the adequacy of the play's defense. They are to think of the play as "no more yielding but a dream," the dream which the play has reminded them might be taken either as untrue or as a vision of the ultimate truths. The epilogue issues a double challenge to the spectators. On the one hand, they can exhibit godlike forgiveness by applauding even though a bad play makes the applause, like grace given humans by God, "unearned." In this case only the pardon can "mend" or absolve the actors or the play. On the other hand, the audience can recognize the play as a vision of a higher truth. Put in terms of Bottom's dream and its allusion to Corinthians, what seems foolish to some, a "weak and idle theme" may actually contain elements of the universal or divine.

A Midsummer Night's Dream, then, examines the poet's role in civil society in a context which gives the politician his due and recognizes the poet's responsibility to the political. At the same time the play points to a vision which extends beyond the politician's in its understanding of the elements of the human soul and of universal truths beyond the domain of the political unit.

Theseus serves as the representative politician, an example of the best of his kind. As the counterpart of the groom for whose nuptial the play was written, Theseus appears as a figure with whom one would desire comparison. He is the model bridegroom who eagerly awaits his wedding and yet has his passions under control. He is the measured statesman who directs the actions of his citizens and upholds the law of Athens.

As a political leader Theseus judges art on the basis of its support of his government. This standard for art is compatible with his view of the poet's capabilities. Works of art are either a poor mirror of the world around them or untrue altogether. They function as mere recreation for those who have time to fill. Thus, as far as Theseus is concerned, the mechanicals' play deserves as much attention as the story of the young Athenian lovers.

Shakespeare as playwright acknowledges the demands of the political and the dangers poetry can pose to the city. His play attempts a reconciliation of poetry and politics which gives the playwright a function compatible with the orderly government of Athens. In A Midsummer Night's Dream Shakespeare points to tragedy's threat to civil society. The inclusion of the Pyramus and Thisbe story along with its parallels with the story of the young Athenian lovers suggests the nature of the threat. Tragic drama reveals the discordence between the natural and the city. The lovers' desire conflicts both with the laws of Athens and with the demands of virtue. The legislator must represent virtue and law as harmonious with human nature and therefore productive of happiness, while the poet represents powerfully a portion of the human soul, the erotic, whose suppression virtue and law sometimes require.

The Pyramus and Thisbe story realizes the potential for violence which desire holds for the city and reminds the audience of the same potential in the story of the young Athenians. The parallels between the two stories and their juxtaposition helps to bring out the relationship between the two. The fate of Hermia, Helena, Lysander and Demetrius could have been similar to the fate of Pyramus and Thisbe, for Helena is alone and unprotected in the wood as is Hermia following Lysander's desertion of her. The attempted duel between Lysander and Demetrius and fight between Hermia and Helena threaten further violence.

Bottom's actions strengthen the case against tragedy by implying that it can lead to tyranny. As the Platonic tradition points out, tragedy is a forerunner of tyranny because it appeals to desires suppressed by other regimes as dangerous to moral virtue. The tyrant is the person whose desires know no limit. He is willing to break law or convention to fulfill them. Bottom shows the same impulses as the tragic poet. He is eager to water the passions, yet his strongest urge is to play the tyrant. Like the tyrant he wants to experience everything: He wishes to play all the parts in the mechanicals' play.

At the same time that Shakespeare illustrates the dangers of tragic drama to politics, he protects the audience from those dangers by revealing desire in the context of the madness, unreality, and artificiality of the wood. Shakespeare's chief protection, however, consists of making a potential tragedy into a comedy which produces ultimate harmony between the lovers' desire and Athens.

The grounds on which the tragedian's understanding threatens the city becomes the grounds also on which the poet can render service to the city. Although Theseus represents the best that politics has to offer, he never fully understands the nature and strength of desire and therefore its danger to the city. Further, he is unable to control desire in his citizens. With the poet rather than the politician rests the ability to understand desire and to control it.

The limitations of Theseus' understanding and

power are made clear in his actions towards the young Athenian lovers. In Athens Theseus cannot resolve the problem of these citizens. When faced with their conflicting loves, he tries to uphold Athenian law and causes their flight from the city to avoid the power of that law. Further, the play suggests that Theseus is inattentive to matters of the heart and their possible disruption of his domain. He admits forgetting to speak to Demetrius about his inconstancy. He may mistake the lovers' reason for being asleep on the edge of the wood on the day he and Hippolyta are to marry. And he certainly is unaware of the lovers' attempt to defy the law.

The fairies have more power than Theseus to produce order in Athens. In fact, during most of the action in A Midsummer Night's Dream Theseus functions as audience rather than as actor. Hippolyta and he comment upon the story of the young lovers in the wood as a work of art whose validity and value they must judge. This creates a strong sense of the playwright's hand in creating the story of the young lover's time in the wood. Thus, from the fairies' power to bring order the viewer can infer the playwright's ordering power.

Critics have often associated the wood where the fairies preside with the irrationality and inconstancy of love as opposed to the rationality of Athens, but inconstancy exists before the lovers enter the wood. In addition, the fairies produce more than inconstancy and madness. Using two herbs, one inducing love and the other removing error, the fairies solve Theseus' problem by altering the young Athenian lovers so that they are mutually affectionate couples. The fairies then guarantee the lovers' continued constancy.

That the fairies rather than Theseus control the reestablishment of order is indicated in further ways. That order has been restored before Theseus enters is implied by the dance of Oberon and Titania, by the restoration of the Indian boy to Oberon and of Titania to Oberon's love which has been said to make "all things . . . at peace," by Titania's and Oberon's earlier control over the forces of nature, and by Oberon's foreknowledge of Theseus' acquiescence in the lovers' choices and of their marriage on the following day.

Shakespeare makes the fairies rather than Theseus responsible for ordering desire because he wants to point out that if it were not for the playwright the story of the lovers could have been a tragedy such as Pyramus and Thisbe's. A tragedy would imply that forces in nature or in the city are hostile to the happiness of the lovers. Shakespeare produces a comedy by making the forces of nature, as represented by Oberon and Titania, harmonize both with the happiness of the lovers and the laws of the city. Titania and Oberon have made desire compatible with the city's laws by sorting out the pairs of lovers and by defending a virtue, constancy, and an institution, marriage, necessary to the city. On the cosmic level they have produced harmony through their renewed friendship.

The quarrel of Titania and Oberon suggests how one must deal with desire. When Titania shuns Oberon's bed, she puts herself in an improper relationship to him by denying the body. Erotic love is necessary to the city if only to reproduce its citizens. Thus it must be recoginzed within the bounds of married love and constancy and with respect to an appropriate object.

If Shakespeare makes the poet superior to the politician in resolving the city's problem, he also recognizes the dubious validity of this solution. It is produced by magic herbs and fairies in a drama which Puck advises the audience to consider a dream. Shakespeare recognizes the intransigent incompatibility of desire and politics. He realizes that desire can disrupt the law and sees that the law is sometimes incompatible with the fulfillment of desire.

Shakespeare's defense of poetry extends beyond the boundaries of Athens and yet occurs always in the context of the critiques of poetry. He expresses this partly in making his play a midsummer night's dream and in insisting on its dreamlike quality through Puck and through the slumbers of the young lovers and of Bottom. This puts Shakespeare in the tradition which allows two possibilities for the dream- that it is a time when one does not see clearly or that it represents the soul leaving the body to gain a vision of truth unhampered.

A Midsummer Night's Dream explains how both categories of dream could apply to poetry. Theseus' speech at V.i.3-22 contains grounds for an attack on poetry as well as implying grounds for its defense. Theseus sees the poet as composed entirely of imagination which can distort reality and lead to misjudgments. One source of such distortion is passion. But, even worse, poets can lie by affirming the existence of something which is untrue. Or, rather than consciously telling untruths, the poet can be governed by madness. Later (V.i.212-13) Theseus allows for poetry as a mirror of reality, but he sees the product of the poet as a shadow--a poor mutation of real things. As the mechanicals' attempt at mimesis illustrates, imitation which attempts to picture actual concrete things is destined to fail.

Theseus' words suggest an alternative view of poetry as imitation--namely, that it imitates essences generalized from particulars and gained through superior vision or inspiration. The "things unknown" are not necessarily untrue. They may have derived from the poet's vision which glances "from heaven to earth, from earth to heaven." The poet may have the ability to recognize the divine pattern in heaven and may attempt to represent that pattern and fulfill it on earth. This may be possible because the poet understands what is on earth--what is godlike or must be encouraged in humans and what is earthly or must be controlled. In other words, the poet may understand both virtue and desire.

In further senses poetry may be both earthly and heavenly. The dramatist say embody an ideal on earth in particular actions and actors. The dramatist can also bring the pattern of virtue to earth through the representation of the gods.

The Renaissance provides two possible sources for the poets' knowledge of universals or of the gods: divine inspiration or the poets' own abilities. Shakespeare considers them both. In A Midsummer Night's Dream what might be called divine inspiration Theseus describes as "frenzy." The idea that the dramatist has reached some knowledge on his own is explained at greater length. One definition of that knowledge appears in Hippolyta's description of the "great constancy" of the lovers' story. This supplies an allusion to Sidney's theory that verisimilitude has more reality than historical fact. The poet is able to frame an example of virtue in its pure form in a way that life is not always able to do. A second definition of that knowledge is inferred by the "strange and admirable" quality which Hippolyta recognizes in the young lovers' story. These words refer to the Aristotelian and Renaissance association of wonder with learning. The theory is made explicit in Quince's injunction to his audience to "wonder on, till truth make all things plain." Again in keeping with Aristotle and Renaissance writers, the learning which wonder teaches concerns the gods. Applied to the story of the wood, wonder arises because the events infer the presence of some divine force. Although Hippolyta hears of no gods, the lovers' fidelity to their original choices seems more than the work of chance. For the audience Shakespeare supplies the gods, not the ones in which his audience believes, but nevertheless beings who carry out the function of deities. Because Hippolyta believes in gods of some sort, she can believe in the truth of the wonderful. In fact, Shakespeare in creating Titania and Oberon may be inventing gods which could be believable to an Athenian.

The words of Theseus' speech as opposed to Theseus' meaning imply a further Elizabethan view giving the poet a claim to knowledge. Theseus' joining of the "lunatic, the lover and the poet" puts his phrases in the tradition deriving from Plato's _Phaedrus_ and the _Symposium_. This tradition defines the lover and the highest kind of poet as those who have seen the "most reality." In the _Phaedrus_, Ficino, Castiglione, and Minturno this vision of reality becomes available by yielding to the rational and checking the bodily. Thus poetic madness becomes in essence a kind of rationality. In the _Symposium_ and Renaissance derivatives such as Castiglione the universal and ultimately the divine become available to the poet as lover by way of a ladder of love climbing from love of the body to love of the mind to love of heavenly beauty. In Castiglione and Ficino love becomes a bond which unites humans to God. This bond provides a further possible gloss on the poet's glance "from heaven to earth, from earth to heaven."

Although it cannot be determined whether Shakespeare read the _Symposium_, the quarrel between Titania and Oberon is close enough to Eryximachus' speech to suggest that its source is either the _Symposium_ or some work which reproduced that part of the _Symposium_ closely. In Eryximachus' speech divination allows man to enjoy earthly love by bringing desire in accord with virtue and sobriety. In so doing the diviner establishes good will between men and the gods. Later the Symposium gives love and the poet the function of divination which mediates between gods and men to produce virtue.

Bottom's speech suggests that Shakespeare may have this in mind. Bottom performs the functions of the poet. First, like the poet, he thinks that he grasps the whole. Believing he understands all kinds of people, he wants to play all of the parts. Second, like the author of A Midsummer Night's Dream and poets in general, Bottom is concerned that the audience will take fiction for truth. Thus he designs a prologue for his play to show the ladies that the actors will not harm themselves with their swords. Third, like Shakespeare and Puck, Bottom and the mechanicals change a tragedy into a comedy. Fourth, just as a dream is the subject of Shakespeare's play, Bottom's dream supplies the subject matter for poetry, for he will have a ballad written about it. Fifth, like the Renaissaince poet-lover, Bottom is enamored.

If Bottom is a poet, then his vision of Titania makes him a diviner. In keeping with the view of the lover as poet, Bottom's vision is beyond the senses, and Titania promises to aid him to a more spiritual existence. The parallel of Bottom's speech with Corinthians reinforces the idea that Bottom's vision is of God's wisdom, not of men's. Bottom's dream would seem foolish to the rulers of the world just as Bottom's play seems foolish to Theseus.

And yet in addition to appearing foolish, Bottom is literally an ass. He is fallen himself and recognizes the limitations of all human understanding. Human knowledge of God comes only through God's grace, for humanity's fallen state makes knowledge undeserved.

The poet as a human has limits to his knowledge, but in A Midsummer Night's Dream the playwright acts like a god in bringing a kind of grace to make things turn out well. Like a god, the poet makes the heavenly relevant to humans. Through his superior vision and the poetry which Theseus attacks, the playwright can bring harmony to Athens in a way denied to Theseus.

90

Puck's epilogue gives the audience the godlike powers exhibited by the poet. Paradoxically, the challenge which Puck issues to the audience to demonstrate godlike forgiveness of a bad play requires acceptance of a vision of the heavenly which _A Midsummer Night's Dream_ has attempted to impart. Taking this part, it would be difficult for the audience to deny that what may seem foolish contains a vision of the highest truth.

Notes

[1]Note that by 1482 Ficino had made Plato available to educated Englishmen by supplying complete Latin translations and introductions to all of Plato's works.

[2]Baldassare Castiglione, The Book of the Courtier, trans. Thomas Hoby (1561) (London and New York, 1928), pp. 318-19. See Jackson Cope, The Theatre and the Dream (Baltimore, 1973), pp. 14-28, for further references to Renaissance views related to the double definition of dreams.

[3]Macrobius, Commentary on the Dream of Scipio, trans. William Harris Stahl (New York, 1952), pp. 87-92.

[4]William Rossky, "Imagination in the English Renaissance: Psychology and Poetic," Studies in the Renaissance, 5 (1958), 51-53. Rossky quotes Sir John Davies, Nosce Teipsum, in An English Garner, ed. Edward Arber (Birmingham, 1877-1896), V, 193.

[5]Rossky, p. 56. Rossky quotes Sir Fulke Greville, A Treatise of Humane Learning, in Poems and Dramas of Fulke Greville, ed. Geoffrey Bullough, I (New York, 1945), 157.

[6]See G. Gregory Smith, I, xxviii-xxix; E. Hoby's translation of Matthieu Coignet's Politique Discourses, in Smith, I, 341-44; Nash, in Smith, I, 323.

[7]Rossky, pp. 54-55.

[8]Plato, Ion, in Phaedrus, Ion, Gorgias, and Symposium, trans. Lane Cooper (Ithaca, New York, 1955); rpt. in The Collected Dialogues of Plato, eds. Edith Hamilton and Huntington Cairns, Bollingen Series, 71 (New York, 1961), 533e-534a. All further references to this work are in the text.

[9]Puttenham, in Smith, II, 3; Chapman, in Smith, II, 298; Sidney, p. 142.

[10]Sidney, p. 129.

[11]Madeline Doran, "A Midsummer Night's Dream: A Metamorphosis," Rice Institute Pamphlet, 46 (1960), 130; Pearson, pp. 279-80.

[12]Sidney, pp. 130, 141-42.

[13]Puttenham, in Smith, II, 3.

[14]Chapman, in Smith, II, 298.

[15]Rossky, pp. 65-67.

[16]Sidney refers here to the common Renaissance idea expressed in Boethius as follows: "Therefore, even though things may seem confused and discordant to you, because you cannot discern the order that governs them, nevertheless everything is governed by its own proper order directing all things toward the good." What seems fortune to humans is really providence which they do not recognize. See Boethius, The Consolation of Philosophy, trans. Richard Green (Indianapolis, 1962), pp. 90-100.

[17]Sidney, pp. 109-11.

[18]Aristotle on the Art of Poetry, trans. Ingram Bywater (Oxford, 1909); rpt. in Rhetoric and Poetics (New York, 1954), 1460b. All further references to this work appear in the text.

[19]Rhetorica, trans. W. Rhys Roberts, in Rhetorica, Rhetorica ad Alexandrum, Poetica, Vol. XI of The Works of Aristotle, eds. J. A. Smith and W. D. Ross (Oxford, 1924); rpt. in Rhetoric and Poetics (New York, 1954), 1371b. See also Epinomis 986d.

[20]J. V. Cunningham traces the idea of wonder from Aristotle through antiquity and the Middle Ages to the Renaissance [Woe or Wonder (Denver, 1951), pp. 62-104]. See also Marvin T. Herrick, "Some Neglected Sources of 'Admiratio,'" MLN, 62 (1947), 222-26.

[21]Cf. discussion of Bottom below, pp. 109-11. Metaphysica, trans. W. D. Ross, Vol. VIII of The Works of Aristotle, eds. J. A. Smith and W. D. Ross (Oxford, 1908), 982b. All further references to this work are in the text.

[22]Cicero, Classification of Oratory, ed. Harris Rackham (Cambridge and London, 1942), pp. 72-73.

[23]St. Albert the Great, _Opera Omnia_, ed. Augustus Borgnet (Paris, 1890), VI, 30a-31b, as quoted in Cunningham, pp. 79-80.

[24]Antonio Minturno, _L'Arte Poetica_, in _Literary Criticism: Plato to Dryden_, ed. Allen H. Gilbert (Detroit, 1962), p. 292. Aristotle says that events appear most astonishing "when they seem to happen as the result of a cause" rather than by chance. Minturno takes the reasonable step of calling the cause divine will.

[25]See, for example, Tasso, p. 479.

[26]Tasso, p. 481.

[27]Jean Seznec, _The Survival of the Pagan Gods_ (New York, 1953), pp. 23, 312-316, 322.

[28]_Marsilio Ficino's Commentary on Plato's Symposium_, trans. Sears Reynolds Jayne, University of Missouri Studies, 19 (Columbia, 1944), pp. 231-33.

[29]_Phaedrus_, trans. W. C. Heimbold and W. B. Rabinowitz (Indianapolis, 1975), 247. All further references to this work are in the text.

[30]Ficino, pp. 231-32.

[31]Castiglione, p. 313.

[32]Antonio Minturno, _L'arte poetica_ (Napoli, 1725), p. A$_3$v, as quoted in Baxter Hathaway, _The Age of Criticism: The Late Renaissance in Italy_ (Ithaca, New York, 1962), p. 435.

[33]Castiglione, pp. 318-21. See Ficino, pp. 213-15 for his version of the ladder and for Pico della Mirandola's version see John Vyvyan, _Shakespeare and Platonic Beauty_ (New York, 1961), pp. 220-21. See also Spenser, _An Hymne of Heavenly Beauty_, ll. 22-56, 71-94.

[34]Castiglione, p. 321.

[35]Ficino, pp. 133-34.

[36]Olson cites a parallel passage in Jonson's _Masque of Queenes_ (1. 221-42) which was written after _MND_ (p. 112).

[37]_Plato's Symposium, or the Drinking Party_, trans. Michael Joyce (New York and London, 1935); rpt. in _The Collected Dialogues of Plato_, eds. Edith Hamilton and Huntington Cairns, Bollingen Series, 71 (New York, 1961), 188a-188b. All further references to this work are in the text.

[38]Vyvyan, pp. 78-79, 83.

[39]Ficino, p. 199. Also see p. 189. The brackets are mine.

[40]See Ch. II, pp. 35-36, for a discussion of parallels between the young lovers' story and the Pyramus and Thisbe play.

[41]Castiglione, pp. 313, 318-319.

[42]The first reference I find to Corinthians is William Burgess, _The Bible In Shakespeare_ (Chicago, 1903), p. 61. Corinthians is also discussed in Olson, pp. 98, 113-14; Kermode, p. 219; Dent, p. 121; Allen, p. 109: R. Chris Hassel, _Faith and Folly_ (Athens, Georgia, 1980), pp. 53-76.

[43]The Tyndale Bible (I cite the 1537 edition.) is closer than the Coverdale or the 1557 Geneva New Testament to Bottom's speech. The Coverdale Bible substitutes "depenesses of the Godheade" for the Tyndale's "botome of Goddes secretes." The 1557 Geneva New Testament substitutes "entred into mans mynde" for the Tyndale's "entred into the hert of mã."

CHAPTER V

THE TEMPEST: THE POET AS POLITICIAN

AND POLITICAL PHILOSOPHER

The Tempest attributes to a political figure the understanding which A Midsummer Night's Dream implies is available only to the poet. As a practical politician concerned with the realities of governing, Theseus is admirable and yet deficient both in attention to the ideal and in recognizing the potency of desire. A Midsummer Night's Dream suggests that a poet is needed to incorporate the ideal with the real[1] and that he can do so partly because he understands the nature of passion. Prospero, on the other hand, is notable for his concern with controlling the passions[2] and for his search for theoretical knowledge at the expense of practical politics. Prospero is so firm with Ferdinand concerning chastity prior to marriage that critics have frequently blamed him for undue harshness or unrealistic attitudes, and his usurpation results from turning over the government of Milan to his brother so that he can continue his studies. The comparison of Theseus with Prospero and the loss of Prospero's dukedom suggest the difficulty of combining theoretical knowledge with practical rule. And yet Prospero eventually applies his knowledge to practical politics to gain true control over Milan and Naples. To do so he calls upon the powers of poetry.

Shakespeare's equation of poet, politician and philosopher is compatible with a general Renaissance association of the three. As argued in Chapter I, poetry's defenders transferred to it the classical claims of politics and political philosophy. Sidney made it the architechtonic discipline whose end was virtuous action stemming from knowledge of "man's self, in the ethic and politic consideration," while other defenders continually referred to the poet as the first philosopher, the first legislator and the first civilizing force. Even poetry's adversaries left a place for a discipline which could support virtue and society.

To understand Prospero's position as a poet who is both ruler and philosopher, one must fill in the Renaissance picture of the poet by reference to

Plato's <u>Republic</u>, for the Renaissance view arose both as a response to Socrates' attack on poetry (pp. 4-6, 46 n. 6 above) and as a modification of Socrates' reform of the discipline. Any Renaissance defense of poetry had either to accept Socrates' reform or to find another method of meeting the grounds of his attack. Poetry's Renaissance defenders found an alternative in the transferral to poetry of philosophy's or politics' claim to being the master discipline. In making the transfer those defenders generally accepted Plato's characterization of the philosopher and of the philosopher-king. But they also added to their description of the model poet the ability to move people to virtue. Prospero in Milan is very much like Plato's philosopher who is unwilling to rule. Later on the island he serves as an effective philosopher-king. In this capacity he has attained knowledge of the mixed nature of himself and others. Like the Renaissance model poet, he uses this knowledge to produce virtue in his citizens. In Miranda and Ferdinand that production of virtue parallels the philosopher-king's education of the city's guardians.

Socrates condemns the poets as dangerous to the city for three reasons. First, they represent the gods as supporting injustice and immorality. Second, they make the city's protectors unduly afraid of death. And, third, they support immoderation through the imitation of evil behavior as well as good. Renaissance writers were correct in arguing that Socrates bans only the abuse of poetry. Socrates gives suggestions for poetry's reform which eliminate those elements potentially harmful to the city.

Socrates' reform of poetry brings it into harmony with politics and philosophy. Since it is necessary for the founders of a city to "know the models according to which the poets must tell their tales" (379a), namely, models for the representation of virtue, the founders must ultimately look to the discipline which studies the beautiful or the good as universals, recognizing them everywhere they exist rather than simply haphazardly in particular examples (473-484). This discipline is philosophy. Finding good in varying examples implies opinion rather than knowledge, which depends upon the recognition of permanent entities. Only the philosopher can attain knowledge, and thus he must rule:

> Unless the philosophers rule as
> kings or those now called kings and
> chiefs genuinely and adequately
> philosophize, and political power
> and philosophy coincide in the same
> place, while the many natures now
> making their way to either apart
> from the other are by necessity
> excluded, there is no rest from ills
> for the cities, my dear Glaucon, nor
> will the regime we have now
> described in speech ever come forth
> from nature, insofar as possible,
> and see the light of the sun.
>
> (473d)

Not only is the best ruler the philosopher, he is
also the poet. Since in the best city only the
rulers and not the private citizens are allowed to
tell tales or lies (389b-d), the rulers ultimately
become poets.

One can see how Socrates' reform of poetry would
lead Renaissance defenders to make the poet the
master of the architechtonic discipline. Instead of
making the philosopher-king take over the functions
of the poet, the Renaissance makes the poet take over
the functions of the philosopher-king. The poet
becomes a philosopher who, unlike the historian, can
present virtue and vice in their pure universal form
as knowledge rather than opinion. The poet also adds
something to the knowledge of the philosopher. He
knows how to move people to act upon that knowledge.
As Sidney argues, the poet can do this because he has
the historian's understanding of the particular as
well as the philosopher's knowledge of the
universal. This allows the poet to render precept in
example to give people a lively understanding of how
they must act, whereas the philosopher's abstraction
is not easily understood or applied. In other words,
the poet knows how best to fulfill the function of
the politician.

Prospero in Milan has the characteristics of
Plato's philosopher without Sidney's additions. In
Milan Prospero is considered "Without a parallel" in
his study of the liberal arts. These he could pursue
in depth because, "neglecting worldly ends"
(I.ii.89), he had turned over the concerns of
practical government to his brother. He dedicates

99

himself "To closeness and the bettering of my mind"
(I.ii.90). Why would Prospero do this? Obviously he
is no Doctor Faustus seeking knowledge for the sake
of power. Rather he is like Plato's philosopher,
whose love of learning makes him turn toward the
universal image of the good and the fair. Such an
image makes him dissatisfied with practical affairs
which can produce at most worldly examples of the
partially good and beautiful:

> a man who has his understanding
> truly turned toward the things that are
> has no leisure to look down toward the
> affairs of human beings and to be filled
> with envy and ill will as a result of
> fighting with them. But, rather, because
> he sees and contemplates things that are
> set in a regular arrangement and are
> always in the same condition--things that
> neither do injustice to one another nor
> suffer it at one another's hands, but
> remain all in order according to
> reason--he imitates them and, as much as
> possible, makes himself like them.
>
> (500c)

Those who have spent their lives in education "won't
be willing to act, believing that they have emigrated
to a colony on the Isles of the Blessed while they
are still alive" (519).

Prospero's study has given him the godlike
characteristics attributed by Socrates to the
philosopher. As in the Republic, "keeping company
with the divine and orderly," the philosopher
"becomes orderly and divine, to the extent that it is
possible for a human being" (500d). The idea that
study of essences or universals approaches divinity
is common in the Renaissance. Castiglione's courtier
ascends the ladder of love towards those truths
available to the eye of the mind through the study of
philosophy, and in approaching God he finds the
heavenly in himself:

> Therefore the soule ridde of vices,
> purged with the studies of true
> Philosophie, occupied in sprituall,
> and exercises in matters of
> understanding, turning her to the
> beholding of her owne substance, as

it were raised out of a most deepe
sleepe, openeth the eyes that all
men have, and few occupie, and seeth
in her selfe a shining beame of
light, which is the true image of
the Angelike beautie partened with
her, whereof she also partneth with
the bodie a feeble shadow.[3]

Renaissance writers also follow Plato in arguing that
knowledge as the pursuit of the eternal leads toward
divinity, while riches have only temporal reality.
Writing eighteen years after Shakespeare's death,
Thomas Heywood puts the idea in a Christian context:

It is a saying of <u>Socrates</u>, That in
war, Iron is better than Gold; And
in the course of a mans life
knowledge is to be preferred before
Riches. Excellent was that
Apothegme of <u>Pythagoras</u>; He that
knoweth no more than he hath need
of, is a Man amongst Beasts; But he
that knowth all that he ought to
know, is a god amongst Men.[4]

Shakespeare, himself, gives explicit expression to
this idea through Cerimon in <u>Pericles</u>:

I held it ever
Virtue and cunning were endowments greater
Than nobleness and riches: careless heirs
May the two latter darken and expend,
But immortality attends the former,
Making a man a god.

(III.ii.27-31)

Many critics have discussed Prospero's godlike
characteristics. He controls the plot like
Providence or an agent of Providence. Ferdinand
believes that the music he hears while sitting on the
bank weeping at his father's death "waits upon / Some
god o' th' island" (I.ii.389-90). "This is no mortal
business, nor no sound / That the earth owes"
(I.ii.407-08). Later the play refers to the events
produced by Prospero as strange, wonderful,
miraculous (IV.i.124; V.i.104-06, 153-62, 178,
227-28, 241-43, 313-15). As Alonso says, "These are
not natural events; they strengthen / From strange to
stranger."

Prospero's forgiveness of those who have offended
him suggests that he is like a Christian god, but his
godlike characteristics also derive from his
knowledge. On the island he has been given the
opportunity to continue his studies through Gonzalo's
provision of books from Prospero's study in Milan.
Prospero sees his exile on the island as a blessed
event as well as the result of foul play: "By foul
play, as thou say'st, were we heaved thence, / But
blessedly holp hither" (I.ii.62-63). On the island
Prospero has gained the godlike control over men that
allows him to recover his dukedom.

Prospero's knowledge provides power in the
practical world once he is on the island. This is a
power which Prospero did not have in Milan where his
brother could usurp him. Somehow Prospero has gained
this power on the island. One of his first actions
upon arrival is to free Ariel from imprisonment in a
tree by an evil spirit Sycorax. Prospero's control
of Ariel then allows him to control the actions of
nature and to orchestrate situations for other
humans. The freeing and control of Ariel must be
symbolic of Prospero's enlargement of his powers.

If Ariel represents poetry, as I argue later
(pp.133-43 below), then Prospero's power over Ariel
makes Prospero a poet. Like a poet, Prospero directs
the production of music and illusions. Before or
after each of Ariel's songs or enactments Prospero
and Ariel confer about Prospero's directives.
Prospero's masque for Ferdinand and Miranda is
perhaps the most explicitly poetic illusion, but
other scenes have a playlike quality. Prospero, for
example, thanks Ariel for his lifelike acting in
playing the figure of a harpy during the banquet
scene (III.ii.83-86), or Prospero creates the
illusion of a tempest which destroys the king's ship
and drowns Ferdinand while actually all are safe. As
Caliban reminds us, only a poet can create such
illusions which "delight and hurt not" (III.ii.140).

Prospero's poetry is not mere illusion. It also
involves magical control over nature. Before his
arrival on the island there is no mention of Prospero
as a magician. To return to Milan Prospero discards
his magician's robes. The control over practical
affairs which Prospero gains on the island, then,
must relate to his role as magician. In this role
Prospero becomes Sidney's poet who has mastered the

102

architechtonic discipline to attain the ability to lead people to virtue.

Shakespeare uses certain NeoPlatonic ideas as a metaphor for the poet who has added to the philosopher's knowledge the ability to direct people's actions to virtue.[5] NeoPlatonic occult philosophers maintain that through attention to the immortal element within him man can attain the powers of causality residing in divinity. These philosophers take from Plato's Timaeus the idea that at creation a part of the "soul of the universe," or an immortal element, is infused by God in various dilutions into every being or object. By infusing the world soul God makes every part of the universe accord with the pattern of the unchangeable and analogous to it. Through participation in the world soul by way of his own soul man is potentially in harmony with everything in the universe. Since the divine pattern is that which is apprehended by reason and mind, the man who has loved knowledge and wisdom and who "has exercised his intellect more than any other part of him, must have thoughts immortal and divine."[6] The NeoPlatonic occult philosophers go a step further than the Timaeus to give man not only the ability to understand the divine, but also the powers of causality residing in divinity. Taking from the Timaeus the idea that all causality is the product of the mind, the NeoPlatonists give to the magician the power to cause things through exercise of the mind. Christian NeoPlatonists emphasize the virtues of religion rather than mind alone as the source of the magician's power.[7]

Cornelius Agrippa who, with Robert Fludd and others, brought NeoPlatonic occult philosophy to the Renaissance describes the process as follows:

> Magicians teach that celestial gifts may, through inferiors being conformable to superiors, be drawn down by opportune influences of the heavens; and so, also by these celestial gifts, the celestial angels (as they are servants of the stars) may be procured and conveyed to us. Iamblichus, Proclus and Synesius, with the whole school of the Platonists, confirm that not only celestial and vital but also

certain intellectual, angelical and
divine gifts may be received from
above by some certain matters having
a natural power of divinity and which
have a natural correspondency with
the superiors, being rightly received
and opportunely gathered together
according to the rules of natural
philosophy and astronomy . . . for
this is the harmony of the world,
that things supercelestial be drawn
down by the celestial, and the
supernatural by those natural,
because there is One Operative Virtue
that is diffused through all kinds of
things . . . .

(I.xxxvii.75)

NeoPlatonic philosophers picture an ascent
through which the magician gains divine powers. As
in the passage from Agrippa cited above, they use the
popular Renaissance view of the great chain of being,
which originates in the Timaeus. According to this
view, there is a hierarchy of intelligences extending
from God to man to the meanest inanimate object. The
closer a being or object is to God the more he
participates in the divine. Everything higher on the
chain is a natural ruler, Agrippa's "superior," of
that which is lower. Agrippa refers to three worlds
or divisions of the chain--the supercelestial, the
celestial, and the natural--which also derive from
the Timaeus. Agrippa pictures an ascent from the
natural to the celestial through attention to the
immortal portion of each natural object as opposed to
its "corporeal qualities." This ascent may continue
to the supercelestial and to God Himself:

Wise men conceive it no way
irrational that it should be
possible for us to ascend by the
same degrees through each World, to
the same very original World itself,
the Maker of all things and First
Cause, from whence all things are
and proceed; and also to enjoy not
only these virtues, which are
already in the more excellent kind
of things, but also besides these to
draw new virtues from above.

(I.i.1)

The magician's power is applied to the natural world through control of those intelligences which in the Platonic universe control the natural world. These are the daemons who serve as middle spirits between gods and men. The idea that God communicates to men through spirits of a middle nature is common in the Renaissance. It is probably expressed most frequently in terms derived from the _Symposium_'s discussion of love as a daemon (quoted on pp. 77-78 above). This is the source of the popular description in Castiglione's _The Courtier_ of love as a binding force, a mean between the heavenly and the earthly.[8]

Identification of Ariel with the daemon as a beneficent spirit and of Prospero with at least the general non-technical understanding of the theurgist, or white magician, is hard to deny.[9] Ariel is clearly a spirit of some sort. Prospero calls him "spirit" (I.ii.194, 207, 215 and V.i.6, 19, 86). Ariel is listed in the cast of characters as an "airy spirit," and Prospero notes of Ariel "thou . . . art but air" (V.i.21). Daemons traditionally inhabited the middle region between the earth and aether, that is, the air. Plato places the daemon between the earth and heavens in the _Symposium_ (202e), and the _Epinomis_ specifically places the daemons in the element of air (984d-e). According to Apuleius, daemons "dwell in the regions of the air, which are adjacent to the earth, and on the confines of the heavens."[10]

Other NeoPlatonists, however, separate daemons into different species arranged in a hierarchy. Each species has control over all of the inferior species. Classified according to habitat, they are celestial, ethereal, aerial, aquatic, terrestrial, and subterranean. The first two of these are intellectual substances.[11] Viewed as part of this system, Ariel becomes a rational aerial daemon who can control aquatic, terrestrial, and subterranean orders of daemons. As a rational substance which can be controlled by the mind, it is appropriate that Ariel should "cleave to" Prospero's "thoughts" (IV.i.164). Ariel's control over other lesser spirits or daemons is explicitly referred to in the play. Ariel first appears with "all his quality" (I.i.193), returns for the banquet scene with his "fellow ministers" (III.iii.65) and works with "meaner ministers" (III.iii.87), his "meaner fellows"

(IV.i.35). Further characteristics which Ariel has in common with the daemon appear in Appendix B.

Prospero's control over Ariel, the rational aerial daemon, implies that he has the qualities of a theurgist. Only the theurgist can command the aerial spirit. The goetist or evil black magician may invoke such a spirit and use it in operations consonant with the symmetry of nature, but he cannot command it or obtain its aid for evil purposes.[12] The "damned witch Sycorax," who was banished "For mischiefs manifold, and sorceries terrible / To enter human hearing," could not as a goetist force Ariel "To act her earthy and abhorred commands." Ariel refused "her grand hests" and was therefore confined by Sycorax in a pine. As a goetist who could deal only with the transitory effluxions of things and whose powers were thus relatively weak, Sycorax "Could not again undo" the charm she laid upon Ariel. Prospero's superior powers as theurgist allowed him to release Ariel.

Some critics have found Prospero's use of magic suspect,[13] but there is little basis for considering it malevolent. Prospero employs his magic only to regain a dukedom rightfully his, to foil two conspiracies to murder, to appeal to the consciences of those who have wronged him, and to make the virtuous Ferdinand and Miranda heirs to the thrones of Naples and Milan. Ferdinand's and Gonzalo's comments on the action contradict the critical view that in doing all this Prospero has exalted himself to a position not rightfully man's. Prospero's control appears as part of a divine plan. Ferdinand tells his father of Miranda that "by immortal providence she's mine" (V.i.189), and Gonzalo attributes the outcome to Providence:

> Look down, you gods,
> And on this couple drop a blessèd crown!
> For it is you that have chalked forth the way
> Which brought us hither.
> (V.i.201-04; see also V.i.205-13)

These comments combined with the play's numerous references to the gods suggest that Prospero's actions have heavenly approval.

Some critics might argue that the final approval of Providence is contingent upon a change in Prospero from vengeful in the early part of the play to forgiving in the final act,[14] but the play does not verify the much-argued view that Prospero changes in this way. Prospero indicates that he has planned all along to free Ariel and that his work as a magician will be completed about the time he forgives his enemies. Prospero and Ariel's first discussion concerns Ariel's promised liberty (I.ii.242-300), a subject to which Prospero refers again even before Act V (I.ii.421; IV.i.263-65). Prospero's entire plan is to be completed within a certain time span: "At least two glasses. The time 'twixt six and now / Must by us both be spent most preciously" (I.ii.240-41). And Prospero's forgiveness occurs just at the point where he has planned to finish his work against his enemies:

> Prospero. Now does my project gather to a head.
> My charms crack not, my spirits obey, and time
> Goes upright with his carriage. How's the day?
> Ariel. On the sixth hour, at which time, my lord,
> You said our work should cease.
>
> (V.i.15)

Prospero's release of Ariel implies an end to Prospero's charms which keep his enemies in torment, and the definite time period assigned to Prospero's dealing with his enemies suggests that some sort of forgiveness or reconciliation has been planned. Further, the positing of a vengeful Prospero leaves no explanation for his arrangement of the union of Ferdinand and Miranda prior to his supposed conversion to forgiveness.[15]

Prospero's magic is not directed towards vengeance as some critics have maintained. He does use it to arouse tempests, to cause hallucinations which put a man out of his wits, and to torment Caliban, Stephano and Trinculo. When viewed as responsible for these activities, Prospero's art seems a "rough magic" directed towards vengeance. And yet Prospero's care that his magic should cause no real harm to those on whom he practices it indicates that he uses magic only to bring about their self-knowledge and repentance, to foil their evil schemes, and to regain his dukedom. Prospero plans that the tempest should hurt no one. During the storm he can tell Miranda that "There's no harm done" (I.ii.13). When Ariel reports his performance of the tempest as "Prospero bade" him, Prospero determines that Ariel has used the appropriate care: "But was not this nigh shore?" Ariel reports that it was "Close by." Prospero then makes certain that the passengers on the ship are safe: "But are they, Ariel, safe?" Ariel's report of the safety of the king's ship is reminiscent of God's protection of Saint Paul at sea in a storm (Acts 27:34): "Not a hair perished. / On their sustaining garments not a blemish, / But fresher than before . . . " (I.ii.217-19). The mariners are safely put to sleep with the ship secure in harbor. In producing these events Ariel has "Exactly . . . performed" Prospero's "charge." In addition, before Prospero frees Ariel and rejects his magic altogether, he uses it to call forth "Some heavenly music" to "cure" the "brains" of the court party and to restore "reason" to an "unsettled fancy."

As a beneficent practitioner of magic acting in accordance with the will of heaven Prospero attains a certain godliness. He can be thought of as a theurgist who attains power not by calling down the celestial, but by raising himself up beyond normal humanity. This reading follows Agrippa's argument that no human spirits can really compel spirits which are incorporeal. Rather we devise symbols "not by which we can in any way couple them to us, but by which we lift ourselves up to them. . . ."[16]

Certain elements of the occult tradition account for the activities of Prospero and Ariel, but Shakespeare is not using the occult tradition for the sake of arguing that certain magical powers are available to humans. The Tempest was produced at court, in the fall of 1611 and during the winter of 1612-1613, before a king who did not believe in the possibility of beneficent magic.[17] As Frank Kermode points out, the situation is analogous to the frequent presentation at court of pagan gods supporting virtues but regarded by James in theory as devils.[18] James would have taken the magical powers of Prospero simply as a dramatic device for representing the embodiment of Prospero's virtue and knowledge in poetry. Seen in 1612-1613 as part of the festivities surrounding the marriage of Princess Elizabeth to the Elector Palatine, the play would have suggested a parallel between Prospero and James. The presentation of knowledge and virtue as the source of true control over one's subjects would have contained an implied compliment to the king. On the other hand, the orthodox opinion that beneficent magic is not possible[19] does make ambiguous the play's position on the ability of knowledge and virtue to attain temporal power.

One would not wish to deny that knowledge and virtue should be the true sources of control over one's subjects, and on the face of it Prospero may have seemed to have gained the requisite knowledge studying liberal arts in Milan. And yet Prospero does not gain control over nature until he is on the island. Perhaps Prospero's knowledge in Milan is incomplete.

Prospero has various experiences on the island which suggest that this is the case. His original treatment of Caliban involves a mistaken view that kindness and education will serve as sufficient means of control. Prospero naively lodges Caliban with Miranda and himself until Caliban tries to rape Miranda. As a result Prospero learns the need for sterner methods--"cramps," "pinches," "stripes." At the same time Prospero acknowledges Caliban as a part of himself--"mine" (V.i.276)--which he and Miranda cannot deny entirely: "We cannot miss him. He does make our fire, / Fetch in our wood, and serves in offices / That profit us" (I.ii.311-13). Caliban represents appetite and the needs of the body which Prospero must recognize and learn to control in others as well as in himself.

A second new experience on the island is the education of Miranda and Ferdinand as future rulers (see below, pp. 113-18). In Milan Prospero had not recognized the need and learned the method to control that aspect of human nature which causes a person to hunger for political power. He had turned over his government to his brother without seeing the danger of putting political power in the hands of such a man. On the island, however, Prospero takes care to mix the desire to rule in Ferdinand and Miranda with a love of virtue which will keep it in appropriate bounds. Miranda and Ferdinand, like Caliban, may represent an element of human nature previously neglected by Prospero (see pp. 131-32 below).

Prospero needs knowledge of appetite and of the desire for political power both as poet and as ruler. In this latter capacity Prospero becomes a philosopher-king of sorts. This is not to say that

The Tempest is a simple embodiment of Platonic ideas, but it does contain obvious elements of many Platonic ideas which had become commonplace in the Renaissance. Shakespeare, of course, puts his own mark on those ideas.

Prospero's attention to his studies in Milan rather than to affairs of state is perhaps most reminiscent of the philosopher of Plato's Republic, and the fact of Prospero's rule brings into effect Socrates' suggestion that philosophers should rule. Moreover, the play begins with the traditional image of the ship of state, a commonplace derived from Plato, and examines the question of who should rule in ways reminiscent of Platonic ideas or Renaissance derivations of those ideas.

According to the tradition, the ruler of the city becomes the ship's pilot.[20] As The Tempest opens Alonso and Antonio appear as ineffectual rulers who have no power to prevent the storm, confusion and ultimate wreck of their ship. In fact, they make conditions worse:

Alonso. Good boatswain, have care. Where's
        the master? Play the men.
Boatswain. I pray now, keep below.
Antonio. Where is the master, bos'n?
Boatswain. Do you not hear him? You mar our
        labor. Keep your cabins; you do
        assist the storm.
                (I.i.9-14; see also I.i.16-51)

Antonio is the false pilot who knows how to gain control through subverting certain people and eliminating Prospero:

Being once perfected how to grant suits,
How to deny them, who t'advance, and who
To trash for overtopping, new-created
The creatures that were mine, I say--or changed
                'em
Or else new-formed 'em . . . .
                (I.ii.79-83)

Antonio views Prospero as useless and incompetent, and yet Antonio's rule is a false one gained only at the expense of Milan's independence:

                                Of temporal royalties
He thinks me now incapable; confederates
(So dry he was for sway) wi' th' King of Naples
To give him annual tribute, do him homage,
Subject his coronet to his crown, and bend
The dukedom, yet unbowed (alas, poor Milan!),
To most ignoble stooping.
                                    (I.ii.110-16)

Prospero is the city's natural ruler as well as
its hereditary leader. Inheritance has much to speak
for it, but, as Miranda points out, "Good wombs have
borne bad sons" (I.ii.119). The boatswain argues
that nature does not recognize the respect due to
kingship: "What cares these roarers for the name of
king?" The implication may be that ordinary kingship
is conventional rather than natural. The waves are
controlled by Prospero who has the natural attributes
requisite to the ruler. In the world of the play
nature recognizes the natural leader of humans. In
NeoPlatonic terms, by virtue of his greater
participation in the divine Prospero is higher on the
chain of being than the rest of humankind and
therefore their natural ruler.

On the level of the family the play presents a
similar issue. The father as the oldest family
member is generally considered the wisest and thus
the natural ruler of the family, and yet fathers are
not always wise. Alonso refers to this difficulty
once he repents for wronging Prospero and accepts
Miranda as his prospective daughter-in-law: "O, how
oddly will it sound that I / Must ask my child
forgiveness!" (V.i.197-98).

Prospero as the true pilot knows something of the
cosmos as a whole. This knowledge is implied by
Prospero's production of music on his island and by
his attention to numerology. In the Republic
(402b-c) the true harmony is available only to the
philosopher who recognizes the universal forms of
things:

                    we'll never be musical--either
                    ourselves or those who we say we
                    must educate to be guardians--before
                    we recognize the forms of
                    moderation, courage, liberality,
                    magnificence, and all their kind,
                    and, again, their opposites,

everywhere they turn up, and notice
that they are in whatever they are
in, both themselves and their
images, despising them neither in
little nor big things, but believing
that they all belong to the same art
and discipline?

The recognition of universals and of their
existence in particulars implies a structure and
harmony in the universe akin to the structure and
harmony of music. In the Renaissance this idea
occurs most frequently in the image of the music of
the spheres, implying an intelligible order in the
universe. Lorenzo describes this music in The
Merchant of Venice:

There's not the smallest orb which thou behold'st
But in his motion like an angel sings,
Still quiring to the young-eyed cherubins;
Such harmony is in immortal souls,
But whilst this muddy vesture of decay
Doth grossly close it in, we cannot hear it.
                        (V.i.60-65)

If humans cannot quite attain this heavenly music,
they can at least reach an imitation of it on earth.
Lorenzo continues,

The man that hath no music in himself,
Nor is not moved with concord of sweet sounds,
Is fit for treasons, stratagems, and spoils;
The motions of his spirit are dull as night,
And his affections dark as Erebus.
                              (V.i.83-87)

The music on Prospero's island, continually
referred to as something more than human, is
suggestive of celestial music or music of the
spheres. It brings order to nature and to man's soul
in allaying the waves of the tempest and soothing
Ferdinand's grief:

                        Sitting on a bank,
Weeping again the King my father's wrack,
This music crept by me upon the waters
Allaying both their fury and my passion
With its sweet air.
                        (I.ii.390-94)

112

The idea that harmony suggests all order, beauty and virtue is common in the Renaissance. Sir Thomas Elyot, for example, asserts that even "a mean musician" could make a "right pleasant harmony" out of Claudian's verses, since "almost every note should express a counsel virtuous or necessary."[21] Prospero's use of music implies his virtue in general as philosopher, poet and politician.

Musical harmonies have a mathematical structure which, as noted above, suggests an order in the universe. Prospero's attention to number implies that he is in tune with this order. His concern to complete his work "on the sixth hour" (V.i.4)[22] is in keeping with the view of six as the number of perfection. This view derives from the fact that six is the only number under ten which is equal to the sum of its parts. Six may be divided by two, three, and six, and the sum of the quotients, three plus two plus one, is six.[23] Six also derives its special virtue from the Pythagoreans' application of it to generation and marriage, from the creation of the world in six days, from Christ's suffering for our redemption on the sixth day, from the six years' service of the Hebrew bondservant, and from the six tones existing in all harmony.[24]

Prospero's emphasis on three--for example, in his dealing with "three men of sin," in his reference to Miranda as "a third of mine own life," and in speaking of "his every third thought"--also has a special significance. The Middle Ages and the Renaissance derived from the _Timaeus_ the idea that two things can be joined together only by a third which acts as a bond. According to Macrobius, the "number three is the first to have a mean between two extremes to bind it together. . . ."[25] The daemon who appears as a middle spirit between God and man is such a bond. In Plato and later writers this triadic pattern is repeated in the state and in the individual. In Plato's ideal city the warriors bind the philosophers and the commons by carrying out the philosopher's orders which the commons obey. In the soul reason and appetite are joined by spiritedness.[26]

As a philosopher-king Prospero is a suitable founder of an ideal commonwealth, and indeed he serves in this capacity. As noted above (p. 1), Northrop Frye has mentioned the allusion to Aeneas as suggestive of Aeneas' trip from Carthage to Rome. Gonzalo's references to the "widow Dido" and to Tunis as Carthage imply, in a general way, a comparison of Aeneas with Gonzalo who imagines being king of his ideal commonwealth and with Prospero who is king of the island. These references are reinforced by a storm which begins both The Aeneid and The Tempest and by a banquet of harpies common to both works.

As philosopher-king Prospero serves as educator of the city's future rulers, Miranda and Ferdinand. Unlike most rulers, they are motivated by a love of virtue which is both compatible with their natures and inculcated by Prospero. Prospero has been Miranda's schoolmaster (I.ii.172) and continues as the educator of both Miranda and Ferdinand. The nature of his teaching is suggested by the masque in which music and the joining of Ceres and Juno to bless the marriage contract of true love suggest the harmony of heaven and earth. Venus, a goddess associated with lust and illicit love, is banned from the masque, and Cupid, Venus' son, agrees to stop shooting the arrows which cause such love. Prospero has become the model Renaissance poet. In explicitly banishing or reforming the immoral, Prospero's actions respond to the accusation that poetry teaches lust (see pp. 4-5 above).

In eliminating immorality Prospero gives Miranda and Ferdinand an education similar to that which The Republic would give the ruling class or, as Socrates calls them, the guardians. As suggested above (pp. 2-3), the education of this class was of greatest concern to the Renaissance. Prospero's concern in the action covered in the play is teaching Ferdinand "to love in a moderate and musical way" (Republic 403a). This entails adjusting the "body's harmony for the sake of the accord in the soul" (591d). Act IV begins with Prospero's warning to Ferdinand not to break Miranda's "virgin-knot before / All sanctimonious ceremonies may / With full and holy rite be minist'red" (IV.i.15-17), and the subject of the masque is the "contract of true love" which bans Venus and Cupid and vows "that no bed-right shall be paid / Till Hymen's torch be lighted" (IV.i.96-97). Given such a contract, Ferdinand and Miranda are guaranteed the blessings of heaven and earth, those of Juno "queen o' th' sky" and of Ceres presiding over earthly abundance:

114

```
Juno.       Honor, riches, marriage blessing,
            Long continuance, and increasing,
            Hourly joys be still upon you!
[Ceres.]  Earth's increase, foison plenty,
            Barns and garners never empty,
            Vines and clust'ring bunches growing,
            Plants with goodly burden bowing;
            Spring come to you at the farthest
            In the very end of harvest.
            Scarcity and want shall shun you,
            Ceres' blessing so is on you.
                            (IV.i.106-17)
```

The nymphs who are called, through the collaboration of Juno and Ceres, to celebrate the contract of true love are "temperate nymphs" who reinforce the impetus to moderation.

In the interest of his guardians' moderation Socrates finds it necessary to ban poetry which represents the gods as performing or rewarding immoral acts (Republic 390-92). Prospero produces an imitation which does not water the passions but orders and controls them. He does this through a reform of poetry of sorts. The ancient pantheon is altered by the exclusion of Venus and the reform of Cupid. Emphasis on the body is thus excluded. Moderation or control of the body by the soul is essential to the love of the beautiful and the good by which the guardian class is to be guided (Republic 401d-402a). Emphasis on the body leads to discord and vice. One cannot drink the same wine or share the same woman or man. Things of the body are subject to scarcity in general, and people cannot have them without excluding others.

Ferdinand and Miranda are motivated by love of the beautiful and the good. Each responds to the beauty of the other and associates that beauty with goodness:

```
Miranda.              I might call him
            A thing divine; for nothing natural
            I ever saw so noble.
                            (I.ii.417-19)
```

```
Ferdinand.            Most sure, the goddess
            On whom these airs attend! Vouchsafe
                my prayer
            May know if you remain upon this island,
```

And that you will some good instruction
                give
           How I may bear me here.
                                    (I.ii.423-26)

Miranda makes explicit the association of the
beautiful with the good: "There's nothing ill can
dwell in such a temple. / If the ill spirit have so
fair a house, / Good things will strive to dwell
with't" (I.ii.457-59). Each is willing to labor for
the beauty he finds in the other. Ferdinand can find
his base logbearing "nobly undergone" and "pleasure"
when it brings Miranda's "sweet thoughts" that "such
baseness / Had never like executor." Miranda mirrors
his sentiment as she offers to carry the logs for him
(III.i.1-31).

The music or poetry which Prospero provides for
Ferdinand and Miranda presents beauty in combination
with virtue. In doing so it leads to a taste for
virtue. It puts into effect Sidney's argument that
the true poetry can best move people to virtue (see
pp. 4-5 above) and Castiglione's that music is
necessary to the courtier's winning the prince's
favor so that he can teach virtue.[27] Such poetry
need not give a rational argument to incite to
virtue. Rather it provides a sense that the good is
beautiful.

In the masque virtue is further supported by
presenting the gods of heaven and earth as rewarding
it. As Socrates argues in The Republic, people
cannot be motivated to virtue if the poets are
allowed to argue "that many happy men are unjust, and
many wretched ones just, and that doing injustice is
profitable if one gets away with it, but justice is
someone else's good and one's own loss" (392b). In
the course of The Tempest Ferdinand learns that
nature and humans are in harmony, that nature is good
to humans. Prospero's control over the seas and over
the action of the play has taught Ferdinand that
"Though the seas threaten, they are merciful. / I
have cursed them without cause" (V.i.177-78).
Nature's harmony with humans, of course, has a
Providential character to it. Twice the play makes
nature's goodness an implication of the validity of
the fortunate fall.[28] Miranda and Prospero's exile
on their island is caused by ill which leads
eventually to the good for them: "By foul play, as
thou say'st, were we heaved thence, / But blessedly

holp hither" (I.ii.62-63). Gonzalo sums up the entire action of the play in terms of _felix_ _culpa_:

> Was Milan thrust from Milan that his issue
> Should become kings of Naples? O, rejoice
> Beyond a common joy, and set it down
> With gold on lasting pillars. In one voyage
> Did Claribel her husband find at Tunis,
> And Ferdinand her brother found a wife
> Where he himself was lost; Prospero his dukedom
> In a poor isle: and all of us ourselves
> When no man was his own.
> (V.i.205-13)

Nature and Providence support the restoration of the dukedom to its true owner and the joining of Naples and Milan under good rulers. Such events, like the harmony of heaven and earth in the masque, suggest the possibility of realizing the ideal on earth.

The vision with which Prospero provides Miranda and Ferdinand transmits harmony, not knowledge. The young lovers are fortunate that Prospero has nurtured their souls to assure correspondence with their beautiful bodies, but their vision of the world contains difficulties. The association of the beautiful with the good indeed provides an impulse to goodness, but in the everyday world the association does not always hold. Miranda, who is motivated by love of virtue but not by a knowledge commensurate with Prospero's, can find a "brave new world" in the attractive appearances of the Machiavellian Antonio and Sebastian. The harmony of heaven and earth produced in the masque has an illusory quality to it, and, as the next chapter will suggest, this everyday world puts limits on the poet, politician, and philosopher.

In the course of The Tempest, then, Prospero comes to fulfill the Renaissance vision combining the poet with the philosopher and politican. Prospero's career in Milan traces this Renaissance formulation to its roots in Plato where the philosopher is so intent on immortal truths that he is unwilling to attend to the practical matters of ruling. But when Prospero arrives on the island he gains poetic and magical powers which enable him to control the natural world to regain political power. Prospero exercises his power through the production of music and illusions, in other words, as a poet. Yet

Prospero also has magical control over nature which extends beyond mere illusion. The NeoPlatonic associations of this magical power serve as a reminder that knowledge and virtue must act as the sources of true control over one's subjects. Prospero's experience on the island also suggests that that knowledge must extend beyond the liberal arts studied in Milan. On the island Prospero recognizes the potency of appetite through his experiences with Caliban; he learns to control it and also accepts it as a part of himself. Prospero also discovers on the island the method to control the hunger for political power, for he educates Miranda and Ferdinand as future rulers of Naples and Milan.

Prospero's philosophic characteristics carry over into the political sphere where, as ruler on the island and rightful ruler of Milan, he becomes a philosopher-king of sorts. Through the image of the ship of state, the play examines the question of who is the city's best ruler. As the true pilot, Prospero shows through production of music and attention to numerology that he knows something of the order of the universe as a whole. This makes him a suitable founder of an ideal commonwealth. He gives his commonwealth's future rulers, Ferdinand and Mirander, an education similar to that which the Republic's philosopher-king would give its guardians: an education which teaches moderation, which presents the gods and nature as rewarding virtue, and which fosters guidance by love of the beautiful and the good.

To give Miranda and Ferdinand this education, Prospero must function as a poet as well as a philosopher-king. The vision which Prospero as poet presents to Miranda and Ferdinand depicts harmony which does not require knowledge of the everyday world. That world puts on poet, politician and philosopher constraints which The Tempest explores.

[1] By "ideal" I mean paradigm of perfection, and by "real" I mean temporal. In Renaissance terms derived from Plato the ideas are more real than any imperfect imitation of them in the temporal world.

[2] Passion in A Midsummer Night's Dream is principally sexual desire, and in The Tempest sexual desire is the passion which Prospero is most clearly concerned to control. In Caliban, Stephano, and Trinculo The Tempest depicts appetite as love of food and drink as well as sexual desire. In addition to the control of appetite, Prospero must deal with ambition in Antonio and Sebastian and, to a lesser extent, in the characters of the subplot. In his own soul Prospero must wrestle with grief and anger.

The Renaissance generally thought of passion as an "infirmity" to which God was not subject. Passion, however, could be acceptable if it were controlled by the mind. Augustine, for example, argues, "Scripture subjects the mind to God for his direction and assistance, and subjects the passions to the mind for their restraint and control so that they may be turned into the instruments of justice. In fact, in our discipline, the question is not whether the devout soul is angry, but why; not whether it is sad, but what causes its sadness; not whether it is afraid, but what is the object of its fear" [The City of God, trans. Henry Bettensen (Baltimore and Middlesex, 1972), pp. 349-50, Bk. 10, Ch. 5].

[3] Castiglione, p. 318; also see p. 77 above.

[4] Thomas Heywood, The Hierarchie of the blessed Angels (London, 1935)--facsimile edition 530 of The English Experience (Amsterdam and New York, 1973), p. 450. Socrates' saying originates in Republic 521a.

[5] Walter Clyde Curry, Shakespeare's Philosophical Patterns (Baton Rouge, 1937) is the first to argue that Prospero is a theurgist. See also Robert Hunter West, The Invisible World (Athens, Georgia, 1939) and D. G. James, The Dream of Prospero (Oxford, 1967) for a more complete exposition of the history of occult philosophy. See also Robert West's Shakespeare and the Outer Mystery (Lexington,

Kentucky, 1968) for reflections on the place of theurgy in The Tempest.

[6]Timaeus 90b-c, trans. Benjamin Jowett, in Plato: The Collected Dialogues, eds. Edith Hamilton and Huntington Cairns (Princeton, 1961).

[7]See Cornelius Agrippa, Three Books of Occult Philosophy, trans. J. F. (London, 1651), III.iii.350. All references in the text to Agrippa are to this work.

[8]Appendix A gives a further history of the Renaissance view of the daemon.

[9]Ariel has been variously identified as a fairy, as eros, as the poetic imagination, as Shakespeare's art, and as the sensitive soul. Describing Ariel as a daemon does not provide a full representation of his function in the play and does not necessarily preclude these further identifications, but any attempts to define Ariel must take into acount his daemonic characteristics. Ariel's function will be discussed again later (pp. 156-65 below).

[10] Apuleius, The God of Socrates, in The Works of Apuleius, trans. Hudson Gurney (London, 1889), p. 357.

[11]This description appears in Curry, p. 175. It derives from Iamblichus, The Mysteries of the Egyptians, Chaldeans, and Assyrians, trans. Thomas Taylor (London, 1821), p. 339, but Curry also cites Proclus, Reginald Scot, and others (p. 241). Robert Burton's classification of daemons according to habitat concurs with this description [An Anatomy of Melancholy, ed. Floyd Dell and Paul Jordan-Smith (New York 1938), pp. 166-71].

[12]Iamblichus, pp. 206-07. Curry makes the following characterization of Sycorax as goetist and Prospero as theurgist.

[13]For example, James Smith, Shakespearian and Other Essays (London, 1974), pp. 234-36; Robert Egan, "This Rough Magic: Perspectives of Art and Morality in The Tempest," SQ, 23 (1972), 175-81; D'Orsay Pearson, "'Unless I be Relieved by Prayer': The Tempest in Perspective," Shakespeare Studies, 7

(1974), 253-82. Numerous critics see Prospero's magic as an indication of his superiority. See, for example, The Tempest, ed. Frank Kermode (London, 1958), p.xli; Herbert R. Coursen, Jr. Christian Ritual and the World of Shakespeare's Tragedies (Lewisburg, 1976), pp. 381-411; Spencer, p. 197.

[14]For example, J. Dover Wilson, The Meaning of the Tempest (Newcastle Upon Tyne, 1936), pp. 13-18; F. D. Hoeniger, "Prospero's Storm and Miracle," SQ, 7 (1956), 35-38; Richard Henze, "The Rejection of a Vanity," SQ, 23 (1972), 433; Egan, pp. 175-82; Pearson, p. 275.

[15]See Rose A. Zimbardo, "Form and Disorder in The Tempest," SQ, 14 (1963), 52.

[16]Agrippa, De occulta philosophia libri tres (Coloniae, 1533), II.xxx.cclxxvii--as translated in Charles G. Nauert, Agrippa and the Crisis of Renaissance Thought, Illinois Studies in the Social Sciences 55 (Urbana, 1965), p. 279.

[17]See Appendix A.

[18]Kermode, p. xli.

[19]See Appendix A.

[20]Although events of The Tempest do not follow precisely the Republic's discussion, the general image of ship as state and ruler as pilot seems applicable. In the Republic the false pilot (or ruler) knows how to gain power, and does so sometimes by killing or exiling his competitors, but he does not understand astronomy or mathematics (i.e., the arts of statemanship) which are necessary to proper navigation (rule). The true pilot or ruler is the philosopher who, with his mind on the good and beautiful, is not interested in fighting for a position in practical politics, and who is thus seen by the sailors or ruling class as useless and foolish:

> they praise and call "skilled," "pilot," and "knower of the ship's business" the man who is clever at figuring out how they will get the rule, either by persuading or by forcing the shipowner, while the man who is not of this sort they blame

as useless. They don't know that
for the true pilot it is necessary
to pay careful attention to year,
season, heaven, stars, winds, and
everything that's proper to the art,
if he is really going to be skilled
at ruling a ship.

(488a-89b)

The circumstances in The Republic and The Tempest
differ somewhat. In The Republic the sailors are
demagogues who subvert the shipowners (i.e., the
people) to gain rule. In The Tempest Antonio
subverts some of the courtiers, but the people still
love Prospero. Antonio gains rule by letting an
outside force enter the city.

The ship of state with a ruler as pilot also
appears in The Laws (709a-712a). There Plato notes
the usefulness of the pilot's art in the midst of a
gale.

[21]The Boke Named the Gouvernour, II, 11.

[22]Shakespeare also uses this reference to point
out that the time which passes in the play
corresponds to the time in which the play is acted.

[23]Macrobius, p. 102.

[24]Agrippa, Occult Philosophy, II.ix.191.

[25]Macrobius, p. 104; Timaeus, 32a-b.

[26]Timaeus, 69c-72d; Republic, 441d; C. S.
Lewis, The Discarded Image (Cambridge, 1971), pp.
43-44, 57, 73-74, 166-69. Lewis cites Apuleius,
Chalcidius, Pseudo-Dionysius, Alanus, and
Bartholomaeus Anglicus. My statement is a somewhat
simplified version of Plato's discussion of eros
which can be love of knowledge as in the Symposium
as well as mere appetite.

[27]Castiglione, p. 279.

[28]Arthur Kirsch argues that such references to
the fortunate fall in the last plays are a direct
result of the Renaissance understanding of these
plays' genre, tragicomedy. Kirsch's development of
this view suits well the idea that Prospero exerts a

godlike and poetic influence on the action of the play. Kirsch argues that in tragicomedy "the genesis of the play becomes wholly and marvellously indistinguishable from the evolution of the providential pattern which it represents." The "unity of the dramatist's creative powers and those of life itself" is "perhaps most perfect in _The Tempest_, where Prospero is both a playwright and a presiding deity . . ." [_Jacobean Dramatic Perspectives_ (Charlottesville, 1972), p. 73].

CHAPTER VI

THE TEMPEST: THE LIMITATIONS OF POETRY,

POLITICS AND PHILOSOPHY

Combining the philosopher with the poet and politician places on the philosopher constraints which are inimical to his search for truth and beauty. The politician must accommodate his rule to his citizens, and the poet must design his work to appeal to his audience. The limitations of citizen and audience require that the politician and poet adjust their goals to everyday, and therefore partial, reality. Further, the politician must respond to exigencies of fortune which do not affect the eternal objects on which the mind focuses.

Machiavelli had instituted a new interest in the limitations of human nature and the constraints which they put on the political leader. He argues that the prince must learn how not to be good since "he that in everie respect will needes be a good man cannot choose but be overthrowne emonge soe many that are ill." Only by recognizing the essential badness of people or how people actually live can the prince maintain control of a stable commonwealth. The ancients' concern for how people ought to live leads only to an imaginary perfection which can never be realized. Further, since how we live is so far removed from how we ought to live "he which respectes, not what is doon, but studies onlie to learne that which shoulde be doon is liker by his knowledge to purchase his owne subvertion, then by his conninge to provide for his safetie. . . ."[1]

Machiavelli's popularity in Renaissance England suggests that his work would have been readily available to Shakespeare. Edward Meyer has listed hundreds of references to Machiavelli in Elizabethan drama and has described Machiavelli's great popularity after 1577.[2] Lily Bess Campbell has found evidence that Machiavelli was popular in England by 1572 and notes recurring references to Leicester and Richard III as Machiavells.[3] Napoleone Orsini and Hardin Craig have discovered at least three distinct translations of The Prince into English before 1600 as well as a manuscript containing a translation of The Discourses.[4] These translations along with the surreptitious Italian editions published by John Wolfe were widely circulated. Moreover, there were printed translations into English of the <u>Arte</u> <u>of</u> <u>Warre</u> in 1563, 1573 and 1588 and of the <u>Florentine</u> <u>Historie</u> in 1595.[5] In 1579 Gabriel Harvey could claim that at Oxford:

> sum good fellowes amongst us begin nowe to be prettely well acquaynted with a certayne parlous booke called, as I remember me, Il Principe di Niccolo Macchiavelli, and I can peradventure name you an odd crewe or tooe that ar as cuninge in his Discorsi sopra la prima Deca de Livio, in his Historia Fiorentine, and in his Dialogue della Arte della Guerra tooe, and in certayne gallant Turkishe Discourses tooe, as University men were wont to be in their parva Logicolia and Magna Moralia and Physicalia of both sortes: <u>verbum</u> <u>intelligenti</u> <u>sat</u>.[6]

Renaissance writers branded Machiavelli as the embodiment of all evil, but nevertheless they were influenced by him. Orthodox writers such as Jean Bodin continued to argue that virtue must be the end of the state but felt compelled to write of things as they are rather than to dream of things as they might be.[7] Respected mainstream writers such as Spenser and Sidney could join in the Renaissance attack on the Machiavell while incorporating in some of their works views derived from Machiavelli or views similar to those of the Florentine. Edwin A. Greenlaw has made a good case for Spenser's use of Chapter III of <u>The</u> <u>Prince</u> in his <u>View</u> <u>of</u> <u>the</u> <u>Present</u> <u>State</u> <u>of</u> <u>Ireland</u>, and Irving Ribner has argued that although Sidney hated Machiavelli, the similarity of some of Sidney's and Machiavelli's views implies that the thinking of Machiavelli was not entirely alien to Elizabethan England.[8] Others such as Montaigne refer to Machiavelli in ways which suggest that they give his views serious consideration.[9]

Whether Shakespeare derives his understanding of Machiavelli directly or through English representations of Machiavelli's ideas, he explores Machiavelli's vision of the world through Antonio and Sebastian. Clearly they have much in common with the typical stage Machiavell. They are characterized by the predominant traits of this figure--underhanded strategem and atheism--and their Italian nationality completes the portrait.[10] Although Antonio and Sebastian are meant to be condemned as Italianate villains, Shakespeare's condemnation is not simple-minded. It reveals an understanding of the bases of Machiavelli's vision.

Antonio and Sebastian contrive their conspiracy against Prospero in terms derived ultimately from Chapter 25 of The Prince where Machiavelli urges man to conquer fortune by force for "fortune is a wooman, and he that will raigne over her, must of force be fayne both to maister her, and quicken her with a Cudgell." Antonio presents to Sebastian the Machiavellian argument that "[t]hou let'st thy fortune sleep," and the interchange continues employing the Machiavellian comparison of fortune to a river which can be controlled:

Sebastian.	Well, I am standing water.
Antonio.	I'll teach you how to flow.
Sebastian.	Do so, to ebb
	Hereditary sloth instructs me.
	(II.i.225-28)

Machiavelli makes the same contrast between fortune which is a fast-moving river and fortune which moves slowly. The Italian applies his river image to foreign invasions. Sebastian and Antonio have translated this into internal rebellion.

> I maie compare fortune to a mountaine flood that beates downe all before it . . . . Notwithstandinge although it be somtymes carried with such violence, yet in calmer tydes may men provide with dammes banckes pyles and such lyke, that att the next invndacion it shall fall downe the right channelles and followe the ordinarie coorse or at the leastwise represse the fury of it in such sorte that it shall neither soe far nor dangerouslie overflowe the bowndes. . . . [Y]f it [Italy] had ben supported with necessarie vertue and valure of the Inhabitantes, as we see Germany, Spayne, & Fraunce, this inundacion had never broken into it, nor the contrie had runn a floate with

such disordred alteracions as it
did.[11]

Depiction of fortune as a river is commonplace in
the Renaissance, but depiction of fortune as a river
which could be controlled by man originates with
Machiavelli. What distinguishes Machiavelli from his
peers is his emphasis on fortune, conceived of as
mutability rather than as the workings of Providence,
in the affairs of state.[12] As Felix Raab points
out, it is the spectre of the secular state which so
horrifies Elizabethan and Tudor England and which
makes Machiavelli the major scandal of European
political thought for two centuries or more.[13]

Antonio goes on, following Machiavelli's fashion,
to urge that caution is apt to cause ruin: "Ebbing
men, indeed, / Most often do so near the bottom run /
By their own fear and sloth." Antonio advocates
temerity, the Machiavellian princely virtue par
excellence. As Machiavelli argues, fortune "yeeldeth
more willinglie to them that use her roughlie and
severelie then to those that intreate her coldie and
fayntelie."[14]

Gonzalo is Antonio's adversary in his belief in
the traditional virtue of prudence. Antonio refers to
Gonzalo as "Sir Prudence" who must be eliminated along
with Alonso. As Gentillet, a Renaissance opponent of
Machiavelli, points out, prudence is suggested by a
belief in a man's limitations along with a sense of
the inscrutability of Providence. For Gentillet the
Italian's emphasis on fortune rather than Providence
contradicts the true view

that the haps which men call Fortune,
proceede from God, who rather blesseth
prudence, which hee hath recommended unto
us, than temeritie: and although
sometimes it happen, that hee blesse not
our counsels and wisedomes, it is because
we take them not from the true spring and
fountaine, namely from him whom we ought
to have demanded it, and that most
commonly wee would, that our owne
wisedome, should bee a glorie unto us,
whereas onely God should be glorified.[15]

128

Antonio's argument stems from the atheism of which Machiavelli was so commonly accused in the Renaissance. As Gentillet puts it, Machiavelli's followers are "enclined to all wickednesse . . . because they are Atheists, contemners of God, neither beleeving there is a God which seeth what they doe, nor that ought to punish them."[16] Antonio's attitude towards his conscience labels him as a nonbeliever:

> If 'twere a kibe
> Twould put me to my slipper; but I feel not
> This deity in my bosom. Twenty consciences
> That stand 'twixt me and Milan, candied be they
> And melt, ere they molest!
>
> (II.i.280-83)

Shakespeare elaborates the Machiavellian view of the world by presenting its representatives as finding nature basically hostile to humans and therefore in need of conquest if humans are to make their place within it.[17] The island which Gonzalo and Adrian find "temperate" and containing "everything advantageous to life" Sebastian and Antonio see as breathing "rotten" air and lacking "means to live." Gonzalo finds the time in the ocean cleansing, while Antonio and Sebastian see it as staining their clothes.

Gonzalo further describes the character of his conspiring companions' attitude toward nature when he complains that they "would lift the moon out of her sphere if she would continue in it five weeks without changing" (II.i.187-88). They assume that they understand nature, and they would oppose it for not meeting their expectations. The moon's continuing five weeks without changing would indicate to them that nature were arbitrary and in need of control. They would go so far as to lift the moon out of its sphere or to try to gain control for themselves over the sphere which, according to the Renaissance, the moon controls--the area of contingency and corruptibility often called nature. This presumption of Antonio and Sebastian recurs when they determine to fight Ariel and his fellow daemons appearing as ministers of destiny (III.iii.103-15).

The implications of Machiavelli's views of nature, fortune and God become clear partly in contrast to their alternatives. The Tempest's virtuous characters find evidence of some divinely established order which

is both beneficent and independent of man's will. The
tendency of all of the play's virtuous characters to
hold this view suggests the dependence of virtue upon
it.

Nature's goodness is expressed by Gonzalo, Adrian,
Prospero and Ferdinand. Gonzalo and Adrian find that
nature provides well for humankind on the island. And
Prospero, Gonzalo and Ferdinand see even the ill which
befalls humans as an ultimate benefit to them (see p.
117 above).

In addition to finding nature beneficent, the
play's virtuous characters agree with the ancient view
of fortune as unconquerable by humans. In the
Renaissance this view would have been strengthened by
the idea that what appears fortune in humankind's
limited view is really an orderly divine plan. As
Boethius puts it, "even though things may seem
confused and discordant to you, because you cannot
discern the order that governs them, nevertheless
everything is governed by its own proper order
directing all things toward the good."[18] This is
the idea inherent in the characters' expressions of
felix culpa (see p. 117 above).

Through his objections to Antonio and Sebastian's
view of nature Gonzalo asserts nature's independence
of human understanding and control, and even Prospero,
who has gained control over certain forces ruling the
lower world, can do so only by being in harmony with
the forces of nature. As argued above, Prospero has
the qualities of the theurgist or white magician of
the NeoPlatonists who, through using his mind and
therefore making contact with the divine pattern which
God has infused in everything, could exercise power
over the natural world. Prospero's control over his
enemies is not the result of control over fortune, but
the result of the capacity to take advantage of
auspicious fortune:

> By accident, most strange, bountiful Fortune
> (Now my dear lady) hath mine enemies
> Brought to this shore; and by my prescience
> I find my zenith doth depend upon
> A most auspicious star, whose influence
> If now I court not, but omit, my fortunes
> Will ever after droop.
>   (I.ii.178-84)

Prospero in taking advantage of fortune through harmony with the forces of nature reveals himself obedient to a divinely established order. This sense of an order beyond humankind is missing in the Machiavellian outlook of Antonio and Sebastian. Machiavelli argues that humans can conquer nature, that nature provides no direction. But before Machiavelli people had an additional understanding of nature. Nature provides an end towards which all natural things are directed, a perfection for which they long. "Nature" used in this sense explains Polixenes' claim in The Winter's Tale that in the improvement of wild flowers the gardener's art "is an art, / That Nature makes" (IV.iv.91-92).

According to Aristotle, a person's nature is realized in understanding and practicing the intellectual and moral virtues.[19] Such a view of nature is implies by Prospero's education of Ferdinand and Miranda. Prospero assumes that a person's nature is best fulfilled by making his or her desire accord with virtue.

When Machiavelli discusses human nature, he considers how people do live rather than how they ought to live. According to Machiavelli's argument, since most people are bad, a ruler can rule only by adapting himself to their badness. Antonio and Sebastian do not state explicitly Machiavelli's assumption that most people are bad, but their general cynicism when they first appear seems to extend to humankind. They treat Gonzalo and Adrian's well-meaning attempts to comfort Alonso with an exaggerated contempt which the audience, having just witnessed Ferdinand's first meeting with Miranda, must view as undeserved.

Any understanding of Shakespeare's attitude towards Machiavelli is incomplete without a perspective on whether Shakespeare sees a viable alternative for a political leader. One alternative to Machiavelli's position involves assuming the goodness of humankind prior to the existence of the city. This is the assumption of Gonzalo. He sees Ariel and his daemons as primitive "people of the island"

Who, though they are of monstrous shape, yet note,
Their manners are more gentle, kind, than of

Our human generation you shall find
Many--nay, almost any.

(III.iii.30-34)

The ideal commonwealth which Gonzalo imagines in terms derived from Montaigne's "Of the Caniballes" consists of people living without the encumbrances of civil society and therefore "innocent and pure":

I' th' commonwealth I would by contraries
Execute all things. For no kind of traffic
Would I admit: no name of magistrate;
Letters should not be known; rights, poverty,
And use of service, none; contract, succession,
Bourn, bound of land, tilth, vineyard, none;
No use of metal, corn, or wine, or oil;
No occupation; all men idle, all;
And women too, but innocent and pure;
No sovereignty.

(II.ii.152-61)

For Shakespeare's audience Gonzalo's ideal commonwealth would call forth a rich tradition surrounding the idea of living outside of civil society. From classical times through the Middle Ages and into the Renaissance people referred to a Golden Age when humans, finding abundance in nature, lived without arts, government, property, clothes, or labor. As Margaret Hodgen notes, almost all of the innumerable Renaissance discussions of the New World and of primitive men consider the question of the value of the pre-civil state.[20] Montaigne claims that the society of his cannibals "doth not only exceed all the pictures wherewith licentious Poesie hath proudly imbellished the golden age, and all her quaint inventions to faine a happy condition of man, but also the conception and desire of Philosophy." Gonzalo himself claims only to govern "with such perfection / T'excel the Golden Age" (II.i.172-73).

Most of the elements of Gonzalo's description may be found in Montaigne, but Shakespeare puts greater stress than Montaigne on the innocence of the people in his commonwealth. According to Montaigne, Plato and Lycurgus

could not imagine a genuitie so pure
and simple, as we see it by
experience; nor ever beleeve our
societie might be maintained with so

little art and humane combination.
It is a nation, would I answer
Plato, that hath no kind of
trafficke, no knowledge of letters,
no intelligence of numbers, no name
of magistrate, nor of politike
superioritie; no use of service, or
riches or of povertie; no contracts,
no successions, no partitions, no
occupation but idle; no respect of
kindred, but common, no apparell but
naturall, no manuring of lands, no
use of wine, corne, or mettle. The
very words that impart lying,
falshood, treason, dissimulation,
covetousness, envie, detraction, and
pardon, were never heard amongst
them. How dissonant would hee find
his imaginarie commonwealth from
this perfection! [21]

Every element of Gonzalo's description matches
Montaigne's with the exception of Gonzalo's exclusion
of war: "Sword, pike, knife, gun, or need of any
engine / Would I not have . . . ." Montaigne's
cannibals do have weapons and do go to war, but Hodgen
finds the rejection of arms frequent in other
portrayals of primitive man.[22] Shakespeare seems to
be completing Montaigne's otherwise utopian vision to
put an emphasis on the absolute purity of Gonzalo's
conception of the primitive man.

Antonio and Sebastian immediately point out the
difficulty of such a conception. Gonzalo has imagined
colonizing the island as "king on't," but in admitting
"no sovereignty" in his domain "The latter end of his
commonwealth forgets the beginning" (II.i.162). The
presumption that humans can be virtuous in a state of
nature outside of civil society is dubious. As
Aristotle points out in his _Politics_ (pp. 15-16),
virtue cannot exist outside of the city. It depends
on the declaration of law and right for which civil
society exists, and only through the establishment of
such institutions and the habituation of the populace
to them can virtue be expected. George Sandys puts it
this way:

> The Cyclops were a salvage people . . .
> unsociable amongst themselves, &
> inhumane to strangers: And no

marvaile, when lawlesse, and subject to
no government, the bond of society;
which gives to every man his owne,
suppressing vice, and advancing vertue,
the two maine columnes of a
Common-wealth. . . . Man is a
politicall and sociable creature: they
therefore are to be numbred among
beasts who renounce society, whereby
they are destitute of lawes, the
ordination of civility. [23]

This is the point of Antonio and Sebastian's criticism
that there would be "No marrying 'mong his subjects."
"None, man, all idle--whores and knaves" (II.i.170-71).

As an example of natural man Caliban provides the
most telling critique of Gonzalo's vision. Caliban's
name is usually thought to come from "Carib," a savage
inhabitant of the New World, or to be an anagram of
"cannibal" which is a derivation of "Carib." This
derivation suits both Montaigne's description of
Brazilians in his essay which is the source of
Gonzalo's speech on an ideal commonwealth and the
material on an English voyage to the New World in the
Bermuda pamphlets, now accepted as a likely source for
portions of The Tempest.[24] Caliban, however,
appears not simply as a native inhabitant of the New
World, but as a representative of primitive man as a
type. He inhabits Prospero's island which is between
Italy and Africa, and although there are references to
the New World in the mention of the "dead Indian"
touted in England (II.ii.34) and of the Patagonian god
Setebos, Caliban appears as the child of an African
witch from Argiers.

Certain events in the play are close enough to the
travel literature's discussion of primitive man to
indicate that Shakespeare meant to evoke these tales.
Sebastian, Antonio, and Gonzalo all refer to the
daemons' banquet presentation as the sort of thing one
would find in travelers' tales. For Antonio and
Sebastian it proves that "Travelers ne'er did lie, /
Though fools at home condemn 'em" (III.iii.26-27).
Trinculo refers to the habit of bringing back strange
specimens for the people at home to observe:

Were I in England now, as I once
was, and had but this fish painted,
not a holiday fool there but would

134

give a piece of silver. There would
this monster make a man; any strange
beast there makes a man. When they
would not give a doit to relieve a
lame beggar, they will lay out ten
to see a dead Indian.
(II.ii.28-34; see also
II.ii.69-72, 78-80)

The early travelers frequently describe curious
creatures. John E. Hankins has found a description in
Purchas which includes some of the characteristics
Stephano observes in Caliban. This monster has the
"eares of a Dog, armes like a Man without haire, and
at the elbowes great Finnes like a fish." The
inhabitants of the land thought the monster the "sonne
of the Devill" because "hee mayde a noyse which might
be heard halfe a league off." Trinculo first thinks
that Caliban is a fish since he "smells like a fish,"
but then he finds Caliban's "fins like arms" and
discovers that this "is no fish, but an islander."
Later Trinculo refers to Caliban as a "puppy-headed
monster," perhaps suggesting the dog ears described in
Purchas, although Pliny and other travel tales and
maps mention dog-headed men reminiscent of Caliban.
As a "howling monster" (III.i.187) and son of a devil
Caliban has other features in common with the monster
of Purchas.[25] Curry's generally accepted identification of Caliban as the product of the union of a
witch with an incubus might also account for his
deformity. An incubus was a devil in the form of a
man who seduced women to illicit sexual relations.
The offspring of such unions were usually deformed or
abnormal.[26]

Discussions of the travel literature have pointed
to other similarities between the activities of
Caliban and those observed by the voyagers. Caliban's
impression that Stephano is a god (II.ii.121-23)
matches an Indian's reaction to the white man, and
Stephano's claim to be descended from the moon
(II.ii.143-44) coincides with the device used by
voyagers who took advantage of the Indians' polytheism
to gain control over them.[27] Caliban's lack of
chastity is reminiscent of that of the European
salvage man, and Frank Kermode finds his love of music
similar to that of the natives described in Peter
Martyr's De Novo Orbe.[28] Some of the foods which
Caliban promises to gather have been recognized to
come from the Bermuda pamphlets. The "scamels from

135

the rock" (II.ii.179-80) are described in William
Strachey's <u>True Repertory of the Wracke</u>, as are the
berries and the fresh springs (II.ii.168).[29] These
foods are the sort which could supply Gonzalo's
commonwealth where there would be no need of
agriculture given the abundance of nature, and they
are the sort of foods Montaigne describes his
cannibals as eating--foods gathered in nature and not
requiring cooking.[30] Caliban's inability to be
improved is suggested by a marginal comment in the
<u>True Repertory</u>: "Can a leopard change his spots? Can
a savage remaining savage be civil? Were not we
ourselves made and not born civil in our progenitors'
days?"[31] Finally, the wine bottle which Stephano
claims to have made out of the bark of a tree is
reminiscent of travelers' stories of their ingenuity
in surviving without the amenities of civilization.

While there is no doubt that Caliban comes from
such Renaissance discussions, his description in the
names of actors suggests that he also derives from
Aristotle's natural slave.[32] As a "salvage and
deformed slave" he fits Aristotle's description of men
"in whom the like difference is to be found as there
is betweene the soule and the bodie, betweene a man
and a beast." Caliban is like the man Aristotle
describes as being in the worst state, with the body
ruling the soul. He has tried to violate Miranda.
Despite Prospero's "humane care" and Miranda's
teaching (I.ii.346, 353-55), Caliban has shown himself
to have a bad nature upon "Which any print of goodness
wilt not take / Being capable of all ill" (I.ii.353-54;
see also IV.i.188-89). His "vile race . . . had that
in't which good natures / Could not abide to be with"
(I.ii.358-59). Caliban also matches the natural slave
by virtue of being a man "which may [has the capacity
to] belong to another man . . . . Whosoever willingly
submitteth himselfe to the power and gouernment of
another man . . . by reason thereof he belongeth to
that other partie, as borne to be in an another [sic.]
mans power" (pp. 30-31). First Caliban becomes
Prospero's slave, and later he willingly enslaves
himself to Stephano (II.ii.159-60). Further, he
serves the function of a natural slave by supplying
his owner with bodily help in meeting his daily
requirements: "We are holpen of each of them by their
bodies (to wit, by servants and tame beasts) in our
necessarie businesse" (p. 30). This is the service to
which Prospero refers: "He does make our fire, /
Fetch in our wood, and serves in offices / That profit

us" (I.ii.311-13). Caliban's deformity also labels him as the natural slave who is "strong for necessarie vses [menial tasks]" but whose carriage is not "straight [upright]" like that of the free man (p. 30).

It hardly seems necessary to point out that The Tempest refutes Gonzalo's presumption of human goodness in the presocietal state as well as any intimations of savage nobility. Caliban's claim to rule "by Sycorax my mother" (I.ii.33) is false both on hereditary grounds and in terms of desert. His mother's right to rule is questionable. It occurs through the usurpation of the authority of others. In celestial terms Sycorax "could control the moon, make lows and ebbs, / And deal in her command without her power" (V.i.270-71). By attempting to exploit Miranda Caliban has shown that he does not deserve to rule, and his exemplification of the natural slave indicates his appropriate position on the island. In Gonzalo's commonwealth with no sovereign above him, no rule of law, and no use of force, Caliban would be free to follow his bodily desires to the detriment of the other citizens. He has shown that he understands only the physical. He is the "lying slave, / Whom stripes may move, not kindness" (V.ii.344-45). He can be controlled only by pinches and cramps. If Caliban seems superior to Stephano and Trinculo in his recognition of trumpery, he merely reveals that they also are debased. If he hopes for grace at the hands of a "brave" master, he merely recognizes the natural superiority of Prospero.

Further suggestions of the problematic nature of Gonzalo's idealistic vision of the world derive from his statements following the court party's arrival on shore. Ariel's report that there is "not a blemish" on "their sustaining garments" (I.ii.218) lends credence to Gonzalo's claim that the drenching of the garments has left them "rather new-dyed than stained with salt water" (II.i.67), and Prospero's reform of Alonso and recovery of his dukedom also imply that the drenching has produced a sort of baptism or purification. On the other hand, to call Dido "widow Dido" is a strange transformation of the relationship of the unmarried Dido and Aeneas. It implies a refusal on Gonzalo's part to accept the fact of vice. Gonzalo's willing metamorphosis of questionable actions also is suggested by his assertion that the garments of the court party are "as fresh as when we put them on first in Afric, at the marriage of the

King's fair daughter Claribel to the King of Tunis"
(II.i.71-74). The wisdom of arranging Claribel's
marriage to the King of Tunis is called into doubt.
Sebastian reports Claribel's "loathness" to wed an
African as well as other Neopolitan advice against it
and relates the shipwreck and loss of son to the loss
of a daughter (II.i.128-39). Although Gonzalo
includes the marriage in his final panegyric
(V.i.205-13), even he has some difficulty with it:

> My lord Sebastian
> The truth you speak doth lack some gentleness,
> And time to speak it in.
>   (II.i.141-43)

Shakespeare puts his message about dreams of the noble
savage and of a Golden Age in the mouth of Trinculo.
Those English who "will not give a doit to relieve a
lame beggar" but "will lay out ten to see a dead
Indian" should forget ideas of primitive nobility and
look to their own morals.

Finding in the natural utopia no viable
alternative to Machiavelli, The Tempest also examines
the introduction of artifice into society as a means
of producing something better. This solution has
defects of its own. The play presents examples of art
corrupting nature. The products of civilization
introduced to a nature inherently bad might allow for
greater ill than if the evil nature were left to
itself. Miranda teaches Caliban to speak, and his
"profit on't / Is, I know how to curse"
(I.ii.363-65). In other words, Caliban reverses what
Aristotle says is the aim of speech--to declare "what
is profitable, what hurtfull, what just; what vnjust"
(p. 15). According to Aristotle, the ability to speak
implies that the city is natural to humans since
speech "was in vaine bestowed vpon them if they should
liue solitarily without companie and conuersation" (p.
12). Speech which should be an indication of people's
natural sociability becomes in Caliban an instrument
for his expression of abhorrence of virtuous humanity.

Certain conventions of society can also corrupt
people. Civilization's elevation of mere appearances
can lead them away from the significant aspects of
life. In The Tempest Stephano and Trinculo are drawn
by the glitter of rich apparel from their intention of
murdering Prospero. They take clothes for the
actuality of rule; they take the outward signs for the

virtues and power which those signs represent. Their rule is a further example of false rule. As Trinculo points out, "They say there's but five upon this isle; we are three of them. If th'other two be brained like us, the state totters" (III.ii.5-7). The stolen clothes later become badges of their rascality: "Mark but the badges of these men, my lords / Then say if they be true" (V.i.267-68). As in Shakespeare's treatment of clothes elsewhere, there is an implied scriptural allusion. In II Corinthians 5 we seek to clothe ourselves with "our house which is from heaven" rather than "our earthly house" so that "being clothed we shall not be found naked." Stephano and Trinculo, on the other hand, find themselves naked being clothed. Their clothes are marks of their attention to the body, to the temporal, to appearances. Caliban, who has not learned to put stock in such superfluities, finds the garments "but trash" and "luggage" (IV.i.224, 230).

Finally, civilization produces men like Antonio and Sebastian who are worse than Caliban. If Caliban is "A devil, a born devil" (IV.i.188-89), Antonio and Sebastian have proved to be "worse than devils" (III.iii.36). Both are governed by a thirst for power and are willing to use any means to gain it. Antonio has learned enough about controlling men to be able to execute his wicked designs successfully.

All of these corruptions of nature by art occur only in natures bad from the outset. Caliban's use of speech indicates the degree of his debasement from the natural or the ideal. In Antonio the exercise of power has merely "Awaked an evil nature" (I.ii.93). And Stephano and Trinculo appear as worthless fellows. Art, however, proves to benefit good natures. Prospero's education of Miranda has given her "more profit / Than other princess' can, that have more time / For vainer hours, and tutors not so careful" (I.ii.172-74).

The variability in education's value to different characters suggests the nature of The Tempest's alternative to Machiavelli. A ruler must be able to distinguish the good natures from the bad. He must nurture what is best in the former and control what is worst in the latter. Neither Antonio and Sebastian nor Gonzalo is capable of seeing the variety in people's natures. Antonio and Sebastian's presumption of human badness and Gonzalo's of human goodness lead to this lack of perception. As far as Antonio and Sebastian are concerned, Trinculo and Stephano are no worse than Gonzalo. Sebastian illustrates this view when he asserts that if Gonzalo were king of the island, he would "Scape being drunk for want of wine" (II.i.151), an accusation more apt to the drunken butler and jester than to the kindly councilor. Gonzalo's view takes no account of Caliban.

Prospero, on the other hand, is capable of recognizing how people differ. He realizes that Caliban is the natural slave who can be ruled only by force. For those members of the court party who recognize the difference between right and wrong Prospero tries an appeal to the conscience and fear of supernatural punishment through the instrument of Ariel and his fellow daemons. Ferdinand and Miranda, however, require mainly an appeal to their love of the beautiful and the good.

Prospero also understands that people have a mixed nature, part body and part soul. The body provides certain limitations which people cannot overcome. Even though Caliban is evil and abhorrent to Prospero and Miranda, they need him to take care of their bodily requirements: "We cannot miss him. He does make our fire, / Fetch in our wood, and serves in offices / That profit us" (I.ii.311-13). In the best of humans the soul rules the body, but even so the body cannot be denied. Prospero recognizes this in his acknowledgement that Caliban belongs to him: "this thing of darkness I / Acknowledge mine" (V.i.275-76). Rationality allows humans to rise to an exalted place within nature, but nevertheless a place circumscribed by human limitations. Because people have such limitations, virtue becomes essentially moderation. Ferdinand and Miranda are not to deny entirely their passion for one another, but simply to place it under the limitations which society imposes upon it in requiring its realization only in marriage.

One of the considerations of The Tempest is how, given human limitations, freedom is to be defined. For Prospero freedom is available through the study of the liberal arts. These are defined by Aristotle in his Politics as those arts appropriate to a free man. Studies are not liberal when done at the instance of others or when directed towards an occupation. Those arts directed towards occupations "are defined as necessary, and in regard of other things," namely, as

140

means. As means they imply an end as yet unattained.
And yet the free man seeks for felicity which is an
end in itself. He looks for the arts which are
studied for themselves, those arts "vndertaken for
their sakes which learn" (p. 384).

Machiavelli's answer to the question of freedom
involves the recognition of human evil. Once the
ruler recognizes this, he can become free from fortune
by gaining control of other people. To do so he has
to adapt himself to the evil of those he rules. This
means that the ruler himself has to be willing to
participate in evil (see p. 125 above).

The Tempest questions Machiavelli's solution to
the problem of freedom by making Antonio its
representative. Antonio's attempts at attaining rule
lead to the enslavement of Milan to Naples. A rule
such as Antonio's can only be false, and the freedom
it represents is not true freedom.

On the other hand, The Tempest also illustrates
the power of the critique of classical philosophy
which underlies Machiavelli's solution. As indicated
earlier, Machiavelli argues that the ancient's concern
for how humans ought to live leads only to an
imaginary perfection which can never be realized and
which, when it becomes the focal point for the ruler,
endangers his survival. Prospero's overthrow by
Antonio would, of course, support Machiavelli's view.
Although Prospero had been reputed "Without a
parallel" in his study of the "liberal arts," his
attention to books had led to his turning over his
government to his brother and to his eventual
overthrow. Interruption of Prospero's masque by
thoughts of Caliban's ill also shows how the reality
of human evil prevents undivided attention to what
ought to be. The masque represents an attempt by
Prospero to bring to fruition a "contract of true
love" between Ferdinand and Miranda. If the young
lovers live up to this contract, Juno and Ceres
promise all of the blessings of heaven and earth,
including the banning of winter: "Spring come to you
at the farthest / In the very end of harvest"
(IV.i.114-15). The impossibility of such an idyllic
life is implied by the inevitability of the seasons as
well as by the intrusion of thoughts of Caliban which
brings an end to the vision presented by the spirits.

If one cannot be free in civil society, perhaps

one can find liberty in the state of nature. Caliban claims that before Prospero came to the island he was free, "mine own king" (I.ii.342), but in a sense Caliban was not free even then. He lived in a bestial condition unable even to speak (I.ii.355-58). Caliban's condition prior to Prospero's arrival suggests that true freedom for humans is available only to those who have received the benefits of civil society.

Caliban's attempts to attain freedom within society also fail. Once Caliban concocts the conspiracy against Prospero, he looks forward to his new condition as freedom:

No more dams I'll make for fish,
   Nor fetch in firing
   At requiring
Nor scrape trenchering, nor wash dish.
   'Ban, 'Ban, Ca--Caliban
Has a new master. Get a new man!

Freedom high day! High day, freedom! Freedom,
   high day, freedom!
                                    (II.ii.188-95)

What Caliban looks upon as freedom is really service to a new master. Although he sings of having no longer to gather food for Prospero, he has already promised to do so for Stephano (II.ii.168-72, 174-80). Caliban proves himself a natural slave, capable only of becoming the property of another. His decision to worship Stephano is based on the effects of his "celestial liquor" rather than on any indication that Stephano's rule will benefit Caliban more than Prospero's.

According to Aristotle the natural slave receives most profit serving a master. For those who are not natural slaves freedom is more than the absence of external restraints. Prospero's warnings to Miranda and Ferdinand make him a likely proponent of the view that freedom involves a positive element. Arguments that freedom results from a life of virtue abound in the Renaissance. Castiglione, for example, argues that "true libertie ought not to be saide, not to live as a man will, but to live according to good lawes."[33] Presumably, living according to good laws gives people a claim to live according to virtue. Herbert Coursen makes this point another way when he argues that Miranda's and Ferdinand's desire to serve each other bearing logs implies that voluntary service can constitute freedom. This is the feeling of Ferdinand who asserts that "most poor matters / Point to rich ends" (III.i.3-4).[34]

In a sense freedom can reside only in the exercise of the mind. As Cerimon argues in _Pericles_, life directed elsewhere is subject to temporal limitations (see p. 101 above). Fortune and human nature limit what people can do in the active life. Stephano's drunken song expresses the same defense of the philosophic life: "Thought is free" (III.ii.128). External realities govern how a person can act, but nobody can control another's thoughts. The philosopher, then, can be free in a way that the politician cannot.

The _Tempest_, then, presents a rather full analysis of Machiavelli and suggests what sort of alternative Shakespeare would formulate. The play rejects Machiavelli's view that nature is hostile, arbitrary, and subject to control by humans. It also finds Machiavelli's emphasis on human evil destructive of the ability to make distinctions among people and to see goodness where it exists. Further, adapting one's self entirely to humanity's evil, as Antonio does, produces a subjugation to evil which calls the whole endeavor into question. On the other hand, naive dependence on nature's beneficence and on the goodness of humankind leads to the foolishness of Gonzalo who could think of a man such as Caliban as "mine own king." Turning to the artifice of society can also be problematic due to the evidence that art both corrupts bad natures further and provides tools for evil men to extend their influence. Still, society presents our only hope, for it offers good natures a degree of release from attention to their bodily needs and the possibility of study of the liberal arts. Shakespeare's alternative to the Machiavellian intent on evil and to the natural utopian intent on nature's goodness is a man such as Prospero who learns to look in both directions, to the higher and to the base, seeking to approach the one and to control the other.

Notes

[1]*Machiavelli's Prince: An Elizabethen Translation*, ed. Hardin Craig (Chapel Hill, 1944), p. 66.

[2]Edward Meyer, *Machiavelli and the Elizabethan Drama* (New York, 1964).

[3]Lily Bess Campbell, *Shakespeare's Histories: Mirrors of Elizabethan Policy* (San Marino, California, 1958), pp. 321-32.

[4]Napoleone Orsini, "Elizabethan Manuscript Translations of Machiavelli's *Prince*," *Journal of the Wanburg Institute*, 1 (1937), 166-69; Napoleone Orsini, *Studi sul Rinascimento Italiano in Inghilterre* (Florence: G. C. Sansoni, 1937); *Machiavelli's Prince: An Elizabethan Translation*.

[5]A. Gerber, *Niccolò Machiavelli, Die Handschriften, Ausgaben und Ubersetzungen seiner Werke* (Gotha, 1913), pt. iii, pp. 93-100--as cited in Felix Raab, *The English Face of Machiavelli* (London and Toronto, 1964), pp. 53, 295.

[6]Gabriel Harvey, *Letter-Book of Gabriel Harvey* (1573-1580), ed. Edward John Long Scott (London and New York, 1965), p. 79.

[7]Jean Bodin, *The six bookes of a commonweale* (1606), ed. Kenneth Douglas McRae (Cambridge, Massachusetts, 1962), preface and Bk. IV, Ch. 4.

[8]Edwin A. Greenlaw, "The Influence of Machiavelli on Spenser," *MP*, 7 (1909-10), 187-202; Irving Ribner, "Machiavelli and Sidney's *Discourse to the Queenes Majesty*," *Italica*, 26 (1949), 177-87; Irving Ribner, "Machiavelli and Sidney: The *Arcadia* of 1590," *SP*, 46 (1950), 152-72; Irving Ribner, "Sidney's 'Arcadia' and the Machiavelli Legend," *Italica*, 27 (1950), 225-35.

[9]Michel de Montaigne, *The Essayes of Montaigne*, trans. John Florio (New York, 1933), pp. 593, 721 (cf. *Prince*, Ch. 18). See also Montaigne on fortune, pp. 120, 160-62, 170.

[10]Raab, pp. 57, 59; Meyer, pp. 30-107.

[11]Machiavelli, pp. 111-14.

[12]Allan H. Gilbert, *Machiavelli's "Prince" and Its Forerunners: "The Prince" as a Typical Book "de Regimine Principum"* (New York, 1938, rep. 1968), pp. 205-19.

[13]Raab, pp. 3, 61.

[14]Machiavelli, pp. 114-15.

[15]Innocent Gentillet, *A discourse upon the meanes of wel governing against N. Macchiavell*, trans. S. Patericke (London, 1602), p. 141.

[16]Gentillet, p. 94.

[17]On Machiavelli's view of nature as hostile to man see Leo Strauss, *Thoughts on Machiavelli* (Seattle and London, 1969), pp. 217-21--reprinted from hardcover edition published in 1958 by The Free Press, Glencoe, Illinois; Harvey Mansfield, *Machiavelli's New Modes and Orders* (Ithaca and London, 1979), p. 191; Leo Paul S. de Alvarez, trans. *The Prince* (Irving, Texas, 1980), p. viii.

[18]Boethius, *Consolation of Philosophy*, trans. Richard Green (Indianapolis, 1962), pp. 109-11.

[19] *Aristotles politiques, or discourses of government*, trans. out of Greek into French by Loys Le Roy, trans. out of French by [I. D.?] (London, 1598), pp. 12, 15. All references in the text to Aristotle are to this edition.

[20]Margaret Hodgen, "Montaigne and Shakespeare Again," *HLQ*, 16 (1952-53), 29f.

[21]Montaigne, p. 164.

[22]Hodgen, pp. 40-41. Hodgen argues that Montaigne omits Gonzalo's support for lack of boundaries on the land, but Montaigne does include this in his "no partitions."

[23]*Ovids Metamorphoses Englished, Mythologized and Represented in Figures* (London, 1632)--rpt. and ed. Karl K. Hulley and Stanley T. Vandersall (Lincoln, 1970), p. 477; see also Aristotle, *Ethics* 1103a.

[24]Geoffrey Bullough, _Narrative and Dramatic Sources of Shakespeare_, VIII (London and New York, 1975), 238-42; D. G. James, pp. 72-122.

[25]See John E. Hankins, "Caliban and the Bestial Man," _PMLA_, 72 (1947), 794-95 and note 8.

[26]Curry, pp. 148-55; R. R. Cawley, "Shakespeare's Use of the Voyages in _The Tempest_," _PMLA_, 41 (1926), 721-22; Hankins, pp. 793-94. Hankins also finds a reference to primitive man as the product of the union of a witch with an incubus.

[27]Cawley, p. 714.

[28]_The Tempest_, ed. Frank Kermode (London, 1958), pp. xxxii-xxxiii, xxxix.

[29]William Strachey, "A True Repertory of the Wracke and Redemption of Sir Thomas Gates" (1610), in _Narrative and Dramatic Sources of Shakespeare_, ed. Geoffrey Bullough, VIII (London and New York, 1975), 283-84.

[30]Montaigne, p. 164.

[31]William Strachey, "True Repertory of the Wrack," in _The Tempest_, ed. Robert Langbaum (New York and London, 1964), p. 133.

[32]See Castiglione's reiteration of Aristotle's natural slave discussion [Baldassare Castiglione, _The Book of the Courtier_, trans. Thomas Hoby (1561) (London and New York, 1928), pp. 275-76]. Kermode mentions Aristotle's natural slave as justification for the enslavement of black men to European gentlemen and of Caliban to Prospero (p. xlii). Hankins suggests that Caliban is the bestial man of Aristotle's _Ethics_ (pp. 797-801). Caliban's inability to be improved matches the bestial man who is lacking the sense of right and wrong. Aristotle's natural slave differs from the beast in being able to recognize reason in another. See Lewis Hanke, _Aristotle and the American Indians_ (Bloomington and London, c. 1955) for a discussion of the sixteenth century application of Aristotle's natural slave to the Indians. Sister Corona Sharp notes some of the same similarities listed below between Aristotle's natural slave and Prospero's view of Caliban ["Caliban," _Shakespeare Studies_, 14 (1981), 267-83].

Sister Corona, however, argues that Shakespeare does not intend the reader to adopt Prospero's view of Caliban. In doing so she takes seriously Caliban's claim to rule which is questioned below, and she omits reference to Aristotle's view that willing submission implies natural servitude. She also tries to rationalize an inconsistent view of Prospero as both cruel tyrant from whom Caliban tries justly to free himself (even through murder) and wise man. To do so she explains Caliban's final recognition of Prospero as a true lord by asserting that Prospero has undergone purification himself, but she does not mention that even after his supposed purification Prospero's characterization and treatment of Caliban remain unchanged.

[33]Castiglione, p. 275.

[34]Coursen, pp. 396-98.

CHAPTER VII

THE TEMPEST: SHAKESPEARE'S DEFENSE OF POETRY

Shakespeare's defense of poetry in The Tempest is partly implicit. By educating Ferdinand and Miranda as ideal guardians Prospero meets the qualifications set down by Socrates and by the Renaissance for the city's proper poet. To become a poet of this sort Prospero had first to be a philosopher so that he would know the model upon which the guardians' education was to be based. To put his knowledge into effect Prospero had to rule.

Prospero teaches the future rulers of Milan and Naples to make their desire accord with virtue, and he gives them a vision of nature as harmonizing both with virtue and with what is good for humans. Gonzalo's view of nature as beneficent contains some of the ingredients necessary to virtue, but it is proved insufficient. Human nature as it exists without the additions of art cannot lead to the ideal commonwealth envisioned by Gonzalo. Prospero who sees a person's nature as his end as well as his original endowment understands the need to educate that person to the nobility of which he is capable. The city needs the poet who is a philosopher.

The difficulty with this defense is the city's inability to offer anything to benefit the philosopher. Given the limitations of fortune and of human nature there is no reason to believe that the philosopher who contemplates eternal truths would be willing to submit himself to working within such limitations. Why should he give up contemplation of the truth in order to rule the city and to educate its guardians? Previously, by turning over his government to Antonio, Prospero has illustrated his lack of interest in exercising leadership in Milan. Why should he now be willing to return to Milan?

If Prospero were pure soul, he would not deal directly with men who are a mixture of body and soul. But Prospero's ascent to the beautiful and the good is only a partial and unfinished ascent. He recognizes his own humanity in admitting that his body is part of him. No matter how much he and Miranda might wish that it were otherwise they need Caliban to take care of their bodily requirements. Partly because of his need for preservation Prospero belongs to the temporal as well as the eternal. Prospero's humanity implies a bond between him and the rest of humankind as part of the same species. That a creature as little tied to the body as Ariel can feel compassion for the inflicted court party suggests the nobility of such a sentiment, but Prospero has all the more reason to be moved:

> Hast thou, which art but air, a touch, a feeling
> Of their afflictions, and shall not myself,
> One of their kind, that relish all as sharply
> Passion as they, be kindlier moved than thou art?
>
> (V.i.21-24)

As a philosopher Prospero is in danger of forgetting the earthly in his own nature. On the island he must face that aspect of himself, for there he meets Caliban, tries to teach him, and learns to control him.

The natural bond between Prospero and the rest of humankind, however, does not explain entirely Prospero's willingness to forgive. Because he is human, the "high wrongs" of Antonio, Sebastian and Alonso have "struck" him "to th' quick." As a human or as a judging god, he has good cause for anger. Nevertheless, Prospero as a philosopher can determine the path where virtue lies: "Yet with my nobler reason 'gainst my fury / Do I take part. The rarer action is / In virtue than in vengeance." Prospero has asserted a kinship with humankind by virtue of his tendency to "passion as they," and the play provides evidence that Prospero's assertion is correct. Upon his and Miranda's abandonment at sea he has shed salt tears into the ocean and "groaned" under his "burden" (I.ii.155-56). And the conspiracy of Caliban and his confederates arouses Prospero to a violent anger which "works him strongly" (IV.i.143). Nevertheless, Prospero's philosophy tells him that his anger is a "weakness," an "infirmity," which must be controlled: "A turn or two I'll walk / To still my beating mind" (IV.i.158-63). Prospero's empathy is insufficient to explain his forgiveness, for the passionate in Prospero leads him to anger as well as compassion. The nobler part of man, his reason rather than his passion, leads him to the forgiveness which is supported by his empathy for humankind.

In this case reason does not deny passion. Rather it distinguishes admirable passions from reprehensible ones. In this it follows what Saint Augustine argues is the position of the Scripture which "subjects the passions to the mind for their restraint and control so that they may be turned into the instruments of justice."[1] Compassion has a special status which places it above the other passions. Pity is a Christ-like sentiment, for Christ pitied man. Guarini worries about Aristotle's description of tragedy as purging pity and fear:

> Now I come to compassion of which I can say that the continual sight of actions that arouse compassion would cause the destruction of the feeling. But I do not see how anyone can be divested of this feeling without divesting himself of humanity, that is, by making himself cruel.

Guarini argues that Aristotle meant only to moderate affections and reduce them "to that proper consistency which can contribute to a virtuous habit." One would not want to purge all compassion but only that directed towards bodily affliction for the sake of the spirit. Compassion is desirable when it is "for a fault which when known and perceived by the sinner becomes pain for his sin."[2] This is precisely the sort of compassion which Prospero expresses at the opening of Act V. As he tells Ariel, repentance has been his end, and when that is accomplished he will turn to forgiveness (V.i.28-30). In fact, in addition to forgiving the penitent Alonso, he forgives Antonio and Sebastian who, although they feel "inward pinches" of conscience, do not exhibit repentance.

Prospero's rational forgiveness is superior to Miranda's compassion for men she views universally as members of a "brave new world." Prospero forgives with full knowledge of human faults. A sense of the uncommon excellence of such forgiveness is sharpened by a parallel action in the Stephano, Trinculo, Caliban subplot. Stephano warns Trinculo that if he should "Interrupt the monster one word further," he will turn his "mercy out o' doors and make a stockfish" of Trinculo. Stephano's mercy is, indeed, shortlived, and upon Ariel's next interruption he strikes Trinculo (III.ii.72-81).

151

Prospero's mixture of humility and godlike forgiveness has a Christian flavor. His acceptance of his humanity despite his tendency to rise above it has intimations of Christ's acceptance of the body. Like a Christian God, he asks only for repentance: "They being penitent, / The sole drift of my purpose doth extend / Not a frown further." His knowledge of Antonio and Sebastian's plot implies to Sebastian that "The devil speaks in him," but Prospero's forgiveness of Antonio makes it clear that his knowledge is heavenly rather than infernal. As I have argued, Prospero's control of the plot and the characters' feelings that his control is Providential, miraculous, and wonderful all make Milan's rightful ruler seem divine.

A man who focuses on the eternal must come to terms with the temporal if he is to rule. He must either accept or attack the elements in humans which tie them to the particular and the transitory. Prospero does both. Human limitations imply the need for forgiveness. The philosopher may understand the end of humankind, but the ruler cannot alter human's natures. Even the best of humans have certain bodily needs. What is most discouraging is education's tendency to enable natures such as Caliban to do greater ill. Society itself produces the thirst for power which makes Antonio or Sebastian even more dangerous than Caliban. In Christian terms, only grace seems sufficient to save them. This is what Caliban suggests when he realizes how foolish he has been to worship the drunken Stephano: "I'll be wise hereafter, / And seek for grace" (V.i.295-96). And even grace may not be enough. Alonso asks for Prospero's pardon, but although Prospero has moved Antonio's and Sebastian's consciences with "inward pinches" (V.i.77), there is no evidence that they actually repent.

Although Prospero's forgiveness may represent an attempt to redeem evil, he himself realizes that it is not a viable political solution to the problem of human evil. Caliban's attempted rape of Miranda is not forgiven. It is treated with confinement, cramps and pinches. And Prospero does not allow the restoration of his dukedom to depend on the repentance of Antonio and Sebastian. Prospero's knowledge of the conspiracy against Alonso gives him leverage which depends only on the conspirators' fear of punishment:

But you, my brace of lords, were I so minded,
I here could pluck his Highness' frown upon you,
And justify you traitors.

                         (V.i.126-28)

Prospero's knowledge gives Antonio no other choice
but to do what Prospero asks:

                         I do forgive
Thy rankest fault--all of them; and require
My dukedom of thee, which perforce I know
Thou must restore.

                         (V.i.131-33)

If the world were peopled only with Calibans,
Antonios, and Sebastians, Prospero's rule could
benefit humankind very little. Prospero does not
return to Milan for the sake of those whose natures
are intransigent to education or to virtue. He
returns for the sake of Miranda and Ferdinand who can
be educated to love the beautiful and the good.
These two superior representatives of humanity embody
Prospero's attempt to make the ideal a temporal
reality, to join heaven and earth. If it were not
for Miranda, Prospero would have turned away from
this world altogether. She gave Prospero fortitude
to get through the storm to which Antonio had
abandoned them:

                         O, a cherubin
Thou wast that did preserve me! Thou didst smile,
Infusèd with a fortitude from heaven,
When I have decked the sea with drops full salt,
Against what should ensue.

                         (I.ii.152-55)

Further, as Prospero tells Miranda, "I have done
nothing but in care of thee" (I.ii.16). To Prospero
Miranda represents "a third of mine own life, / Or
that for which I live" (IV.i.3-4). She is the bond
which holds him to this life. In terms of the
Platonic triad (see p. 113f. above) she is the third
which holds together the other two portions of
Prospero. As an ideal guardian she would bind the
people to the philosopher. She could reconcile
Prospero to Caliban or Stephano and Trinculo. As a
guardian she would represent spiritedness or the part
of man's soul which ties him to the city. Although
Miranda's upbringing does not tie her to any
particular state towards which her spiritedness would
be directed, Prospero does give her the education of

153

the ideal guardian. This education moderates spiritedness with a love of the beautiful and the good which makes the guardian more open to rule by reason and the philosopher. Prospero's control over Ferdinand represents the relationship between spiritedness and reason. When Prospero threatens to manacle Ferdinand, the young prince draws his sword and resists Prospero's control. Prospero assuages Ferdinand's anger by producing Ferdinand's love for Miranda which is a love for the beautiful and the good (see pp. 115-16 above). This love makes Ferdinand submit to Prospero's rule:

> My father's loss, the weakness which I feel,
> The wrack of all my friends, nor this man's threat
> To whom I am subdued, are but light to me,
> Might I but through my prison once a day
> Behold this maid.
>   (I.ii.487-92)

In the triadic pattern spiritedness joins reason to appetite. Put in other terms, Miranda is the part of Prospero which binds that in him which yearns for the eternal with that in him which holds him to the earth.

Prospero's renunciation of his magic implies his willingness to return to humanity. The changing of his magician's robes for his ducal attire after V.i.89 symbolizes his return to Milan and to the everyday world. That Prospero's ability to forgive is a necessary condition of this return is indicated by the sequence of events concerning forgiveness and renunciation of magic. First, Prospero states his intention to forgive. His announcement directly afterwards of his plan to turn away from his magic implies that his plan is the result of forgiveness. Next he carries out his intention to forgive before a court party restored to its senses by heavenly music called forth with the aid of magic. Then comes the symbolic alteration of attire.

As argued above (pp. 106-08), Prospero's abjuration of his magic does not signal an alteration in his character from vindictive to forgiving as so many critics have argued.[3] First, from the outset of the play Prospero applies his magic with the limited purpose of regaining his dukedom while foiling the conspiracies of Antonio and Sebastian and of Stephano, Trinculo and Caliban. Second, Prospero's abjuring of his magic occurs at the sixth hour which he had set for the completion of his plan and which, indeed, brings the accomplishment of his end. Third, a vengeful Prospero would not arrange the union of Ferdinand and Miranda prior to his supposed conversion to forgiveness.[4] Fourth, Prospero sometimes uses his magic for purposes which can only be related to his kindness: to ensure that the ship's passengers come to no harm and to cure the brains of the court party.

Prospero's return to humanity involves leaving the sphere in which his magic operated. He has come to possess magical powers through knowledge derived from study of the liberal arts and through virtue. On the island he has added the knowledge of appetite and of desire for political power so necessary to the ruler. There he has also come to possess poetic powers. Surely his removal of his magician's robes cannot mean that he will lose all this. It could mean, however, that to the extent that he focuses on the world of practical affairs he must turn away from the study of universals required by NeoPlatonism for control over the natural world which is in tune with higher forces. In this sense turning toward Milan means turning away from philosophy.

Prospero's renunciation of his magic also suggests a turning away from poetry. As argued later, however, Shakespeare's play ultimately qualifies the implication that a return to humanity necessitates a partial denial of philosophy and of Prospero's poetry (see pp. 169-75). Association of poetry with magic implies a renunciation of poetry along with magic. Prospero's use of magic to direct the events of the play implies the poetic character of that magic, but The Tempest explicitly relates Prospero's magic to poetry both in the masque and in the epilogue. Furthermore, Ariel who as daemon has carried out Prospero's magical commands may represent poetry or the poetic imagination.

Prior to the masque Prospero tells Ariel that he must produce for Ferdinand and Miranda "Some vanity of my art" (IV.i.41). In this passage "art" means "magic," but the vanity which Prospero's magic produces is a masque. The daemons who have been the instruments of Prospero's art become actors in the masque (IV.i.39, 148-50).

The epilogue makes Prospero the magician speak as

Shakespeare the playwright:

> Now my charms are all o'erthrown,
> And what strength I have's my own,
> Which is most faint. Now 'tis true
> I must be here confined by you,
> Or sent to Naples. Let me not,
> Since I have my dukedom got
> And pardoned the deceiver, dwell
> In this bare island by your spell;
> But release me from my bands
> With the help of your good hands.
> Gentle breath of yours my sails
> Must fill, or else my project fails,
> Which was to please. Now I want
> Spirits to enforce, art to enchant;
> And my ending is despair
> Unless I be relieved by prayer,
> Which pierces so that it assaults
> Mercy itself and frees all faults.
> As you from crimes would pardoned be,
> Let your indulgence set me free.

As playwrights Prospero and Shakespeare must appeal to their audiences, and hence their intention is "to please." In this sense Prospero or Shakespeare is the slave of the audience, in "bands" and under its "spell." In this respect the audience becomes godlike and replaces Prospero as the controlling force who judges, shows "mercy," and possesses magical powers. Like the court party whose only recourse is to petition to Prospero for forgiveness, Prospero and Shakespeare are those who must petition the audience for forgiveness. Otherwise they must "despair" as Alonso does upon the accusation of Ariel. This final humility presents only a partial view of the poet's position in relation to his audience. Formerly Prospero has possessed magical charms and has controlled the action of the play. Poetry traditionally had the dual function of pleasing and teaching, and Cicero had expanded this to include the power to move. Prospero has attempted not only to please Miranda and Ferdinand with his art but to teach them. The poet's "charms" perhaps are most suggestive of the poet's power to move, and certainly Prospero exhibits this power in his use of magic to control the court party and the clownish conspirators.

Since Ariel carries out Prospero's magical

commands, identification of Ariel with poetry or the poetic imagination suggests a further connection of magic with poetry. Along with the renunciation of magic, the freeing of Ariel suggests a turning away from poetry. If one is to make an identification of Ariel beyond his function as a daemon, he seems closest to poetry or the poetic imagination. The variety of interpretations of Ariel's role suggests the difficulty of applying an exact allegorical significance to Ariel. Ariel has been identified as a daemon, a fairy, the fancy, Shakespeare's art, the sensitive soul, and as man's higher imaginative powers.[5] And Paul Cantor has suggested to me that Ariel might represent spiritedness.[6] On the other hand, some of these identifications are not mutually exclusive, and elements of others can be rationalized to accord with a different interpretation.

Certain aspects of <u>The Tempest</u> do suggest that Shakespeare intended Ariel to function as more than a daemon. The opposition of Caliban and Ariel implies that they are contrary aspects of man. Ariel is "spirit," "air," "delicate," as opposed to Caliban who is body, "earth," "monster." Ariel is "too delicate" to enact the "earthy and abhorred commands" of Caliban's mother. Caliban is Sycorax's son—"hagseed" and a base thing which crawls on the earth, a "tortoise." He is characterized by base appetite—lust and love of drink. After Prospero arrives on the island, he frees Ariel from a pine and confines Caliban in a rock. If humans are between gods and beasts, Ariel as daemon is closer to the gods, and Caliban as monster and "tortoise" is closer to the beasts.

The identification of Ariel as spiritedness is compelling in certain ways, but the difficulties with this identification outweigh its advantages. If Caliban is appetite and Prospero is reason, the third part of the soul, spiritedness, remains for Ariel. Ariel's desire to be free of Prospero would represent the difficulty of getting reason to rule anger in the soul and in the state. Prospero's ability to control Ariel would be illustrative of his learning to control spiritedness on his island, whereas earlier in Milan he could not understand spiritedness as embodied in Antonio. Ariel's control of Caliban would parallel the control of appetite by spiritedness in the triadic pattern, and the use of dogs to chastise Caliban and his cohorts would be suggestive of the guardian dogs of the <u>Republic</u> (375-76).

The most obvious difficulty with this identification is Ariel's failure to exhibit warlike characteristics. One would expect a representative of spiritedness to be a discordant element exhibiting hardness and toughness such as Shakespeare's other representatives of spiritedness--for example, Coriolanus. But Ariel, although perhaps "moody" at times (I.ii.243), is never angry; he feels compassion. He is not hard and tough, but a "spirit" who is "delicate," "gentle," "kind" and who "lives in cowslips bells." He does not produce discord, but harmony, music, and love. Further difficulties with making Ariel spiritedness are the lack of explanation for his production of illusions and for Prospero's freeing him before returning to Milan. In the world of practical politics of all places Prospero would need to maintain his control over spiritedness.

The more generally accepted interpretation of Ariel as poetry or as the poetic imagination makes more sense, can subsume most of the other identifications of Ariel, and can be rationalized with the most compelling aspects of the spiritedness identification. Making Ariel the poetic imagination provides the most plausible explanation for his ability to produce music and illusions. Ariel controls Ferdinand, Caliban, Stephano, and Trinculo with music. In the masque he "enacts" Prospero's "fancies" as poetry would. And elsewhere he produces actions which Prospero has desired: In creating the tempest and its effect on the court party Ariel's "charge / Exactly is performed" (I.ii.238-38), and in playing the harpy Ariel has "nothing bated" of Prospero's "instruction" (III.iii.85). As G. Wilson Knight points out, Ariel's element of air is reminiscent of <u>A</u> <u>Midsummer</u> <u>Night's</u> <u>Dream's</u> "airy nothing."[7] This is reinforced by Trinculo's reference to Ariel as "Nobody" (III.ii.132).

Ariel as the poetic imagination correlates nicely with Ariel as daemon. Ariel as daemon represents a high form of the poetic imagination. The daemon as a bond between man and the gods might, like the poet of <u>A</u> <u>Midsummer</u> <u>Night's</u> <u>Dream</u>, glance "from heaven to earth, from earth to heaven" (see pp. 64-66, 75 above). Such a poet would recognize the ideal in heaven and try to find a way to fulfill it on earth.

He would recognize the godlike in humans and try to reinforce it. In order to do so he would have to understand entirely what he sees on earth, including human limitations.

The Renaissance daemon derived from the _Symposium_ is associated with love. Both bind earthly and heavenly things. Once the daemon becomes the poet or the poetic imagination he calls forth all of the Renaissance ideas concerning poet as lover (discussed on pp. 72-79 above). These ideas suggest that the true poet possesses superior knowledge. According to the _Phaedrus_ and Renaissance versions of its ideas, the poet is the "follower of the Muses" who, along with the lover, has seen the most "reality" in heaven. The true poet is a man who writes only after he knows the truth. In other words, he is a philosopher poet such as Prospero.

Ariel's role in causing the love of Ferdinand and Miranda makes explicit the relation of daemon and love (see Appendix B). It also explains his opposition to Caliban. Caliban represents base love or appetite, while Ariel represents noble love or love of the beautiful and the good. The play's songs repeat the opposition. Caliban's cohort, Stephano, sings songs expressing appetite, both for sex and for drink, while Ariel's songs suggest the transformation of humans into something higher.

Seeing Ariel as representing not just poetry, but poetry of a divine and noble sort is compatible with Ariel's constant urge to be free of Prospero's control. Ariel is willing to obey Prospero for a time, for Prospero is a philosopher, if only an earthly one. Still, poetry which seeks a vision of divine essences must be subject to the philosopher's urge to turn away from the temporal. Even Prospero has a body, and Ariel longs for freedom from it as much as Prospero does (see pp. 167-69 below). Ariel partakes too much of spirit to accept a commission much mixed with earthiness.

Making Ariel a poet with a vision of essences or of the divine also explains the limits of Sycorax's power over him. It is the spiritual nature of Ariel, the fact that he is "dainty" and "too delicate," which makes him refuse to grant her "earthy" requests. As a goetist or evil black magician (pp. 105-06 above), Sycorax would be unable to control an

aerial daemon for her purposes. The most she can do
is to imprison Ariel in a pine.

    The sort of poetic imagination which Ariel
represents is elaborated in Ariel's songs. It is
tempting to accept Harry Berger's suggestion that
Ariel's last song, "Where the bee sucks there suck
I," is reminiscent of Plato's comparison of the poet
to a honey-gathering bee in the garden of the
Muses.[8] On the face of it Ariel seems like the
poet in Ion 543b--"a light and winged thing, and
holy." In this section of the Ion Socrates tells the
rhapsode that poetry has its source in divine power.
Ariel's position as daemon and bond between gods and
men would make him seem to be like one of the rings
of the magnet who, inspired by the deity, imparts
inspiration to men. And yet Socrates also tells Ion
that the poet is "never able to compose until he has
become inspired, and is beside himself, and reason is
no longer in him." Ariel produces illusions for
Prospero who is controlled by reason, and thus
Ariel's poetic productions in The Tempest are not the
result of simple divine inspiration. Socrates also
tells Ion that poetry cannot be an "art" if it is
divinely inspired. If it is based on faith, it
cannot depend on rational knowledge of the poet.
Shakespeare's point would be just the opposite.
Ariel's control by reason implies that poetry can be
an art. It is an art based on Prospero's
knowledge--knowledge of the philosopher who both
studies universal essences and knows the nature of
humans.

    Ariel's songs present an image of the way that
Prospero's and Shakespeare's art works:

    Where the bee sucks, there suck I;
    In a cowslip's bell I lie;
    There I couch when owls do cry.
    On the bat's back I do fly
    After summer merrily.
    Merrily, merrily shall I live now
    Under the blossom that hangs on the bough.
                            (V.i.88-94)

Prospero and Shakespeare are aware of the evil in the
world--both in humans and in nature. They understand
owls and bats, symbols of night and darkness and
evil. And yet despite that evil they present humans
with a picture of sweetness, of summer and light and

virtue. The vision of summer derives from a depiction of the gods as beneficent to humanity. This is the honey which the bee sucks in the garden of the Muses and which has its source in an inspiring divinity. Ariel represents the comic spirit but is more comprehensive than comedy alone, for his comedy includes an understanding of tragedy.

Ariel's daemonic image of Prospero's and Shakespeare's art is further elaborated in an earlier song:

> Come unto these yellow sands,
>   And then take hands.
> Curtsied when you have and kissed
>   The wild waves whist,
> Foot it featly here and there;
> And, sweet sprites, the burden bear.
>   Hark, Hark!
>   Burden dispersedly. Bow, wow!
>   The watchdogs bark.
>   [Burden dispersedly.] Bow, wow!
>   Hark, hark! I hear
> The strain of strutting chanticleer
>   Cry cock-a-diddle-dow.
>   (I.ii.377-83)

Again Ariel appears as the comic spirit whose music can chase away evil, as watch dogs chase away prowlers and as the rooster chases away night to bring the day. The harmony of the dance and love can calm the wild waves produced by the tempest, a symbol of tragedy and of the difficulties of this life.

In this song Shakespeare presents the poet as lover. Ariel's control by Prospero or reason suits the image. In the Phaedrus 247 the reality which both poet and lover see is "visible only to reason, the soul's pilot; and all true knowledge is knowledge of her [reality]." The true poet again is the philosopher-poet. Ariel's music can calm Ferdinand's passion as well as the fury of the waves. As in Ficino, poetry can produce harmony in the human soul, for poetic madness separates "reason and opinion . . . from confused fancy and sense desire." It does this by arousing the soul, calming the discords of the body, and producing harmony between body and soul (see p. 73 above).

In Ariel's song nature responds to the harmony of

dance and of love in humans. The poet must
illustrate a harmony of nature with virtue if he is
to lend support to virtue. This is what Ferdinand
learns in the course of the play: "Though the seas
threaten they are merciful. / I have cursed them
without cause" (V.i.178-79). This harmony implies
the existence of a divinity which punishes evil and
supports good. For Ferdinand Ariel's music suggests
the existence of "Some god o' th' island"
(I.ii.390). The major poetic production for
Ferdinand and Miranda, the masque, preserves a vision
of nature rewarding virtue (see pp. 114-16 above).

Later when Ariel plays the part of destiny's
minister, he gives the court party a description of
nature's, and the gods', rejection of vice:

> But remember
> (For that's my business to you) that you three
> From Milan did supplant good Prospero;
> Exposed unto the sea, which hath requit it,
> Him and his innocent child; for which foul deed
> The pow'rs, delaying, not forgetting, have
> Incensed the seas and shores, yea, all the
> creatures,
> Against your peace.
>   (III.iii.68-75)

What Ariel teaches in effect is to believe in the
gods. Earlier Antonio has told Sebastian that he
does not believe in the gods: "Twenty consciences /
That stands 'twixt me and Milan, candied be they /
And melt, ere they molest!" (II.i.282-84). But the
appearance of the strange shapes bringing a banquet
makes Sebastian "believe / That there are unicorns;
that in Arabia / There is one tree, the phoenix'
throne, one phoenix / At this hour reigning there"
(III.iii.21-24). And Antonio adds that he will
"believe both." The phoenix and the unicorn are both
symbols of immortality and thus suggestive of the
existence of gods.

Shakespeare's play in general teaches the
existence of beneficent gods. A parallel to
Shakespeare's method in The Tempest appears in King
Lear in simplified form. Both Shakespeare and Edgar
produce imaginary evidence of the gods' concern for
humans. In Lear Edgar teaches the blind Gloucester
not to despair by having him leap off of Dover Cliffs
in his imagination. Gloucester, who is in a field

and not on a cliff at all, has not fallen, but Edgar,
pretending that his father has fallen, argues that
Gloucester's survival reveals the existence of gods
offering aid to men: "Think that the clearest gods,
who make them honors / Of men's impossibilities, have
preserved thee" (IV.vi.73-74). The injustices which
Gloucester and Lear have suffered make life seem
unbearable and suggest that the gods do not care
about men. Gloucester needs belief in the gods to
give meaning to his existence and to accept his
sufferings as part of a larger scheme. To believe
that the gods care is a precondition to bearing life
with "free and patient thoughts."

In The Tempest Shakespeare presents the audience
and Prospero presents the court party with what seems
miraculous--the vision of Ferdinand and Miranda at
chess. Both Edgar's pretended miracle and Prospero's
seeming miracle involve the preservation of life when
death seems certain. Like Edgar, Prospero preaches
patience to Alonso: "I rather think / You have not
sought for help . . . " (V.i.141-44). But unlike
Edgar, Prospero can also remove the cause of
despair--Ferdinand's death. His ability to do so
seems "A most high miracle" to Sebastian and
"strange" or "not natural" to Alonso. Ferdinand's
belief in nature's beneficence also derives from a
restoration of what seemed dead--of Alonso.

Ariel's third song is an image of art
transforming the brazen world of nature into Sidney's
golden world:

        Full fatham five thy father lies;
            Of his bones are coral made;
        Those are pearls that were his eyes;
            Nothing of him that doth fade
        But doth suffer a sea change
        Into something rich and strange.
                                (I.ii.397-402)

Alonso is to become an art object--with bones of
coral and eyes of pearl. That Alonso does become
more virtuous through Ariel's appeal to his
conscience suggests that art can to some extent
improve the world in actuality as well as in writing.

Ariel as poetic imagination, then, represents the
highest form of poetry, that available to the poet as
philosopher. This form of poetry is comic in spirit,

but it is broad enough to include tragedy within its vision. Such poetry manages to chase away evil and darkness and tragedy through its representation of nature as in harmony with man.

Most of the identifications of Ariel accord easily with this one. Ariel's fairylike characteristics are incorporated into his appearance as daemon. To give Ariel the qualities of one part of a tripartite division of the soul does seem problematic, since the three portions seem to have been fulfilled by other characters. Miranda is "one third" of Prospero's life. Prospero acknowledges Caliban as "mine." And Prospero himself seems the most likely representative of reason or of the rational soul. Furthermore, any allegorical identification of a character must be qualified somewhat. Miranda's and Ferdinand's spiritedness has been moderated by a love of the beautiful and the good. Prospero, like the human philosopher, is controlled by reason, but he exhibits anger and reports grief. Still, the characterization of Ariel as the sensitive soul makes sense but rests largely in its function as the part of the soul to which imagination belongs.[9] Calling Ariel poetry, Shakespeare's art or the poetic imagination is to refer to the same subject. Poetry would exhibit the same qualities as the poetic imagination which produced it. To limit Ariel to spiritedness would limit the implications of his songs, and yet to have the poetry or poetic imagination of the philosopher-politician perform some of the salutary functions of the spirited element of the city seems entirely reasonable.

The most difficult question to answer concerning Ariel is why Prospero frees him when he returns to Milan. Some time ago G. Wilson Knight argued that Prospero's rejection of his magic and his freeing of Ariel represented Shakespeare's farewell to his art.[10] Such an explanation is incomplete unless it can also explain why Shakespeare would turn away from poetry and how a farewell to art is appropriate to Prospero and to the rest of The Tempest. Why would Prospero have to leave poetry to return to Milan? If he returns to Milan for the sake of Miranda and Ferdinand, guardians educated to love of the beautiful and the good, he will need the sort of poetry Ariel represents to continue their education. Prospero frees Ariel even though he loves him

(IV.i.47-49) and will "miss" him (V.i.95). The duke looks upon the freeing of Ariel with regret. The explanation, then, must lie in the impossibility of taking Ariel to Milan. Ariel as poetry or the poetic imagination represents a high form of poetry which depends on knowledge derived from philosophy, on knowledge of eternal things as well as of the temporal. Insofar as Prospero's return to Milan is a return to practical politics, he will have less time for philosophy, and return to the temporal world means return to a life which cannot always effectively deal with its tragic elements and which cannot always embody the comic spirit.

The alteration in Prospero once he renounces his magic and returns to humanity suggests that there is a distinction between art and life. Art can be assumed to be natural to the extent that it educates humans to fulfill their end. But art differs from life when it provides an incomplete vision to people, although one supportive of virtue, as does Prospero's masque. Miranda's view that the world is a "brave new world" has definite limitations which have been discussed earlier. Prospero provides Ferdinand and Miranda with a sense of the harmony of humanity and nature and a taste for the beautiful and the good, but he must exclude certain facts of life to do so. Prospero's masque can depict nature in harmony with humans because it moves from autumn to spring, omitting winter. Art forgets mortality in its focus on the eternal, but The Tempest as a whole, a work of art itself, reminds the reader of mortality and death as the thought of Caliban and his conspiracy interrupts the masque. Furthermore, the play begins with a dramatization of what Prospero's control over nature eliminates--tragedy and death. Only magical control preserves the members of the court party and transforms them. To explain to Miranda his former life in Milan Prospero must remove his magical robes, for there he has not had the powers of magic. As a human Prospero has been subject to evil along with the rest of men. Antonio's evil designs are successful then. Even the masque makes clear what its blessing has rejected: illicit love as represented by Venus and the unreformed Cupid (IV.i.92-101) and the "Scarcity and want" characteristic of winter (IV.i.116-17).

Other elements in the play suggest that there is a distinction between art and life. The Tempest

165

continually attracts attention to its own art. Miranda, for example, refers to Renaissance ideas on verisimilitude. Sidney argues that the "truth of a foolish world" often contradicts the perfection which a poet might wish to present (see pp. 67-68 above). Nature presents a brazen world, whereas art presents a golden one. Miranda, however, argues that life in the form of Ferdinand cannot be improved upon: "Nor can imagination form a shape, / Besides yourself, to like of" (III.i.56-57). But, since Miranda's statement appears in a work of art, it suggests that The Tempest presents a golden world which is superior to life.

The Tempest's emphasis on its conformity to the unity of time indicates that it is lifelike, but such an emphasis also calls attention to the poet's artistry in producing verisimilitude. Early in the play Prospero points out to the audience that the play will take place during the same time that it will be viewed: "At least two glasses. The time 'twixt six and now / Must by us both be spent most preciously" (I.ii.240-41). In the last act Ariel and the boatswain again remind the audience of the play's unity of time: "On the sixth hour, at which time, my lord, / You said our work should cease" (V.i.4-5, see also V.i.222).

The Tempest's references to dreams and sleep also suggest that the world of the play may not be like life, and these references raise questions about where humans should look to find the truth--to art or to life. First, there is actual sleeping induced by Ariel and Prospero in Miranda, in the court party, and in the mariners. If Ariel represents poetry or the poetic imagination, the implication would be that poetry produces dreams. The same holds for Prospero as poet. This calls forth questions about the quality of a dream. As in A Midsummer Night's Dream, the tradition of two senses of dream becomes relevant (see pp. 61, 62, 67 above). Is the dreamer he who does not see clearly what is true? Or is he the one who has left his body behind so that his soul can see the truth unhampered?

Second, various characters in The Tempest refer to its events as dreamlike. These references make one wonder which is a dream--art or life.[11] The play makes the audience ask whether life in Milan was actually a dream or whether life on the island is the

166

dream. Miranda refers to her memory of her past life in Milan as "rather like a dream than an assurance / That my remembrance warrants" (I.ii.45), whereas Ferdinand finds that on Prospero's island "My spirits, as in a dream, are all bound up" (I.ii.487).

References to the play's events as dreamlike also evoke the dual senses in which dream might be taken. On the face of it Prospero's famous revels speech suggests that human life and death as well are insubstantial and insignificant:

> We are such stuff
> As dreams are made on, and our little life
> Is rounded with a sleep.
> (IV.i.156-58)

And yet the play earlier has evoked another attitude toward the dream--the view that it is a means of viewing eternal truths unhampered by the body. This view is described by an unlikely source, Caliban:

> Sometimes a thousand twangling instruments
> Will hum about mine ears; and sometimes voices
> That, if I then had waked after long sleep,
> Will make me sleep again; and then, in dreaming,
> The clouds methought would open and show riches
> Ready to drop upon me, that, when I waked,
> I cried to dream again.
> (III.iii.142-48)

Caliban's dreams have given him a vision of the eternal--"riches" ready to drop from the heaven. These dreams have been induced by Ariel's music, which is remininiscent of both celestial music and of poetry.

The Tempest's references to "nothing" and to "nobody" reinforce a sense of dual possibilities. Ariel's invisible playing on the tabor reminds Trinculo of the "picture of Nobody" (III.ii.131). "Nobody" may, of course, imply nonexistence. But it may also imply the existence of something unseen. It is tempting to apply II Corinthians again (4:18): "The things which are seen are temporal; but the things which are not seen are eternal." Gonzalo's talk to Alonso of "nothing" and Sebastian's and Antonio's habit of laughing at "nothing" contain the same possibilities. Gonzalo speaks of a vision of the ideal which the others reject as impossible.

Although Miranda and Ferdinand tie Prospero to this world, he persists in longing for emancipation from its limits. Prospero's willingness to rule is tenuous, for his desire for the eternal continues. Milan's rightful duke admits that once he returns to his dukedom "Every third thought shall be my grave" (V.i.311). He longs to escape the body for the world of pure spirit. In Platonic or NeoPlatonic terms, Prospero is the philosopher whose soul focuses on the imperishable realm and is never willingly connected to the body. The practice of philosophy is "meditation upon dying" in the sense that "the soul, still residing in his body, spurns all bodily allurement under the guidance of philosophy, and frees itself from the tempting devices of the lusts and all the other passions."[12] For the philosopher the creature's death is the soul's life since the soul is released from the body to return to the immortal world. The soul which has shunned the body

> departs to that place which is, like itself, invisible, divine, immortal, and wise, where, on its arrival happiness awaits it, and release from uncertainty and folly, from fears and uncontrolled desires, and all other human evils, and where . . . it really spends the rest of time with God.[13]

Lear speaks of this set of ideas as he and Cordelia are captured:

> Come, let's away to prison:
> We two alone will sing like birds i' th' cage:
> When thou dost ask me blessing, I'll kneel down
> And ask of thee forgiveness: so we'll live,
> And pray, and sing, and tell old tales, and laugh
> At gilded butterflies, and hear poor rogues
> Talk of court news; and we'll talk with them too,
> Who loses and who wins, who's in, and who's out;
> And take upon's the mystery of things,
> As if we were God's spies: and we'll wear out,
> In a walled prison, packs and sets of great ones
> That ebb and flow by th' moon.
>
> (V.iii.8-18)

Lear speaks of himself and Cordelia as two souls, "two birds" (a Christian icon for the soul), imprisoned in the body and in the temporal world.

Even so they will make their cage superior to the temporal by focusing on something better—on the bond between them, on God, on the old tales which are an improvement on life. Lear expresses no confidence that they will attain knowledge of the eternal, but at least they can pretend to understand "the mystery ot things" by standing back from the world and observing it.

Even though Prospero returns to Milan, his art has been directed towards the eternal. He has taught Ferdinand and Miranda to subordinate body to soul by controlling their passion for the sake of virtue. Earlier he had ignored worldly matters almost entirely when in Milan he had studied the liberal arts, and the island has provided a degree of isolation from practical affairs which has enabled him to continue his study. Prospero's emphasis on the mind has led to control of Ariel whose airy nature makes him even less a creature of the body than humans. How Prospero applies to poetry his emphasis on the eternal is made clear in his characterization of his masque for Ferdinand:

> Our revels now have ended. These our actors
> As I foretold you, were all spirits and
> Are melted into air, into thin air;
> And, like the baseless fabric of this vision,
> The cloud-capped towers, the gorgeous palaces,
> The solemn temples, the great globe itself,
> Yea, all which it inherit, shall dissolve
> And, like this insubstantial pageant faded,
> Leave not a rack behind. We are such stuff
> As dreams are made on, and our little life
> Is rounded with a sleep.
>
> (IV.i.148-58)

As Stephen Orgel has noted," revels" is a technical term which means "masque," and this passage applies to Prospero's art as well as to life.[14] In words reminiscent of II Peter 3:10-11 Prospero alludes to the Last Judgment as a comment on the transitory nature of both this world and his art. Prospero's actors have melted into the air like the earth at the Last Judgment or humans at death. All that which seems substance shall dissolve in the end. The Last Judgment means the end of the body and a turning to pure soul. Man's body disappears at death so that he can be no more than spirit. Life is ended with the sleep which releases the soul from the body so that it can view the truth unhampered (see pp. 61-62 above). Life and the world in general, then, have their end in the eternal. In this sense both philosophy and the art which focuses on virtue, harmony, the beautiful and the good are like life.

Shakespeare brings art and life together in other ways. As suggested earlier, The Tempest as a work of art, although comic in spirit, includes a sense of the tragedy, mortality and winter which it transcends. Shakespeare also brings art and life together in his epilogue where Prospero speaks as both actor and character to an audience which is asked to participate in the outcome of the story. The audience's approval in applauding the play will send Prospero to Naples. Otherwise he will remain "confined" on the island by the audience, and his "project fails." The audience's approval could also suggest that the play will participate in their lives. Their acceptance of Prospero means that they approve of the poetic philosopher-king. Their rejection means that the philosopher poet will remain isolated from his audience and from rule.

Act V of The Tempest combines a strong sense of the eternal with Prospero's return to the temporal world of Milan. Alonso, Gonzalo, and Sebastian all suggest that the events which they observe originate in the divine. For Alonso "These are not natural events; they strengthen / From strange to stranger" (V.i.227-28; see also V.i.241-43). Sebastian calls the discovery of Ferdinand and Miranda at chess "A most high miracle" (V.i.178). Chapter V discusses Gonzalo's opinion that the events of the play are an illustration of the idea of the fortunate fall. Prospero extends the allusion to the divine beyond immediate events. His earlier reference to his and Miranda's arrival at shore "by Providence divine" (I.ii.159) is reiterated as he explains to the court party that he was "most strangely . . . landed" upon the island (V.i.160-61).

Act V is packed with references to the play's events as "strange," "wonderful," or "admirable." The abundance of these references suggests that Shakespeare has in mind the Renaissance view derived from Aristotle that the end of poetry is the production of wonder.[15] Renaissance theories of romance and tragicomedy emphasize admiration as their chief end. Shakespeare, therefore, might have had in mind the theories about these two genres in particular. Renaissance poetics relates the romance to the epic, the Aristotelian genre with which it has most in common. Attacks on the improbabilities of romance could be answered by referring to Aristotle's allowances for improbabilities in the epic. A drama could not justify its improbabilities by applying the _Poetics_' argument that the improbable is more acceptable in epic than in tragedy because the agents are not visibly before one. But one could use Aristotle's argument that the improbable is the chief factor in the marvellous which is a cause of pleasure (1460a). Impossibilities in poetry are justified in the sense that they serve the end of poetry by making the work more astounding (1460b). Simone Fornari makes this argument in his _Spositione sopra l'Orlando Furioso_ (1549). Fornari uses Aristotle's argument to justify the presence of the improbable, the marvellous, and the supernatural in Ariosto.[16]

Theories of the tragicomic also derive their discussion of wonder from Aristotle. Guarini seems to have in mind Aristotle's opposition of the probable and the marvellous when he argues:

> Thus in the _Pastor Fido_ one action is so ingrafted with the other, and with so much necessity and verisimilitude, that if what Messer Giasone says is true, that the marvelous in poems springs from the enrichment of the subject with such episodes as do not offend its unity, it seems to me that the poem can be called marvelous.[17]

Guarini's characterization of imitation as a "marvelous and truly divine activity"[18] also has its roots in Aristotle, in the _Rhetoric_'s discussion of imitation as a cause of wonder and learning (quoted on pp. 68-69 above). The significance of wonder as the end of tragicomedy for Guarini may derive chiefly from his association of the tragicomic peripeteia with the Christian idea of _felix culpa_. Arthur Kirsch has argued that Guarini suggests this in his _Compendium_ when he denies the need of a tragic catharsis for an audience living by the Holy Gospel. Kirsch also cites passages in the _Pastor Fido_ which make explicit the view that joy derives partly from suffering.[19] Further support of this characterization of Guarini's poetics lies in Guarini's argument that the happy ending of tragicomedy is made more delightful because it follows upon sad moments.[20] Making the tragicomic pattern correspond to workings of Providence recalls the Aristotelian and Renaissance idea that wonder in poetry results from wonder about the gods.

Whatever the emphasis, all of these theories of poetry lead to the same implications concerning wonder. Further references in The Tempest are reminiscent of these implications. Most important is the view that wonder in poetry results from wonder about the gods. The wonder associated with the divine is produced in poetry when the events in the work of art seem the result of a divine plan, namely, in Minturno's words, "when they come about with probability." Prospero promises to make the incidents of the play fit this description when he tells Alonso that his explanation will make every incident "seem probable" (V.i.249). In his promise to explain the events on the island Prospero replaces "Some oracle" which Alonso has felt "must rectify our knowledge" about the strange occurrences. Prospero serves the function of the oracle which appears in tragicomedy and in romance. An oracle usually presents the word of a god in hidden or metaphorical form. In this way the oracle meets the traditional Christian requirement that divine things be hidden from the vulgar. Thomas McFarland notes a reference to this tradition in Prospero's continual prodding of Miranda: "Dost thou hear?" (I.ii.106). "The very minute bids thee ope thine ear" (I.ii.37). "Hear a little further" (I.ii.135). McFarland suggests that these passages all allude to Jesus' signal that special attention is required to uncover the truth which parable has veiled: "He that hath ears to hear, let him hear."[21]

The Tempest also contains reminders of Saint Albert's definition of wonder in poetry which arises from wonder about the divine. References to the incidents of the play as "strange" suggest Saint Albert's definition of wonder as the result of a "desire to know the cause of that which appears unusual and portentous." In Renaissance discussions of poetry it had become a cliché to say that the unusual or the unexpected caused admiration.[22] This is the view to which the Friar refers at the conclusion of Much Ado About Nothing when he promises

172

to explain how Hero could return to life: "Meantime
let wonder seem familiar" (V.iv.70). Hamlet also
refers to the Renaissance cliché when he discusses
Gertrude's reaction to his peculiar behavior: "O
wonderful son, that can so astonish a mother! But is
there no sequel at the heels of this mother's
admiration?" (II.ii.335-37). The Tempest's representation of events as "not natural," as "more than
natural," as "no mortal business" also has ample
theoretical support in the Renaissance view that
admiration in poetry derives from what is outside of
nature. As Benedetto Varchi puts it,

> Poets must not consider in the main
> how things are done by men, but how
> they should be done, although many
> things are permitted to them even
> outside nature; and even outside the
> reasonable or the verisimilar, so
> that they may bring not only greater
> utility for this mortal life but
> also greater delight and admiration
> to men.[23]

According to Minturno's version of Aristotle's views,
a further cause of astonishment in poetry is the
introduction of events arousing "compassion or
horror." Gonzalo's characterization of the island
implies that it contains this further cause of
wonder: "All torment, trouble, wonder, and amazement /
Inhabits here" (V.i.104-05).

Prospero as poet creates wonders or works of
art. The events of the play, of course, are
wonderful, but Prospero's principal poetic creations
are people. He transforms Alonso into "something
rich and strange" (I.ii.375), an art object with
coral bones and eyes of pearl. He creates the
"admired Miranda" (III.i.37) whose name itself means
"the wonderful." In Miranda Prospero has produced
the ideal guardian for the city; in other words, the
poet has become the creator of virtuous citizens.

Both Alonso and Miranda are educated by poetic
creations within the play. These creations in turn
evoke wonder which, in accord with Renaissance poetic
theory, causes learning. This learning concerns the
gods (see pp. 69-71 above). Prospero alters Alonso
by teaching him that gods reward virtue and punish
vice. The rightful duke of Milan produces the

banquet with Ariel cast as minister of fate, a representative of the gods, to chastise Alonso for wronging Prospero.

The Tempest makes Miranda's education through wonder more explicit. Miranda attributes her sleep to the unusual nature of Prospero's story about their life in Milan and their exile: "The strangeness of your story / Put heaviness in me" (I.ii.306-07). The unusual nature of Prospero's story makes it seem wonderful. This in turn produces sleep in Miranda. If sleep can be taken as turning toward the eternal and away from the body, then the ultimate result of Prospero's tale is to teach about the eternal, or the beautiful and the good.

That Alonso and Miranda themselves become wonderful after being taught by that which is itself wonderful implies that Prospero has taught them to partake of the divine. As wonders they in turn become sources of learning for the audience which might also learn to become closer to the divine or the perfect image of goodness.

The wonderful and the strange in The Tempest appear more generally as an indication of the degree to which humans can participate in the divine. That Ferdinand has "strangely stood the test" (IV.i.5-7) of his love suggests the divine quality of that love. Prospero's ability to call forth spirits for the production of a majestic vision implies to Ferdinand that Miranda's father is like God, a "wond'red father and a wise" who "Makes this place a Paradise" (IV.i.123-24). That the incidents which produce wonder in Act V have been initiated and controlled by Prospero would indicate that wonder should be directed toward the rightful duke of Milan. Renaissance poetics provides justification for viewing Prospero the poet in this way. First, from Cicero the Renaissance derives the view that the poet seeks to induce admiration for his own genius as well as for what is depicted in his poetry.[24] Second, Renaissance poetic theory supports the idea that the poet's divinity is implied by his ability to produce wonder. Benedetto Varchi puts it this way:

> The poet, in addition to well-composed and sententious verse, has a greatness, a majesty more divine than human, and not only

teaches, delights, and moves, but engenders admiration and wonder in the minds of the listeners, if they are noble and gentle, and in all those who are naturally disposed, for imitation and consequently poetry is (as Aristotle shows in the <u>Poetics</u>) most natural for man.[25]

Prospero as a poet, politician and philosopher has been the godlike cause of wonders. The climax of the play is the production of wonders which are like miracles, the wonders of God. For Alonso and the court party Prospero's display of Ferdinand and Miranda at chess is like a resurrection from the dead. Alonso's appearance to Ferdinand has the same effect. Prospero's powers as a divine poet have been expounded. One need not go too much further to attribute the wonders of <u>The</u> <u>Tempest</u> to Shakespeare's godlike powers.

In <u>The</u> <u>Tempest</u>, then, Shakespeare presents the ultimate defense of his art. This accords with the general Renaissance defense of poetry in making the poet both the philosopher who knows what virtue is in its universal form and the politician who educates citizens to virtue. The Renaissance view arose as a response to Plato's attack on poetry and as a modification of his reform. Plato made philosophy the highest discipline and gave to the philosopher the functions of the politician and the poet, but poetry's Renaissance defenders made it the master discipline and had it subsume the functions of the philosopher and the politician. In doing this, the Renaissance accepted Plato's characterization of the philosopher as unlikely to be willing to rule. This characterization matches Prospero as he appears in Milan. The Renaissance also found virtue in the argument for the philosopher-king. Prospero becomes a philosopher-king of sorts on the island where he controls the actions of the other characters and gives Ferdinand and Miranda the education of Plato's ideal guardians.

When poetry's sixteenth and seventeenth century defenders made poetry instead of philosophy architechtonic, they were attuned to possible defects in philosophy. In attending to universal essences, philosophers might lack understanding of particulars. A key figure making this argument is

Machiavelli whose ideas Shakespeare explores in depth. Machiavelli argued that the classical philosophers had spent too much time attending to imaginary commonwealths rather than to how people actually live. While recognizing the force of the Machiavellian argument that inattention to evil can be unwise, Shakespeare rejects the foundations and outcomes of Machiavelli's thinking. The Tempest denies that nature is hostile, arbitrary and subject to control by men and women. The play also points out that an emphasis on recognizing evil people can eliminate the ability to distinguish among them and to see goodness where it exists. On the other hand, Gonzalo's naive dependence on nature's beneficence and the goodness of humans is also viewed as foolhardy. At the same time, The Tempest suggests that attempts of civilization to reach beyond the primitive can also be problematic. Artifice can make bad natures worse and can provide opportunities for evil to extend its influence. Society's only hope is someone such as Prospero who, recognizing both the noble and the base, seeks to reach the former and to control the latter.

Machiavelli was not the only one to argue that the philosopher might not be able to see things as they are. Sidney had pointed out that those who seek knowledge alone might be lacking in understanding of life on earth. His characterization of the astronomer as looking at the heavens only to fall into a ditch is reminiscent of Aristophanes' attack on philosophers as falling into holes while observing the heavens.[26] Plato himself had admitted that the philosopher might have difficulty understanding the particular, for in developing his well-known image representing how people live as a cave, Plato pointed out that the philosopher who had seen the light of the sun would have difficulty adjusting his eyes to the darkness of the cave upon his return. The Republic, however, is a book about politics, about how the philosopher must operate in the cave.

Prospero in Milan is subject to the criticism that he pays insufficient attention to people as they are. He does not recognize Antonio's evil, and this leads to his overthrow. On the island, however, Prospero shows that he understands the desire for power and knows how to control it. Prospero on the island also learns to understand the force of the passions, for there he comes to know Caliban and to make him serve the higher ends of Prospero. The knowledge which Prospero gains on the island is essential if the philosopher is to rule. Its most important function is in the education of the ruling class, represented in The Tempest by Ferdinand and Miranda. Prospero makes Ferdinand place his willingness to serve the beautiful and the good as embodied in Miranda above his desire to challenge Prospero. Miranda is equally willing to serve her image of the beautiful and the good in Ferdinand. Prospero reinforces the lovers' service to what is good by teaching them to moderate their passions.

As the Renaissance saw, in attempting to understand humans in general, philosophers were most apt to miss weakness in themselves. As Sidney argued, the philosopher "might be blind in himself," "sophistically speaking against subtlety, and angry with any man in whom [he sees] the foul fault of anger."[27] Prospero of the island does not have this fault. Shakespeare puts particular emphasis on Prospero's understanding of his own frailty. Prospero, for example, recognizes Caliban as "mine," and the philosopher sees the need to control his own passion with his reason.

Although attention to the particular was an important consideration, what enabled Sidney to make poetry the prince of all skills, including philosophy, was poetry's relevance to "well-doing" over "well-knowing only."[28] The difficulty with philosophy is its attention to knowledge for its own sake. Like Plato's philosopher, Prospero in Milan studied knowledge with no eye to action. The combination of philosopher with poet and politician is tenuous, for the philosopher might be unwilling to attend to action. Indeed, Plato finds that his philosopher would not wish to rule and must be compelled to do so. Shakespeare's joining of poet, politician and philosopher is more tenable and strengthens his defense of poetry, for Shakespeare finds reasons why the philosopher might be willing to rule. First, recognizing the nobility of forgiveness could help the philosopher to forgive human faults. Second, the philosopher's knowledge of his own weakness suggests a common bond between himself and the rest of humankind. Third, recognition of the good of which human beings such as Ferdinand and Miranda are capable ties him to politics. Even in The Tempest, however, the longing to be free of the earthly continues in the philosopher's "every third thought."

If poetry is to offer anything beyond philosophy, it must add to philosophy's knowledge. Sidney's addition, the ability to act upon that knowledge, is the most compelling one. Shakespeare uses elements of the NeoPlatonic occult tradition as a metaphor for poetry's ability to use knowledge to control what happens on earth. Prospero as magician represents Prospero as poet, and Ariel as daemon represents poetry in its noblest form. This poetry would support virtue by representing the gods as beneficent and nature as in harmony with virtue. Unable to deny the existence of evil, the highest poetry, while comic in spirit, would contain a vision of tragedy as well as comedy. Not only would poetry represent the world as it is, then, it would also transform that world into a golden one. Poetry's transformation gives the audience cause to wonder at the seeming existence of a divine hand in governing the actions of the play. This wonder educates to virtue and is indicative of the degree to which humans can partake of the divine. Prospero's poetry does, in fact, transform human nature into something higher: Alonso repents. Miranda and Ferdinand follow virtue. And yet Antonio and Sebastian are unrepentant, and Caliban remains in need of grace. The dependence of Prospero's art upon magic, the recalcitrance of certain members of society, and the impossibility of taking Ariel to Milan suggest the difficulty of realizing the ideal. In denying evil, poetry would remain distinct from life. As Shakespeare's revels speech suggests, both this world and Prospero's poetry are transitory. And yet Shakespeare's reference to the Last Judgment implies that poetry's end would parallel the end of life in the eternal. In this sense both philosophy and the art which focuses on virtue are like life. If Caliban, Antonio and Sebastian remain, so also do Alonso, Ferdinand and Miranda.

Notes

[1]*The City of God*, p. 349, Bk. 9, ch. 5.

[2]Giambattista Guarini, *The Compendium of Tragicomic Poetry* (1599), as trans. by Alan H. Gilbert, *Literary Criticism: Plato to Dryden* (Detroit, 1962), pp. 516-23.

[3]For example, J. Dover Wilson, *The Meaning of The Tempest* (Newcastle Upon Tyne, 1936), pp. 13-18; F.D. Hoeniger, "Prospero's Storm and Miracle," *SQ*, 7 (1956), 35-38; Richard Henze, "The Rejection of a Vanity," *SQ*, 23 (1972), 433; Robert Egan, "This Rough Magic: Perspectives of Art and Morality in *The Tempest*," *SQ*, 23 (1972), 175-81; D'Orsay W. Pearson, p. 275.

[4]Rose A. Zimbardo, "Form and Disorder in *The Tempest*," *SQ*, 14 (1963), 52.

[5]For references to the discussion of Ariel as a daemon see pp. 102, 105-06 above. Kermode discusses the various identifications of Ariel (pp. lxxxi-lxxxviii, 142-45). See also Robert R. Reed, "The Probable Origin of Ariel," *SQ*, 11 (1960), 61-65; Phillips, pp. 147-59; W. Stacy Johnson, "The Genesis of Ariel," *SQ*, 2 (1951), 205-10; G. Wilson Knight, *The Crown of Life*, pp. 222, 232-35, 208-11; G. Wilson Knight, *The Shakespearian Tempest* (London, 1932), p. 257. Appendix B presents the daemonic characteristics of Ariel.

[6]Paul Cantor has since published a discussion of Ariel as spiritedness: "Prospero's Republic: The Politics of Shakespeare's *The Tempest*," in *Shakespeare as a Political Thinker*, ed. John Alvis and Thomas G. West (Durham, 1981), pp. 245-47.

[7]Knight, *Crown*, p. 210.

[8]Harry Berger, "Miraculous Harp: A Reading of Shakespeare's *Tempest*," *Shakespeare Studies*, 5 (1969-70), 255.

[9]Phillips, p. 153.

[10]Knight, *Crown*, pp. 252-53.

[11]For other discussions of this point see Reuben Arthur Brower, The Fields of Light (New York, 1962), pp. 104-22; Barbara Mowat, The Dramaturgy of Shakespeare's Romances (Athens, Georgia, 1976), pp. 64-67; Cope, pp. 239-44; Alvin Kernan, The Playwright as Magician (New Haven and London, 1979), pp. 135-45.

[12]Macrobius, pp. 138-39. See also the source in Plato's Phaedo 80e-83a.

[13]Phaedo, trans. Hugh Tredennick, in The Collected Dialogues of Plato, eds. Edith Hamilton and Huntington Cairns (Princeton, 1961), 81a, p. 64. Castiglione also sees death as release from the body following purification of the soul and as a coupling with God (p. 322). See also Macrobius, p. 127.

[14]Stephen K. Orgel, "New Uses of Adversity: Tragic Experience in The Tempest," In Defense of Reading, ed. Reuben A. Brower (New York, 1962), p. 129. This essay includes an especially illuminating discussion of Prospero's masque.

[15]The discussion which follows relies on an earlier description of Renaissance views of wonder (pp. 68-71 above).

[16]Weinberg, II, 956.

[17]Giambattista Guarini, Il Verato secondo (1593), as trans. by Weinberg, II, 1088.

[18]Giambattista Guarini, The Compendium of Tragicomic Poetry (1599), as trans. by Alan H. Gilbert, Literary Criticism: Plato to Dryden (Detroit, 1962), pp. 505-06.

[19]Kirsch, pp. 10-11.

[20]Il Verato secondo (1593), paraphrased in Weinberg, II, 1087.

[21]Thomas McFarland, Shakespeare's Pastoral Poetry (Chapel Hill, 1972), pp. 150-53.

[22]Weinberg, I, 1973, 188, 239, 397.

[23]Lezzione seconda, pp. 616-17, as translated in Weinberg I, 430. See also Weinberg, I, 202; II, 739, 761.

[24]Weinberg, I, 129, 151.

[25]Benedetto Varchi, _Hercolano_ (Florence, 1570), p. 279, as translated by Weinberg, I, 149.

[26]Sidney, p. 104.

[27]Sidney, pp. 104-05.

[28]Sidney, p. 104.

CHAPTER VIII

SHAKESPEARE'S REVELS: THE TEMPEST'S DEVELOPMENT

OF A MIDSUMMER NIGHT'S DREAM AND FURTHER THOUGHTS

ON THE POET IN CIVIL SOCIETY

In A Midsummer Night's Dream and The Tempest Shakespeare has considered the problem of the poet in civil society and has attempted to resolve it insofar as resolution is possible. A Midsummer Night's Dream most clearly indicates a conflict between poetry and politics by keeping the poet and the politician separate, whereas The Tempest resolves the conflict by joining the two in a poetical philosopher-king. The potential conflict is made apparent in both plays' concern with the poet's ability to support the morality necessary to civil society. A Midsummer Night's Dream further explores the conflict by examining the limitations of the politician's view of art, while The Tempest eliminates any contradictions between the views of politician and poet by combining the two.

The possibility that poetry could support immorality is made apparent in the Pyramus and Thisbe type of situation which the young Athenian lovers face in A Midsummer Night's Dream and in the Platonic backgrounds of The Tempest. The potentially tragic situation of the young Athenian lovers suggests the potential incompatibility of poetry and politics. Tragedy is dangerous to the city because it makes apparent the conflict of the natural with the city. Love can conflict with the laws of the city as it does in both the Pyramus and Thisbe story and in that of Demetrius, Helena, Lysander, and Hermia. Love can conflict with virtue necessary to the city as Lysander's desire to sleep next to Hermia and Hermia's dream suggest. Finally, love can become the source of discord within the city as in the attempted duel between two of Athens' citizens, Lysander and Demetrius. The legislator must represent virtue and the law as harmonious with human nature. He must argue that virtue and obedience to the law produce happiness. A story such as Pyramus and Thisbe reveals an unresolved conflict between love and the city which leads to tragedy for the lovers. Neither the city nor the world outside offer any comfort to Pyramus and Thisbe.

The _Tempest_ contains reminders of the dangers of poetry to civil society in its Platonic backgrounds. Prospero's similarity to Plato's philosopher-king along with his operation as a poet recall the Platonic critique of poetry in the _Republic_. The grounds of Socrates' attack concern poetry's threat to virtue. He accuses the poets of representing the gods as rewarding injustice and as exhibiting vices.

Poetry and politics clash again in _A Midsummer Night's Dream_'s examination of the politician's view of art, while _The Tempest_ makes the two harmonize in the poet-politician. In _A Midsummer Night's Dream_ the politician, Theseus, judges art according to its indication of loyalty to the city's ruler. But the mechanicals' play demonstrates that not all art which meets Theseus' standard is adept. And the "story of the night" told by the young Athenians reveals that some art which does not meet Theseus' standard can be appealing. Theseus' standard puts the loyal inept work of art before the dangerous but charming work.

In rejecting Theseus' standard the poet might point to limitations in the politician's vision which would make him a poor judge of even that art which might benefit the city. First, Theseus lacks the poet's understanding of the nature of desire. He does not realize that the love of Hermia and Lysander is strong enough to make them oppose the laws of the city. Second, Theseus does not recognize the possibility that poetry might present a vision of perfection which could benefit the city. Theseus views poetry as mere shadows, or poor imitations of the temporal world.

In _The Tempest_ Prospero the politician does not have the deficiencies of Theseus the politician. Since Prospero produces the play's art, all art accords with the will of the politician. As a philosopher Prospero would have a vision of essences which could aid the city, and as one who has experienced the defects of human nature he would understand passion.

In both plays Shakespeare's defense of poetry lies in its ability to deal with the problem of human morality. Both plays recognize the need to bring sexual desire in accord with virtue. _The Tempest_ adds the need to deal with real viciousness--rape, murder, treason--as well as the general problem of educating citizens to virtue. A Midsummer Night's Dream, although recognizing that poetry can be dangerous to civil society, represents the poet as society's benefactor. The poet understands human sexual passion in a way which the politician does not. He sees the need to recognize desire and to come to grips with it. In terms of the play the poet makes desire orderly by sorting out the pairs of lovers and by giving this order the support of nature as represented by Titania and Oberon.

The Tempest expands the possibilities for support of virtue by giving the politician the understanding of the poet. As in A Midsummer Night's Dream, the forces which rule nature are represented as supporting virtue. Just as the deities of the wood, Titania and Oberon, reward orderly married love, in Prospero's masque the gods of heaven and earth reward temperate married love. And in The Tempest as a whole Ferdinand finds nature in harmony with humans. As the teacher of Ferdinand and Miranda Prospero can go further in the support of virtue by making moderate love beautiful as he does in the masque. In doing so Prospero develops a taste for virtue in the future rulers of Milan and Naples, thus giving Ferdinand and Miranda an education similar to that of the Republic's ideal guardians. Prospero recognizes the insufficiency of an appeal to love of the beautiful and the good in controlling the passion of some people, and he provides pinches and cramps to control the natural slave Caliban and appeals to the conscience to control members of the court party other than Ferdinand.

Both plays leave questions about poetry's ability to produce in life what it has done on the stage. In both plays the reality of the poet's solution is called into doubt by its reliance on magic, dreams, and fairies or daemons. The Tempest also questions the validity of its own solution by making it depend on the unlikelihood of the rule of a poet-philosopher and on the eventual rule of a virtuous but naive Miranda. On the other hand, in the course of resolving the play's moral dilemmas Shakespeare explains why poetry might also have the power to resolve them in the temporal world outside the drama.

Similarities in Shakespeare's defenses of poetry in A Midsummer Night's Dream and The Tempest imply that Shakespeare held certain views about the role of the poet throughout his career. The former is a relatively early play (1594-96), while the latter is one of the last plays (1611). In addition, these views are corroborated in other plays. On the other hand, The Tempest's greater recognition of human evil along with its suggestion of poetry's ability to transform people to some extent implies that development of Shakespeare's views also occurred.

Shakespeare argues that the poet is able to produce virtue because he has knowledge both of essences or ideals and of temporal reality. The poet sees the perfection which is a human's end, and he understands the temporal both in recognizing the godly in humankind and in realizing human limitations. In A Midsummer Night's Dream Theseus represents the poet as glancing "from heaven to earth, from earth to heaven." The poet recognizes the vision of harmony and virtue towards which people should be directed, and yet he understands the power of desire to disrupt that vision. In The Tempest the double aspect of the poet's vision is included in Ariel. As daemon Ariel is an intermediary between gods and humans who would have knowledge of both. Prospero as philosopher-poet also has a dual vision. Through his study of the liberal arts he has gained knowledge of essences, and on the island he has reached an understanding of human nature. He realizes that even the best of people are a combination of body and soul: He acknowledges that Caliban is "mine." And Prospero also sees that different people have different natures: Caliban who is ruled by bodily desires requires physical punishment. The court party can be controlled by an appeal to their consciences. Ferdinand and Miranda are moved by a love of the beautiful and the good.

Both The Tempest and A Midsummer Night's Dream represent the poet's knowledge of essences in terms of the Renaissance theory of the poet as lover--he who has seen the most reality in heaven. Theseus in arguing that the "lunatic, the lover and the poet / Are of imagination all compact" unwittingly presents the grounds of the poet's defense. In The Tempest Ariel recalls the association of poet as lover by producing love in Ferdinand and Miranda. In addition, Ariel as daemon would be associated with love and a closeness to the gods. These qualities in Ariel help to identify him as some aspect of a higher poetic vision. The two plays also refer to the understanding of essences in their reference to dream in the sense of depiction of the soul leaving the body behind to gain a pure vision of the eternal.

Along with his representation of the poet's inclusive vision, Shakespeare suggests that the alternatives are lacking in attention to the ideal, in knowledge of temporal reality, or in both. A Midsummer Night's Dream illustrates the limitations of the practical politician, who recognizes neither the strength of desire nor the possibility of representing the ideal. The Tempest questions the vision which attends to the ideal while ignoring the practical difficulties inherent in human nature. In Milan Prospero's attention to theoretical studies has led him away from practical affairs and has eventually led to his overthrow. Gonzalo's picture of a commonwealth in the state of nature proves problematic in its blindness to the problem of vice and prevents people from recognizing virtue where it exists.

The dual vision of the poet is repeated in Shakespeare's view that poetry should be inclusive--that it should subsume both tragedy and comedy. In A Midsummer Night's Dream Shakespeare plays on the idea of turning a potential tragedy into a comedy. The mechanicals turn their Pyramus and Thisbe drama into very "tragical mirth." Puck turns the aunt's "saddest tale" into a comedy by pretending to be a footstool and slipping out from under her. And Shakespeare turns the potential tragedy of the Athenian lovers into a comedy by sorting out the lovers and preventing them from fighting. In The Tempest Ariel's songs point to the comic vision which includes a sense of the tragic. This pattern is repeated in the masque which refers to the winter which it omits and in the play as a whole which includes evil characters who are either transformed or brought under control.

In both plays Shakespeare uses the poet's knowledge of the ideal and the real to make the ideal a reality. A Midsummer Night's Dream establishes order and harmony in Athens and in nature and promises future happiness. Miranda, in The Tempest, represents Prospero's attempt to make the ideal a reality. She has given him the strength to bear the

187

evils of the world, and he returns to Milan for her sake.

How poetry can do this is explained by Shakespeare's references to Renaissance poetic theory. Poetry teaches through wonder. Since wonder is directed towards what seems divine, poetry teaches about the gods. This teaching about the gods makes people virtuous. A nature which both works for human happiness and rewards virtue can support human attempts at morality. Both plays allude to theory concerning wonder and depict nature and the gods in a manner designed to make people virtuous. In A Midsummer Night's Dream the "story of the night" is "strange and admirable." The wonder which it produces results from the sense of some deity or divine plan preventing discord and sorting out the lovers to produce harmony. The story also brings forth a harmony in nature as associated with Titania and Oberon. This harmony is mirrored in the harmony produced in the Athenians. Finally, nature or deity, Titania and Oberon, support virtue in their guarantees of fidelity and promise happiness in their blessing of the marriage beds.

The Tempest is even more insistent about the theory of wonder. The frequent allusion to the play's events as causing wonder calls forth a whole series of Renaissance views. In the masque the gods of heaven and earth, or Juno and Ceres, function in the same way as Titania and Oberon in A Midsummer Night's Dream. They also reward virtue, in this case chastity prior to marriage, with promises of fertility. The harmony which they promise parallels the harmony of the dance of "temperate nymphs." The relation of wonder to the works of gods is made even stronger in The Tempest than in A Midsummer Night's Dream. The principal wonder-evoking event, the revelation of Ferdinand and Miranda at chess, is like a miracle—the resurrection of the dead. The views of Prospero as godlike and as a poet, or producer of wonders, go hand in hand. Prospero causes wonder through his tale to Miranda, and he produces wonderful objects—Alonso transformed into "something strange and rich" and the "admired Miranda."

Shakespeare's drama suggests that poetry produces virtue by creating a golden world. As Sidney argues, many things occur which people do not understand and therefore attribute to fortune rather than to a divine plan which supports virtue and wisdom. The "truth of a foolish world" often argues against the perfect pattern which a poet might present. The poet, however, can depict a world which for the reader presents a clear support for virtue. Both plays' references to dream call forth ideas about a golden world. The dual sense of dream in the Renaissance left open the possibility that the dreamer was the person who had left the body to view the things of the soul unhampered. In A Midsummer Night's Dream Puck's epilogue relates the whole play to such a dream, while Bottom's dream and that of the young lovers refer to specific portions of the play as a dream, i.e., those portions which involve the gods, Titania and Oberon. In The Tempest Ariel's and Prospero's ability to produce sleep implies that they as poets are creating a dreamlike vision for the play's characters, and Ariel's song of Alonso's transformation implies that he is to become an art object which is superior to life. Prospero's revels speech refers again to the sleep which implies a vision of a higher reality than the temporal. Life ends in death which is a sleep, and the temporal world dissolves at the Last Judgment. In both plays, however, Shakespeare is playful in his evocation of the idea of dream. In addition to including suggestions of the dream as a higher vision, he also tells his audience to dismiss his play as a dream if they dislike it, i.e., to consider it of no significance.

Although certain elements of Shakespeare's view of the poet's role in civil society persist throughout his career, the more powerful defense of poetry in The Tempest implies a development of Shakespeare's understanding of the poet's role. The Tempest contains a real recognition of the problem of human evil along with a sense of the superiority of the poet's vision in dealing with it. While A Midsummer Night's Dream includes a representation of human limitations in Bottom's metamorphosis into an ass, those limitations are no more serious than right-minded foolishness. The Tempest, however, comprehends murder, treason, and rape. The issue becomes one's method of dealing with evil. Alternatives to the poet's method are Antonio's Machiavellian approach and Gonzalo's technique of considering evil the result of civilization. Antonio's approach leads only to evil and prevents him from recognizing Gonzalo's virtues. Gonzalo's view, while producing a kind and virtuous citizen, is insufficient for a political leader who must understand that vice is inherent in human nature even without the additions of art. Only the poet can direct people toward the ideal in a manner consonant with their limitations. He can use his art to bring people's bodies in accord with virtue and to direct their souls to the good. To forget Caliban as Gonzalo does is to forget the possibility that he can destroy an attempt at perfection. To ignore Miranda and Ferdinand as Antonio does is to forget the possibility of working toward the good in the city.

Along with the recognition of human evil, _The Tempest_ presents the possibility that poetry can transform and educate human beings. Although the final vision of _A Midsummer Night's Dream_ defends virtue in depicting nature's beneficence and reward of virtue, the poet's solution to the play's problem seems a mere trick. The love juice transfers the lovers' affections from one to another without any other alteration of character. _The Tempest_, however, using magic as an image of poetry, suggests that it has the ability to transform people through appeals to the conscience and to create virtuous citizens through directing good natures towards the beautiful and the good. Alonso's transformation is the result of an appeal to his conscience through Ariel's enactment of destiny as punishing unrepentant sinners against Prospero. In other words, art can alter people through its depiction of gods and of nature. The creation and education of Miranda and the later education of Ferdinand represent the poet's creation of virtuous citizens through an art such as the masque which directs them towards the beautiful and the good.

Discussing Shakespeare's view of the poet's role in civil society on the basis of two plays can represent only a beginning of a full consideration of the question. Other plays deal with the problem, raise the same issues as _A Midsummer Night's Dream_ and _The Tempest_, or elaborate certain ideas found in these two plays. A full survey of the way Shakespeare's plays do all of the above is a project too large to address here, but some brief examples from each of the major genres might suggest the validity of that project. One such example, _Love's Labor's Lost_, presents an early discussion of the philosopher-king's relation to the poet, considers

190

the attack on the poet as liar, examines the limits and the possibilities in the poet's creation of a golden world, and implies that the best poetry is inclusive of more than tragedy or comedy alone.

That _Love's_ _Labor's_ _Lost_ is one of Shakespeare's earliest plays suggests that from the outset of his career Shakespeare considered the best poetry to contain an understanding of both the temporal and the eternal. In terms of the play, focusing either on the eternal alone or on life alone is problematic. The difficulties of the philosophic vision are represented in the problems faced by the "little academe" set up by the King of Navarre. As T. W. Baldwin has noted, Navarre's establishment of an academy parallels La Primaudaye's _French_ _Academy_ which sets up a Platonical school for four young men of the nobility of Anjou. The _French_ _Academy_, translated into English in 1586, had praised Henry III's court for its wisdom and had suggested that a king should be a philosopher and his court an academy:

> Sir, if we credit the saying of _Plato_, Commonwealths begin then to be happy, when Kings exercise Philosophie, and Philosophers raigne. The wise man speaking more diuinely, exhorteth kings to loue and to seeke after wisdome, that they may raigne vpon earth righteously and in heauen eternally.[1]

As Berowne points out, a principal difficulty with a general attempt at philosophizing is most people's incapacity to do so. Berowne makes his point in Platonic terms. People who attempt to come out of the cave where most people live are blinded by the light of the sun, unable to look on the truth directly:

> Light seeking light doth light of light beguile;
> So, ere you find where light in darknees lies,
> Your light grows dark by losing of your eyes.
> (I.i.77-79)

> Study is like the heaven's glorious sun,
> That will not be deep-searched with saucy looks.
> (I.i.84-85)

191

As in the _Republic_ (493b) most of those who pretend
to know the truth take the commonly held opinion for
the truth: "Too much to know is to know nought but
fame" (I.i.92). Astronomers may give names to the
stars, but they live as much in the darkness and know
as little about the stars as anyone else. What the
astronomers are doing is mistaking the names for a
kind of truth or knowledge about the stars in the
same way as those pretenders to the truth in the
Republic (515b) give names to shadows projected on
the cave's walls and take those shadows for truths:

> Small have continual plodders ever won
> Save base authority from others' books.
> These earthly godfathers of heaven's lights,
> That give a name to every fixèd star
> Have no more profit of their shining nights
> Than those who walk and wot not what they are.
> Too much to know is to know nought but fame;
> And every godfather can give a name.
>   (I.i.86-93)

Furthermore, people lack power to conquer their
affections on their own. Navarre has set up his
academe to direct his court towards things of the
mind rather than the body. The lords are to swear
not to see ladies, to fast and to sleep only three
hours. But Berowne argues that "every man with his
affects is born, / Not by might mast'red, but by
special grace" (I.i.150-51). Berowne points out that
humans have a dual nature which cannot be denied. If
one is to take the easiest and surest path to living
well, one must take account of people's natural
propensities--including a young man's desire to
associate with women:

> At Christmas I no more desire a rose
> Than wish a snow in May's new-fangled shows,
> But like of each thing that in season grows.
> So you--to study now it is too late--
> Climb o'er the house to unlock the little gate.
>   (I.i.105-109)

Even if one could truly philosophize and had
attained knowledge of how people should live their
lives, in doing so he would have turned away from
life and thus would have lost the ability to put his
knowledge into action. Put in Platonic terms, the
philosopher who has looked directly on the light of

the sun would have difficulty seeing if he returned
to the darkness of the cave:

> So study evermore is overshot
> While it doth study to have what it would.
> It doth forget to do the thing it should;
> And when it hath the thing it hunteth most,
> 'Tis won as towns with fire--so won, so lost.
> (I.i.141-45)

Berowne, of course, is proved correct in the
course of the play. The King and the young lords are
all foresworn, and they fall in love. Even in this,
however, they are seen faulty in experience of life.
When the ladies exchange gifts, each lord worships
the sign of his love rather than his love herself.
Love itself must be recognized as something of a
compromise between the ideal and the real. The
distance between Berowne's love, the dark Rosaline,
and the ideal beauty testifies to this:

> Berowne. Beauty doth varnish age as if new-born,
>   And gives the crutch the cradle's infancy.
>   O, 'tis the sun that maketh all things shine.
>
> King. By heaven, thy love is black as ebony!
>
> Berowne. Is ebony like her? O wood divine!
>   A wife of such wood were felicity.
>   O, who can give an oath? Where is a book?
>   That I may swear beauty doth beauty lack
>   If that she learn not of her eye to look.
>   No face is fair that is not full so black.
>   (IV.iii.243-252; ll. 253-80 go
>   on in the same vein.)

Even the Princess recognizes that she is the
"thickest and tallest." Although the Princess jests
that "my beauty will be saved by merit," she
recognizes that to some extent love must be seen as
grace in the eyes of the lover.

While pointing to the difficulties of a simple
philosophic outlook, the play also suggests that
attention to the eternal is necessary to living
well. Berowne has been able to consider the
difficulty with single-minded philosophy only because
he is "well . . . read to reason against reading"
(I.i.94). In addition, the Princess's trial of the
King implies that proof of one's value in this world

requires focusing to some extent on what is beyond. The King must prove his love by spending a year in a hermitage where he will turn away from the pleasures of the world.

For Shakespeare the best poetry directs humans toward the eternal with some sense of what life is like. Satire like Berowne's is insufficient because it causes pain without being able to direct humans towards what is good in life. If people were willing or able to turn away from this world altogether, focusing on the foibles of this world might make them laugh. But people are not willing to do so. And thus satire cannot have a salutary effect. This argument is implied by Rosaline's trial of Berowne--to spend twelve months trying to make the dying sick laugh:

> Why, that's the way to choke a gibing spirit,
> Whose influence is begot of that loose grace
> Which shallow laughing hearers give to fools.
> A jest's prosperity lies in the ear
> Of him that hears it, never in the tongue
> Of him that makes it. Then, if sickly ears,
> Deafed with the clamors of their own dear groans,
> Will hear your idle scorns, continue then,
> And I will have you with that fault withal;
> But if they will not, throw away that spirit,
> And I shall find you empty of that fault,
> Right joyful of your reformation.
>   (V.ii.859-70)

Satire leads people only to "shallow laughter" which lacks true understanding. Such laughter is given with "loose grace" which implies that the approval is undeserved. A profound laughter, that of philosophy, would allow people to turn away from this life and from the things of the body altogether. Philosophizing in the sense of turning toward the soul is "learning how to die" (see pp. 167-69 above). If people could philosophize, they could laugh at death. Even Berowne, however, is incapable of this. He has as much difficulty keeping his oath as his three companions. He has the fault of the satirist and his audience who can see the weaknesses of the rest of the world without recognizing their own: "But I believe, although I seem so loath, / I am the last that last will keep his oath" (I.i.158-59). Berowne and most people are incapable of turning away from life altogether. The dying wish

to live. They care about their bodies and "their own
dear groans." Given that characteristic of most
people, satire which focuses on the evils of the
world can only cause pain without curing the world of
its vices.

Presenting a simple golden world, however, is
insufficient as well. Shakespeare creates in Armado
a poet whose work contains the difficuties of a
vision directed only toward ideal types. Such poetry
might delight, but it must be accounted a lie:

> This child of fancy, that Armado hight,
> For interim to our studies shall relate
> In high-born words the worth of many a knight
> From tawny Spain, lost in the world's debate.
> How you delight, my lords, I know not, I,
> But, I protest, I love to hear him lie,
> And I will use him for my minstrelsy.
> (I.i.169-75)

Shakespeare makes it clear that his play intends to
do more. If Love's Labor's Lost were a simple
comedy, it might be subject to the objection that,
like philosophy, it turns away from life and, thus,
in some ways makes it more difficult to live well.
Berowne complains that

> Our wooing doth not end like an old play;
> Jack hath not Jill. These ladies' courtesy
> Might well have made our play a comedy.

The King points out that "it wants a twelvemonth and
a day, / And then 'twill end," but Berowne realizes
that "That's too long for a play."

As You Like It is another play dealing with the
problem of the poet in civil society. It presents a
serious elaboration of the question of the poet's
ability to support morality. In this play the poet's
problem is the defense of virtue in the face of
adverse fortune. The play refers to alternative types
of poetry which are ineffective in their attempts at
producing virtue.

Jaques suggests that he will act like a satiric
poet to cure the world of its ills. He will "Cleanse
the foul body of th' infected world, / If they will
patiently receive my medicine" (II.vii.60-61). Such
a poet might be "full of matter," as Duke Senior puts

it, but there are problems with Jaques' position. First, he must leave for romantic love and harmony to survive. Jaques departs in order for Orlando to woo Rosalind. Romantic love must bid "adieu" to "good Monsieur Melancholy" (III.ii.290), and Jaques insists on leaving once Orlando starts talking "in blank verse" (IV.i.30). At the conclusion of the play where the lovers are brought together Jaques once again departs claiming, "I am for other than dancing measures" (V.iv.193).

Second, Jaques focuses on the faults of the world rather than on his own soul. As Rosalind points out, he is like the man who sells his "own lands to see other men's" (IV.i.21-22). He has no time to attend to his own riches, his soul. Orlando, on the other hand, will "chide no breather in the world but myself, against whom I know most faults" (III.ii.277-78). Duke Senior argues that Jaques' satiric impulse derives from his past life as a libertine. Jaques sees his own evil, and he projects it on the world: "All th' embossèd sores and headed evils / That thou with license of free foot hast caught, / Wouldst thou disgorge into the general world" (II.vii.67-69). Jaques argues that his satire hurts no one if it is inapplicable since it is directed toward the world in general, not to one person. But Jaques' inattention to his own soul suggests satire's difficulty in convincing the audience to relate faults revealed in poetry to their own souls.

The third and major difficulty with Jaques' vision is its inability to recognize virtue where it exists. His speech on the seven ages of men presents only man's riping and rotting: bawling infants, unwilling schoolboys, foolish lovers, jealous and overeager soldiers, pseudo-intellectuals, ridiculous old men, and senility. Immediately following this passage Adam enters representing a contradiction to it--aged virtue half-starved in service to his master. Jaques sees ill everywhere. He "mars" Orlando's verses by reading them "ill-favoredly" (III.ii.260). He "can suck melancholy out of a song as a weasel sucks eggs" (II.v.10-12).

Orlando and Silvius both represent the conventional romantic view. Their excessively idealized outlook is problematic because it makes their vision cloudy and their expectations too high.

Silvius obviously does not see clearly, for, as Rosalind reminds Phoebe, she is not "for all markets." There is something to Phoebe's feeling that Silvius lies when he says that she has wounded him with her eyes. As Rosalind points out, "the poor world is almost six thousand years old, and in all this time there was not any man died in his own person, videlict, in a love cause" (IV.i.89-93). A lasting love requires more moderation, for man's idealized view of his love cannot persist: "Men are April when they woo, December when they wed" (IV.i.140).

Touchstone makes no claim to write verses, but he does compare himself to Ovid exiled among the Goths for his immorality. Touchstone offers another alternative opposite to the romantic vision. By reducing love to the lowest common denominator, he makes it devoid of sentiment altogether:

As the ox hath his bow, sir, the horse his curb,
And the falcon her bells, so man hath his desires;
And as pigeons bill, so wedlock would be nibbling.
(III.iii.76-79)

Touchstone accepts the inevitability of cuckoldry and turns it into a joke. Man marries to cope with his desires, and therefore his horns are horns of defense. Touchstone reduces everything to the corporeal. He announces after his journey to Arden, "I care not for my spirits, if my legs were not weary" (II.iv.2). His claims as a romantic poet are limited by his emphasis on bodily needs. He tells Rosalind of Orlando's verses, "I'll rhyme you so eight years together, dinners and suppers and sleeping hours excepted" (III.ii.96-98). Further, he defines humans merely in terms of growth and decay:

And so, from hour to hour, we ripe and ripe,
And then, from hour to hour, we rot and rot;
And thereby hangs a tale.
(II.vii.26-28)

Touchstone's view of love is at least as defective as the romantic view. Love devoid of all sentiment cannot last. Jaques notes that Audrey and Touchstone's marriage "Is but for two months victualled" (V.iv.192), and Touchstone himself finds Sir Oliver Mar-text's defects as a clergyman advantageous in that "not being well married, it will be a good excuse for me hereafter to leave my wife" (III.iii.88-90).

If satiric and romantic poetry are defective in their support of virtue, at the outset of As You Like It the politically powerful have proved unreliable as well. Shakespeare examines the poet's possibilities as the "right popular [moral] philosopher" by moving to Arden where he can substitute his own support of virtue for that of civil society. He does this by providing models whose virtues are independent of fortune, by examining the nature of the view of the world which will provide such independence, and by making fortune commensurate with virtue in the course of the play.

In Acts I and II the virtuous are dispossessed by fortune. Oliver has denied Orlando his education and his fortune. Duke Ferdinand has usurped his brother's kingdom, has banished Rosalind because of his jealousy of her virtues, and has failed to reward Orlando's victory over Charles because of his enmity to the deceased Sir Rowland de Bois. This is a world where "what is comely / Envenoms him that bears it" (II.iii.13-14). Those who "sweat . . . for promotion" (II.iii.60) get ahead. The danger in the existent civil society is the spoiling of nature by fortune. Celia suggests this when in her discourse with Rosalind she asks, "[W]hen nature hath made a fair creature, may she not by Fortune fall into the fire?" (I.ii.42-43)

To combat this danger to virtue Shakespeare provides models whose virtue is independent of fortune. Rosalind and Orlando maintain their virtues despite their fortunes. Orlando refuses to become a highwayman. Celia is true to her sisterly love rather than her own comfort. And Adam serves his master out of a sense of obligation rather than for material reward: "Yet fortune cannot recompense me better / Than to die well and not my master's debtor" (II.iv.75-76). The play provides in Oliver an example of the conversion to virtue by such models.

The proper vision of the world is embodied in the play's highest ranking nobility--Duke Senior and Rosalind. As Touchstone points out, since any sort of life has characteristics which can be accounted an advantage or a disadvantage, one situation provides

198

the possibility of contrary outlooks. Of a shepherd's life he says:

> Truly, shepherd, in respect of itself, it is a good life; but in respect that it is a shepherd's life, it is naught. In respect that it is solitary, I like it very well; but in respect that it is private, it is a very vile life. Now in respect it is in the fields, it pleaseth me well; but in respect it is not in the court, it is tedious. As it is a spare life, look you, it fits my humor well; but as there is no plenty in it, it goes much against my stomach.
>
> (III.ii.13-21)

Jaques finds life in Arden as melancholic as life anywhere. He grieves for a wounded deer deserted by its companions and looks on the Duke and his men as usurpers in the forest. Duke Senior, on the other hand, "Finds tongues in trees, books in running brooks, / Sermons in stones, and good in everything" (II.i.15-17). The Duke has seen adversity and flattery and recognizes that there is "much matter" in Jaques, and yet he insists upon an optimistic vision: "happy is your Grace / That can translate the stubbornness of fortune / Into so quiet and so sweet a style" (II.i.18-20). Rosalind maintains the same sort of vision. She is realistic about the excesses of romantic love, and yet she continues to love. Her realism makes her love independent of illusions which could endanger it.

Not everyone in the play is capable of sustaining the vision of Duke Senior and Rosalind or of maintaining a virtue independent of fortune. Shakespeare offers a further support for virtue--its reward by fortune. Duke Senior regains his dukedom. Orlando recovers his fortune and is given his love. Rosaland finds a tested love and is restored to her proper position in society. Celia is married to a converted Oliver. The play, then, fulfills in this life religion's promise to reward virtue in the next life. In producing harmony between virtue and fortune the playwright would receive approval from heaven:

Then is there mirth in heaven
When earthly things made even
Atone together.

(V.iv.108-10)

The play, then, represents a literalization of what religion offers abstractly. While Duke Frederick is being converted by an old religious man, the playwright is offering his inducement to virtue.

References to the poet's role in civil society appear in the tragedies as well as in the comedies. Hamlet may provide one of the most obvious examples, for it refers explicitly to a play's ability to appeal to the conscience:

I have heard that guilty creatures sitting at a play
Have by the very cunning of the scene
Been struck so to the soul that presently
They have proclaimed their malefactions.

(II.ii.601-04)

O. B. Hardison locates Hamlet's theory in Thomas Heywood's An Apology for Actors. There Heywood defends drama's social utility by reference to its ability to attack "the consciences of the spectators, finding themselves toucht in presenting the vices of others." In particular tragedies can move the audience to divulge "notorious murders, long concealed from the eyes of the world."[2] Hamlet, of course, employs this theory in producing The Mousetrap to discover whether Claudius is guilty of the murder of Hamlet's father. Although The Mousetrap does not induce a confession, it does effect the desired appeal to Claudius' conscience. Claudius attempts to pray, but he knows that one cannot truly repent if one retains what he has gotten through sinning. Without repentance there can be no pardon, and Claudius cannot pray " Though inclination be as sharp as will" (III.iii.39).

Shakespeare generalizes drama's ability to appeal to the audience's conscience through Hamlet's directions to the players, through extended references to the world as a stage, and through the device of the play within the play. Not only is Claudius to see his own crime enacted in the drama, but the audience of any play should see itself reflected there. As Hamlet tells the players, they should hold "the mirror up to nature; to show virtue her own feature, scorn her own image, and the very age and body of the time his form and pressure" (III.ii.23-25). The audience of Shakespeare's play is given ample illustration of how this works with respect to the players of The Murder of Gonzago and Claudius, for Hamlet draws a number of parallels between the actors and the court. He welcomes in particular the actor who plays the king and asks for a recital of a passage on a king's (Priam's) killing and a queen's grief. Hamlet furthers the equation of actors with court by relating the rise in popularity of the child actors to the rise in popularity of Claudius. Then Hamlet summarizes the situation for Polonius by describing the players as the "abstract and brief chronicles of the time" (II.ii.535-36). Later the "bravery" (V.ii.78) of Laertes' grief for Ophelia and of his desire for revenge rivals the sort of overacting which Hamlet asks the players to avoid (III.ii.1-15).

The image of the world as stage and the stage as world is carried out by the device of the play within the play. The play within the play makes the stage a world by involving the spectators in the same dilemmas as the characters. The audience watches Hamlet and Horatio watching Claudius watch a play in order to determine Claudius' guilt or innocence, but this series of watching and being watched may perhaps be moved back one step to make the audience actors beings watched by someone else,[3] possibly Providence. This, of course, would be supported by the appearance of Providence in Act V. When related to the idea of the play within a play, the other instances of spying, watching and acting reinforce the sense of world as play and play as world. Hamlet, for example, becomes an actor when he puts on an "antic disposition" for an audience consisting of the spying Polonius and Claudius. Or Claudius becomes a player when with smiles he hides his guilt from his audience, the court. The operation of the play within the play also gives one a sense both of the limited vision of man and of the unlimited vision of Providence. The various characters must spy or watch to determine what is going on, and yet at different times each character in varying degrees is unaware of the true state of affairs. Recognition of the limitations of human vision and of the infinite vision of Providence is supported in Act V by Hamlet's acceptance of his own inability to foresee events ("we defy augury") and by his placement of events in the hands of Providence. The audience, then, must be aware of the play's characters' difficulty in determining the true nature of affairs and, consequently, of its own difficulty in doing so.

Another tragedy, Lear, provides an interesting point of comparison for The Tempest's treatment of the role of the poet in civil society, for Edgar, although not another Prospero, is like Prospero in combining the functions of politician and philosopher with those of poet. Edgar as the play begins is like Hamlet as well as Prospero. Both Edgar and Hamlet are so open and honest that they do not suspect treachery in another. Edmund tells us that he can deceive Edgar because his "nature is so far from doing harms / That he suspects none" (I.ii.193-94). The result of Edgar's virtue is the same as that attendant upon Prospero's focus on universals at the start of The Tempest. Both fail to recognize evil.

While Prospero establishes his philosophic credentials through the study of the liberal arts and completes his understanding of humanity on the island, Edgar becomes a philosopher by virtue of his experience of humanity in the state of nature. Thus Lear first recognizes Edgar as a philosopher on the heath at the point where Lear finally realizes that he has entirely deprived himself of the political role which has defined him in the past. Goneril and Regan's maltreatment of Lear and reductions in Lear's train on the principle of "necessity" enact what the Fool has called Lear's foolish reduction of himself to "nothing" (I.iv.200). Lear's tearing off of his clothes at III.iv represents his final reduction of himself by ripping off the last vestiges of civilization. Now Lear's task is to find out what he is outside the city. His reaction to Edgar gives two possibilities: Either "unaccommodated man is no more but such a poor, bare, forked animal" (III.iv.109-10), or he is a "philosopher" (III.iv.157, 160, 179, 183). In Aristotelian terms, outside the city man is either a god or a beast. This disjunction is what Lear is left with in the end. He seems content to be imprisoned with Cordelia to look down on the political world of "gilded butterflies" while he and Cordelia play the part of "god's spies" who "take upon's the mystery of things" (V.iii.16-17). And yet on her death he sees only beasts remaining: "Why should a dog, a horse, a rat,

have life, / And thou no breath at all?"
(V.iii.308-09).

The Aristotelian definition of man in the state
of nature is also reflected in <u>The</u> <u>Tempest</u>. Caliban
as man in the state of nature is a deformed and
beastlike creature. Prospero, on the other hand, is
godlike.

Edgar as philosopher, however, never attains the
godlike characteristics of Prospero, and <u>Lear</u> is thus
much less optimistic than <u>The</u> <u>Tempest</u> about the
viability of the philosopher's vision in supporting
virtue. Lear looks to Edgar to explain the fact of
evil: "Is there any cause in nature that make those
hard hearts?" (III.vi.76-77). And yet Edgar can
illustrate for Lear no true justice in nature. Evil
persists and goes unpunished: "False justicer, why
hast thou let her [Goneril] 'scape?" (III.vi.55).
Edgar can argue that "the gods are just" when Edmund
dies, but his words cannot explain the death of
Cordelia. Ultimately one must ask whether there is
any support for virtue rather than following virtue
for its own sake. No one gives a better argument for
virtue than the Fool:

> That sir, which serves and seeks for gain,
> And follows but for form,
> Will pack, when it begins to rain,
> And leave thee in the storm.
> But I will tarry; the Fool will stay,
> And let the wise man fly,
> The knave turns Fool that runs away,
> The Fool no knave, perdy.
> (I.iv.76-84).

Unlike Prospero's philosophy, Edgar's always seems
subject to limits. As soon as he develops an
argument for rising above fortune, the play calls it
into question. Just after he reconciles himself to
being at the bottom of the wheel of fortune where one
need fear sinking no more, Gloucester enters blinded
to show Edgar that he can always be worse off.
Prospero's philosophy, on the other hand, is
effective because, unlike Edgar's, it operates under
the aspect of beneficent fortune.

Edgar and Prospero as politicians both learn to
operate in a world in which they need to recognize
and control evil. Prospero, however, takes on the

political as a compromise with his vision of the eternal. For Lear the fact of evil has destroyed the possibility of the political. For him that "a dog's obeyed in office" (IV.vi.161) suggests the impossibility of the justice for whose sake the political exists. That the judge could be more evil than those he judges destroys the rationale behind judging at all. Edgar recognizes this view as "matter and impertinency mixed." One must establish some standards of human behavior and support for them even if those standards are not always met.

When functioning as poets both Edgar and Prospero recognize the need to represent the gods as supporting virtue. Although not operating as poet as consistently as Prospero does, Edgar does teach Gloucester that the gods care about him by having Gloucester jump off a Dover cliff in his imagination. He also represents the actions of the gods as just even though the events of the play do not represent them in that way. In contrast to Prospero's poetry, however, Edgar's seems like a sterile trick. Because Prospero obtains control over The Tempest's events, his art seems to accord better with actuality, at least as he has created it with the help of fortune.

There is a kind of poetry which escapes the necessities of this world. It is the poetry of "old tales" such as Lear and Cordelia will tell one another in prison. That poetry looks down on politics from above. And there is some question as to whether it can ever be fully integrated with the political. In The Tempest Ariel as the highest form of poetry is always longing to be free.

The history plays also contain significant references to poetry. The Henry plays, for example, raise several issues which bear on the question of poetry's role in civil society. They consider the relationship of poetry to courage, to justice and to truth. Civil society often requires armed defense and thus needs courageous citizens, but 1 Henry IV suggests that poetry is at odds with courage and spirit in their extreme form.

Hotspur, of course, is the embodiment of the man of spirit, "the theme of honor's tongue" (I.i.80) which Henry IV would wish for Hal rather than for Henry Percy. Hotspur is all made up of the roughness and disharmony of soldiery which allows for no attraction to the meters of poetry:

> I had rather be a kitten and cry mew
> Than one of these same meter ballad-mongers.
> I had rather hear a brazen candlestick turned
> Or a dry wheel grate on the axletree,
> And that would set my teeth nothing on edge,
> Nothing so much as mincing poetry.
> 'Tis like the forced gait of a shuffling nag.
> (III.i.126-34)

If the play questions poetry's appeal to the soldier, it also calls into question the value of unmediated spiritedness. Hal is reluctant to give himself up entirely to the pursuit of honor in Hotspur's fashion: "I am not yet of Percy's mind, the Hotspur of the north: he that kills me some six or seven dozen of Scots at a breakfast, washes his hands, and says to his wife, 'Fie upon this quiet life! I want work'" (II.iv.103-06). A warlike nature can lead to gratuitous killing.

Moreover, courage in its pure form may lead to the loss of battles. Hotspur's eagerness for battle leads him to fight imprudently, against Worcester's and Vernon's advice, before all of his troops have arrived and while some are not yet rested (IV.iii). This same eagerness may have led to what the rebels of 2 Henry IV see as Hotspur's mistaken reliance on "aids incertain" in going to battle (I.iii.23-26). In addition, although the Archbiship attributes Glendower's absence to prophecies, Hotspur's angry, mocking treatment may have convinced him to stay away. As Worcester argues, wilfullness can be seen as courage and spirit, but it can also indicate "harsh rage, / Defect of manners, want of government, / Pride, haughtiness, opinion and disdain; / The least of which haunting a nobleman / Loseth men's hearts" (III.i.182-86).

Hal, himself, is courageous, but his position as king demands far more. Political success requires qualities often at odds with courage--calculation and understanding of the body. In 2 Henry IV calculation is symbolized by coldness, the coldness which Falstaff finds in John of Lancaster and which Falstaff says Hal "did naturally inherit from his father" (2 Henry IV, IV.iii.121-22). Henry IV corroborates Hal's coldness in a warning to Thomas that when Hal is angry, "he's flint / As humorous as winter and as sudden / As flows congealed in the spring of day" (IV.iv.33-35). According to Falstaff, this coldness of blood produces cowards, although in 1 Henry IV John is courageous, Shakespeare seems in support of Falstaff elsewhere. In Antony and Cleopatra Mark Antony's courage, when undiminished, compares favorably in battle with Octavius' coldness. Just as with Hal and John, the former drinks heavily, while the latter refuses to drink. To the extent that courage requires irrational overcoming of the fear of death, or, as Falstaff puts it, "inflammation" (2 Henry IV, IV.iii.98), courage is at odds with calculation.

A king must understand the body if he is to rule effectively. Hal knows the call of appetite within himself, although ultimately he must deny it. Hal's tavern companions have a strong appeal for him, and even after he leaves them to overcome Hotspur the desire for "small beer" lingers. Appetite, of course, looms largest in the body of Falstaff. It is no surprise that Falstaff illustrates how attention to the body is at odds with courage in the sense that fighting threatens bodily harm and, even in the absence of harm, offers no reward to the senses:

> Can honor set to a leg? No. Or an arm? No. Or take away the grief of a wound? No. Honor hath no skill in surgery then? No. What is honor? A word. What is in that word honor? What is that honor? Air--a trim reckoning! Who hath it? He that died a Wednesday. Doth he feel it? No. Doth he hear it? No. 'Tis insensible then? Yea to the dead. But will it not live with the living? No. Why? Detraction will not suffer it. Therefore I'll none of it. Honor is a mere scutcheon--and so ends my catechism.
> (1 Henry IV, V. i. 131-42)

Falstaff himself is a coward, but Falstaff teaches the king much that he needs to know. Serving as "father ruffian" to Hal, Falstaff teaches through experience rather than through books. Although one might argue that secretly learning while seeming to lead a low life is just part of Hal's plan,

Canterbury seems to take note of the tavern as the source of Henry's much-admired learning:

> the art and practic part of life
> Must be the mistress to this theoric;
> Which is a wonder how his Grace should
>   glean it,
> Since his addiction was to courses vain,
> His companies unlettered, rude, and shallow,
> His hours filled up with riots, banquets,
>   sports;
> And never noted in him any study,
> Any retirement, any sequestration
> From open haunts and popularity.
>   (Henry V, I.i.51-59)

As many critics have noted, Hal uses his time with Falstaff to make himself familiar with the conditions of his future rule. Following Henry IV, Hal will have to learn to win the hearts of the people. To do this he must learn to speak to the people, and in the tavern, as Hal says, he learns to "drink with any tinker in his own language" (1 Henry IV, II, iv. 17-18). Warwick corroborates this analysis when he describes Hal's companionship with low characters as an attempt to learn a foreign language which must be known (2 Henry IV, IV.iv.67-73).

With Falstaff Hal also learns of the nobles, for the tavern life reflects on the life of the nobles. As many critics have noted, the disorder of tavern life reflects disorder in the kingdom. The highway robbery, for example, parallels both Bolingbroke's taking the crown from Richard and Percy's plot. The imaginary deeds of Falstaff parallel Hotspur's description of the fight of Glendower and Mortimer.

Hal's time with Falstaff also teaches him that he has a body like other men. Unlike Richard II, Henry V will not depend on the idea of divine right to protect himself from harm. Hal has nothing but mockery for Falstaff's story that after the robbery he ran away from Hal and Poins because instinct kept him from attacking the true king.

Another skill which Hal learns from Falstaff is how to play a part, for the two continually play English political figures in order to mock either one another or the condition of the political figure.

207

Falstaff playing the king, for example, pretends to virtue while berating Hal for his dissolute life. This comes uncomfortably close to the nature of Bolingbroke's action on his return to England from banishment. Then, as Henry IV tells Hal, "he stole all courtesy from heaven, / And dressed myself in such humility / That I did pluck allegiance from men's hearts" (III.ii.t0-52). When Falstaff tells Hal that as king he must make thieving seem admirable (I.ii.27-28), his advice seems again to parallel the condition of Henry IV's rule. Although Hal will inherit the crown, he will still need to know both how to display virtue and how to make subjects support a succession based on his father's abrogation of divine right. Hal illustrates his ability at the former in his plan to associate with low companions in order to make his character seem more brilliant by contrast when he gives them up. Hal attempts the latter, of course, by fighting "foreign wars," by gaining the Church's sanction for his actions, and by attributing his victories to God.

Pure spirit, then, is not sufficient for a king or even for a soldier. In addition to learning cold calculation, the king must gain an understanding of the body, of appetite. The association with appetite, however, must not extend too far. Otherwise, Falstaff's claim that the "laws of the kingdom are at my commandment" (2 Henry IV, V.iii.139) might be accurate. In that case thieves and prostitutes would receive offices from Falstaff, and justice would be undermined. In other words, monarchy would become tyranny, for the tyrant is the rule who uses his power to fulfill his appetites, however unjust, at the expense of his citizens. Falstaff, then, seems to threaten more than honor.

Is the threat simply from Falstaff as appetite? Or does it come from poetry as well? The similarity of the names "Shakespeare" and "Falstaff" has been noted often enough. If Falstaff stands for Shakespeare as poet as well as for appetite, then poetry seems to threaten just rule. This recalls Bottom's enthusiasm for acting the tyrant (pp. 41-44 above). Tyranny and poetry are alike in their emancipation of the passions.

Through allowing free rein to fear of death poetry also dissuades citizens from displaying the courage required in war (pp. 41-42 above). Attention to the body leads to the cowardice of Falstaff and his low life companions. Honor is "insensible," as Falstaff puts it. It cannot supply the body. On the contrary, the winning of it may require pain or death.

The argument, then, takes us full circle to Hotspur's dislike of poetry. Its threat to martial virtue is real. Beyond that, poetry as represented by Falstaff supplies the king with valuable lessons, but it also threatens just rule.

Henry V raises the question of justice and poetry in another way. This play asks to what extent the images of poetry reflect what is just. Pistol introduces the question when he refers to Bardolph's arrest for stealing a pax in terms of fortune's wheel. Describing in detail the blindness and mutability of fortune, Fluellon approves of the image: "In good truth, the poet makes a most excellent description of it; Fortune is an excellent moral" (III.vi.37-39). And yet when Pistol explains Bardolph's situation, Fluellen is forced to take a stand suggesting that assuming a de casibus model conflicts with the administration of justice: Although Bardolph is Pistol's friend, in Fluellen's eyes even if "he were my brother, I would desire the Duke to use his good pleasure and put him to execution; for discipline ought to be used" (III.vi.55-57).

If poetry's correlation with principles of justice is questioned, its correlation with truth is also placed under suspicion. Henry V opens casting doubts on the playwright's, actors' and threatre's ability to match the greatness of their subject, but as usual the play also provides suggestions of a possible defense. All of the previously discussed allusive qualities of the word "nothing" (pp. 64-68 above) come to bear as Shakespeare refers to his stage as a "wooden O" which could turn 100,000 into 1,000,000 when properly placed. The play will not present a literal presentation of its subject, and yet the imagination might supply a superior understanding, one involving essential truths.

On the other hand, the play records enough examples of innacurate tales of past exploits to make the audience develop some suspicions about the literal truth of any epic. Pistol lies about his deeds in battle. Falstaff of 1 Henry IV produces

fantastic tales of his battle with thieves and with
Hotspur. Even Henry V describes how the soldier
retelling the story of Crispin's day will "remember
with advantages, / What feats he did that day"
(Henry V, IV.iii.50-51).

The accuracy of epic comparisons also becomes an
issue. Fluellen is the character prone to drawing
epic parallels which are inappropriate. He compares
Pistol's bravery with Mark Antony's (III.vi.13-16)
although he comes to see that Gower's assessment of
Pistol as a "counterfeit rascal" (III.vi.63) is
accurate. Later Fluellen matches Henry V with
Alexander the Great, but the comparison is strained:
Both were born in a town on a river, and the rivers
are alike in that "there is salmons in both"
(IV.vii.32).

Although Shakespeare may raise doubts about the
truth of some poetry, he always seems to have in mind
a higher form of poetry wich correlates with the
highest truths. The unlikely vehicle for this higher
poetry is Falstaff, for that "father ruffian's" death
associates him with the true poet who is also a
philosopher. Falstaff's death is reminiscent of
Socrates' death in the Phaedo (117e-118):

> The man--he was the same one who had
> administered the poison--kept his
> eyes upon Socrates, and after a
> little while examined his feet and
> legs, then pinched his foot hard and
> asked if he felt it. Socrates said
> no. Then he did the same to his
> legs, and moving gradually upward in
> this way let us see that he was
> getting cold and numb. Presently he
> felt him again and said that when it
> reached the heart, Socrates would be
> gone.

Falstaff also dies from the feet up:

> I put my hand into the bed, and felt
> them [his feet], and they were as
> cold as any stone. Then I felt to
> his knees, and so upward, and
> upward, and all was as cold as any
> stone.
>
> (Henry V, II.iii.24-27)

Is Falstaff really the true poet who is also the philosopher, as the above passages imply? Henry V rejects Falstaff, and given Falstaff's threat to justice, the rejection seems appropriate. Does the attention to the political, then, involve a loss--denial of the philosophical? The tetralogy of history plays seems to raise these questions through the humorous, and apparently low, life of Falstaff.

The last plays are all obvious choices in a further consideration of Shakespeare's views of the poet's role. Their common reference to wonder in particular calls forth Renaissance theories. Exploration of Shakespeare's views on poetry's inclusiveness immediately bring to mind The Winter's Tale where Shakespeare is explicit about bringing tragedy and comedy together in a play ultimately comic: As in A Midsummer Night's Dream and The Tempest this play evokes magic and dreams to make the audience ask questions about the reality of the poet's vision. In Sicily where the play is turned to comedy "sleepy drinks" make people forget where actual magnificence is lacking (I.i.12). But such a dream is possible only by awakening "faith" (V.iii.95). And even though belief might "sleep" (V.ii.66), an old tale continues to have "matter to rehearse." Poetry is like magic because it charms the audience into believing that it is life. Shakespeare plays on this idea by having Leontes fear that the living Hermione is but a production of art: "If this be magic, let it be an art / Lawful as eating" (V.iii.110-11). In the play Hermione is actually alive and pretending to be a statue sculpted by a man who makes lifelike statues, and yet Hermione is actually an art object created by Shakespeare.

Shakespeare again examines the limits of art. It cannot alter the world merely by lying. The clown might declare that Autolycus is an honest man, but such a declaration cannot transform Autolycus. On the other hand, art can improve upon nature by recognizing the best elements of nature and capitalizing on them: "This is an art / Which does mend Nature, change it rather; but / The art itself is nature" (IV.iv.95-97). It does so in humans by presenting them with objects of wonder which can serve as models and offer evidence of the gods' beneficence. In The Winter's Tale such causes of wonder are Perdita and Florizel, the discovery that

Perdita is Leontes' daughter, and the statue of Hermione.

Much remains to be done with these and other plays. Certain constant elements from one play to the next tend to reinforce some general ideas about Shakespeare's views of the role of the poet. In *As You Like It* and *Love's Labor Lost*, for example, Shakespeare criticizes satire in common terms which suggest that Shakespeare believed that there were limits to the sort of truth which poetry ought to admit. There is "much matter" in both Berowne and Jaques, but the truths which they understand are not salutary for their audiences. Neither can relate satire to his own soul, a fault of the satirist and perhaps of his audience in general. Given man's desire to live in this world, emphasis on its foibles can only cause pain. Furthermore, such an emphasis makes it difficult to recognize goodness where it exists.

On the other hand, a number of plays suggest that poetry which represents a simple golden world is insufficient. Armado's vision in *Love's Labor's Lost*, Silvius's and Orlando's in *As You Like It*, or Gonzalo's in *The Tempest* are fragile because they are over-idealized. Ultimately they must be accounted lies. *The Winter's Tale* makes the argument most explicit. As the clown's remarks on Autolycus illustrate, one cannot change the world by lying.

In play after play the best poetry and the truest vision arises out of an understanding of both the eternal and the temporal. The difficulty of limiting the understanding to one or the other is depicted repeatedly. The "little academe" of *Love's Labor's Lost*, for example, shows the problem with most people's attempt to philosophize and the foolishness of neglect of one's own body and of the temporal in general. Even those capable of philosophy such as Prospero cannot function well until they understand the elements in human nature which tie humans to the earthly. Those who limit their vision only to the lowest in humanity, however, destroy the possibility of virtue altogether. *The Tempest*'s Antonio and Sebastian or *As You Like It*'s Touchstone can see no virtue in the world and exhibit none themselves. In the former the attitude leads to attempting the worst of crimes, while in the latter it leads to infidelity. The truest vision manages to combine a

picture of the ideal with a sense of realism.
Rosalind is one of Shakespeare's most appealing
heroines because she can love intensely while
remaining realistic. Prospero's philosophizing in
Milan must be completed by his coming to grips with
the body and with spiritedness. As A Midsummer
Night's Dream suggests, looking from heaven to earth
and from earth to heaven makes the truest poetry.

A further constant quality of the highest poetry
as Shakespeare represents it is the combining of both
tragedy and comedy. In addition to appearing in A
Midsummer Night's Dream and The Tempest this theme
recurs frequently in the last plays. It also arises
elsewhere, such as in As You Like It's reminder that
it is more than a typical comedy in that its heroes
and heroines are not married in the end.

In producing poetry or referring to it,
Shakespeare repeatedly invokes Renaissance theories
of wonder and of dream. The Harvard Concordance
includes references to "wonder" or "wonders" in all
of the plays, in all of the narrative poems, and in
several of the sonnets. Every play except for 1
Henry VI contains a form of the word "dream".

Repeated and playful allusions to "dream" suggest
that Shakespeare has in mind Renaissance theory
recognizing the dual possibilities in the word:
Poems which are dreams could be distortions of
reality or untruths. Or they could be embodiments of
higher truths. The poet could be capable of
illustrating these higher truths either because he is
inspired or because he has some knowledge. Both
possibilities are recognized in Shakespeare's plays.
The former is alluded to in Theseus' discussions of
poetry and in Ariel's song "Where the bee sucks."
The latter is alluded to in Hippolyta's mention of
verisimilitude, in the plays which associate the poet
with the philosopher, and in the references to
wonder. These references to wonder recall Aristotle
and Renaissance derivations on wonder in poetry as a
source of learning and on that learning as involving
the gods.

In addition to containing certain recurring
attitudes about poetry, the plays repeatedly raise
certain issues concerning poetry. Poetry's ability
to support morality appears in many different forms:
The dichotomy between poetry and courage crops up in

1 _Henry_ _IV_. The question of how one should defend virtue in the face of adverse fortune is an issue in _As_ _You_ _Like_ _It_ and in _Lear_. A statement of poetry's ability to appeal to the conscience is made literal in _Hamlet_. The viability of a poetic form such as the _de_ _casibus_ in defining justice is questioned in _Henry_ _V_. The possibility that poetry can lead to tyranny is suggested in _A_ _Midsummer_ _Night's_ _Dream_ and in the Henry IV and Henry V plays. The chance that poetry could lead to other sorts of immorality is examined through the Pyramus and Thisbe play of _A_ _Midsummer_ _Night's_ _Dream_. The relative value of poet and politician in supporting morality is explored in _A_ _Midsummer_ _Night's_ _Dream_, in _As_ _You_ _Like_ _It_, in _Lear_, and in the _Richard_ _II_ to _Henry_ _V_ tetralogy.

Another recurrent issue is the accuracy of poetry and the related consideration of the poet as philosopher. The poet as liar appears in preceding discussions of _A_ _Midsummer_ _Night's_ _Dream_, of _Henry_ _V_, and of _The_ _Winter's_ _Tale_. The possibility of having a poet-philosopher arises in _The_ _Tempest_, in _Lear_, and in _Henry_ _V_.

Still another question of continued concern to Shakespeare is what sets the poet's vision apart from the politician's. In a number of plays by turning to a place geographically separate from the city, such as the wood in _A_ _Midsummer_ _Night's_ _Dream_ or the forest of Arden in _As_ _You_ _Like_ _It_, Shakespeare suggests that the poet observes some areas not available to the politician. Lear can examine the state of nature only on the heath after he has removed all vestiges of rule and of civilization. _The_ _Tempest_ addresses the issue of the state of nature more directly through Gonzalo's imaginings of a land with no government and through a study of Caliban.

Whether the politician's or the poet's vision is superior is naturally of concern to Shakespeare. No judgment of Shakespeare is single-minded. He admits the danger of poetry to civil society--in terms of possible distortions of truth and possible support of immorality. But he also sees deficiencies in the politician's view--for example, Theseus' misunderstanding of the power of desire or Edgar's inability to extend justice to include Cordelia's death. Shakespeare also intimates at times that poetry can reach higher than politics--in Lear's "old tales" or in Prospero's and Ariel's longing to be free.

Changes in Shakespeare's attitude are more difficult to explain than elements which persist. The Tempest, for example, contains a greater sense of human evil coupled with a greater sense of poetry's ability to transform than A Midsummer Night's Dream. At this stage I can only speculate upon the reasons for this. It seems to me that Shakespeare increasingly recognized the inadequacies of the temporal world but never gave up poetry's attempt to direct it toward something better. Most of the tragedies concern heroes whose virtues are inappropriate to the world in which they live. In every case the play contains a vision of a superior world lost or of a world ultimately set in order. Brutus, Coriolanus, and Antony, to a lesser degree, embody republican virtues in a world where republicanism is no longer possible. Hector represents the heroic in a Greek world ruled by craft. Hamlet cannot avoid the taint of an evil world, but his actions restore order. Romeo and Juliet bring the warring factions of a city together with a love which transcends the family. Even Lear leaves Edgar to rule with a sense of justice and of the gods' beneficence, although Cordelia's death might suggest that she is too pure for the world.

Another alteration seems to occur in Shakespeare's attitude toward philosophy. Love's Labor's Lost forcefully raises doubts about the study of philosophy as a goal for young men and their ruler, but The Tempest contains an ideal poet-philosopher-king. The explanation for this may lie in the difference between the philosophy of Prospero on the island and that of Love's Labor's Lost. In Love's Labor's Lost philosophy is speculation upon eternal truths as opposed to actual life. Prospero's philosophy in Milan is similar. It focuses on the liberal arts to the neglect of human nature. Prospero does not understand human ambition and thus loses control over his government. Prospero of the island, on the other hand, understands human limitations. He knows that Caliban is part of him and of humans in general, and he can recognize the ambition of Sebastian and Antonio. Prospero seems to have gained the virtues of the poet's vision in A Midsummer Night's Dream. He can look "from earth to heaven, from heaven to earth."

The above survey suggests the pervasiveness of Shakespeare's concern with the poet's role in civil society. Although modern neglect of such a broad Shakespearian concern is surprising, certain modern tendencies serve to explain that neglect. The main critical approaches to the plays discussed have been based on the assumption that literature is distinct from politics, ethics, and philosophy. Even those critics interested in Renaissance ideas have been influenced by the view that literature is *sui generis*. Moreover, that recent critical theory which does not see literature as different from other forms of discourse has been based on a determinism which leads away from the political or which represents a view of the political alien to Shakespeare. In addition, the modern tendency to reject virtue and the political as sources of happiness reinforces the literary-critical predisposition to neglect moral and political questions in the plays.

As Chapter I argues, the Renaissance did find the poet's ability to produce moral humans critical in any assessment of poetry in general. Furthermore, as the chapters on *A Midsummer Night's Dream* and *The Tempest* argue, Shakespeare was concerned with both poetry's danger to civil society and its ability to make a salutary contribution. Shakespeare's views of the role of the poet are important to us not simply because they are Shakespeare's but also because they might be correct.

Notes

[1]T. W. Baldwin, *Shakespeare's Five-Act Structure* (Urbana, 1947), pp. 579-80.

[2]O. B. Hardison, "Three Types of Renaissance Catharsis," *Renaissance Drama*, n. s. 2 (1969), 4.

[3]Maynard Mack makes a similar point in "The World of Hamlet," *Hamlet*, ed. Edward Hubler (New York, 1963), p. 246. Also see Maynard Mack, "Engagement and Detachment in Shakespeare's Plays," *Essays on Shakespeare and Elizabethan Drama* (Columbia, Missouri, 1962), p. 281.

APPENDIX A

THE RENAISSANCE VIEW OF THE DAEMON

In the Renaissance daemons were viewed by most as evil spirits alone, but the NeoPlatonists revived the ancient view that daemons could be beneficent.[1] In the Middle Ages the view had gained ground that all daemons are bad. Associating daemons with fallen angels, the church fathers in general saw the daemon as evil. Augustine, for example, says that wherever _daemon_ appears in the Bible "it always refers to malignant spirits,"[2] and Aquinas sees demons as equivalent to devils.[3] The extent to which the word _daemon_ came to be associated with _devil_ is illustrated in the _Anatomy of Melancholy_ where Burton points out that "Separate essences and intelligences are the same which Christians call Angels, and Platonists Devils, for they name all Spirits daimons, be they good or bad Angels, as Julius Pollux observes."[4] The orthodox opinion agrees that middle spirits exist, but good spirits of this sort are called _angels_ and have some functions similar to Socrates' daemon, such as guarding man from harm and conveying messages from God. Burton sees the difference as partly a matter of terminology, but others such as Jean Bodin insist that the Sorbonne was correct in condemning as heretics those who say that there are good daemons.[5] Certain Renaissance NeoPlatonists, however, deny that all daemons are evil. Cornelius Agrippa defines daemons as beneficent in his _Occulta Philosophia_: "By daemons I do not mean here those beings we call devils, but I understand thereby in the true meaning of the word spirits as it were wise, understanding, and sage."[6]

A controversy raged in the Renaissance over man's ability to control unbodied spirits. The orthodox view is that a man can at will deal with spirits, but only with evil ones through alliance with the devil. James I, for example, argues that none can use "the circle and arts of _Magie_ without committing an horrible defection from God."[7] Occult philosophers admit that spirits can be controlled for evil purposes, but they defend themselves by making a distinction between white magic or theurgy and black magic or goety. The theurgist is the magician described by Agrippa who, through a virtuous and exalted life, controls good spirits for appropriate ends. The goetist, on the other hand, is the magician who, attending to the flesh rather than the soul, attracts evil spirits by similitude with them. His power is weak since he can deal only with devils and lower orders of spirits. This distinction is not limited to the occult philosophers. Shakespeare, himself, makes it in As You Like It: "I have since I was three years old, conversed with a magician, most profound in his art and yet not damnable" (V.ii.60-62).

Notes

[1]Lewis, p. 118.

[2]St. Augustine, The City of God, pp. 365-66 (Book IX, Chapter 19).

[3]All references in the text to Saint Thomas Aquinas are to Summa Theologiae, 60 vols. (New York and London, 1964-1976), 1a.64, 114.

[4]Burton, p. 158.

[5]Jean Bodin, La Demonomanie (Paris, 1958), I.i.50-51; Heywood, p. 447.

[6]Cornelius Agrippa, De occulta philosophia libri III (Paris, 1567), III.xvi. West points out that the 1651 English translation has angels for the Latin daemons.

[7]James I, Demonologie (London, 1597), I.v.15--reprinted by Bodley Head Quartos, ed. G. B. Harrison (London, 1924). See also Burton, p. 173; Heywood, pp. 469, 471.

DAEMONIC CHARACTERISTICS OF ARIEL

The daemon's substance allows him to become invisible, protects him from harm, and permits motion unbounded by time and space. Because the daemon is formed of "the most pure serene element of air," it is "not visible on every occasion to the human eye."[1] This accords with Ariel's invisible presence as he sings to Ferdinand (I.ii.375-405), when he puts the court party to sleep (II.i.189-202), when he warns Gonzalo of the conspiracy (II.i.301), as he causes trouble among the conspirators by seeming to be Trinculo refuting Caliban (III.ii.44f.), and as he retains his "shape invisible" to catch Caliban, Stephano, and Trinculo (IV.i.185). The daemon's invisibility allows him to trick people, as Ariel does Stephano and Caliban, by counterfeiting voices.[2] As an immortal being made of air, the daemon is not subject to harm. Some Renaissance sources on daemons such as Michael Psellus argue that daemons can be hurt, but most agree with Scaliger and Burton that "if their bodies be cut, with admirable celerity they come together again."[3] As Ariel says to the court party,

> The elements
> Of whom your swords are tempered, may as well
> Wound the loud winds, or with bemocked-at stabs
> Kill the still-closing waters, as diminish
> One dowle that's in my plume. My fellow ministers
> Are like invulnerable.
>
> (III.iii.61-66)

The daemon's substance also allows him to move unbounded by the restrictions on time and place which obtain to the corporeal world. He can be one place at one instant and another in the next. A daemon's "movement is discontinuous, it may happen that he passes from one point to another without crossing a place between."[4] Again the characteristics of the daemon are those of Ariel. He arrives instantly whenever Prospero calls, and when sent to fetch the master and the boatswain of the ship, Ariel claims, "I drink the air before me, and return / Or ere your pulse twice beat" (V.i.102-03).

Ariel's representation of himself and his fellow spirits as "ministers of Fate" (III.iii.61) recalls the ancient characterization of daemons as distributors of destiny. Such daemons could be either beneficent or malignant. In Plato the daemon appears as a beneficent spirit who favors the good and produces peace, mercy, justice, harmony and happiness among men (Statesman 271d-274b, Epinomis 985a-986d, Cratylus 398a-b, Laws 713d). He is the god who is "the master of rational men" (Laws 713a). Later the daemon is again the more general arm of destiny who conducts all natural phenomena in accordance with the will of the gods.[5] Ariel's principal role in the banquet scene concerns the execution of justice and the ministration of mercy. He reminds Alonso, Sebastian and Antonio of their wrongs to Prospero and Miranda:

> But remember
> (For that's my business to you) that you three
> From Milan did supplant good Prospero;
> Exposed unto the sea, which hath requit it,
> Him and his innocent child; for which foul deed
> The Pow'rs, delaying, not forgetting, have
> Incensed the seas and shores, yea, all the creatures,
> Against your peace.

> (III.iii.68-75)

Corresponding to the daemon's control over fate is his clairvoyance. The popular Symposium passage on the daemon (pp. 77-78 above) includes divination as a power of the daemon, and later Christian NeoPlatonists accept the notion of a daemonic clairvoyance somewhat more limited than God's. According to Aquinas, who sees the daemon as a fallen angel, daemons maintain the knowledge which comes through nature, because such knowledge "is a direct consequence of their angelic nature which is essentially intellectual" (1a.64.1). Since angelic natures administer things on earth, the "demons know what happens among men eternally. . . " (1a.114.2). Ariel has the ability to know and control simultaneously what happens in more than one place. He reports, for example, that he has seen the King's ship safely to harbor and has put its crew to sleep, noting that in the meantime the remainder of the fleet which he had dispersed had met again and, supposing the King's ship wrecked, had turned towards Naples (I.ii.227-37). Ariel appears with the court party, with Prospero, and with Ferdinand following the wreck, and he keeps track simultaneously of the

224

activities of the court party, of Prospero, and of Caliban, Trinculo and Stephano. It should be noted that since Prospero directs Ariel and since Prospero can call forth Ariel "with a thought" (IV.163) at times Ariel's clairvoyance could originate with Prospero as it does at II.i.299: "My master through his art foresees the danger . . . ." But the above-mentioned report of Alonso's ship and fleet is made in response to Prospero's request for fuller knowledge.

Perhaps the daemon's aerial nature and his association with divination led to an emphasis on his ability to produce storms and thunder. According to Apuleius, daemons can administer things of nature such as "launching thunders, or causing lightning to flash in the clouds." Randall Hutchins writes of daemons that they "often disturb the air, stir up tempests and thunder," and Robert Burton mentions that they "cause many tempests, thunder, and lightning." Thomas Heywood refers to "spirits of th'Aire" who cause "thunders and Tempestuous showers."[6] Again the characterization of the daemon fits Ariel.

Ariel's performance of the banquet scene and his cure for Caliban, Stephano and Trinculo demonstrate the powers of good and bad angels to change a person's imagination and move his senses. Aquinas argues that angels, including fallen ones, can produce "local changes in our animal spirits and humours" to induce "imaginary appearances" in us. The disturbance of the "spirits and humours may be so great that hallucinations of this sort may occur even in those of us who are awake, as, for example, in the insane and the like" (1a.11.3). Angels can change the senses by altering the bodily spirits and humours or by presenting "objects to the senses externally-- either natural objects or something quite new as when an angel takes on a bodily form . . . " (1a.111.4). Ariel exhibits this last power by taking on the body of a harpy and by appearing with his fellow daemons as hounds to those who conspire against Prospero. Ariel presents objects to the senses externally by producing the feast and its disappearance for Alonso, Sebastian and Antonio. Sebastian and Antonio recognize that the shapes they have seen exhibit the powers of angels, and they assume that Ariel and his cohorts are fallen angels:

```
Sebastian.                    But one friend at a time,
            I'll fight their legions o'er.
Antonio.                      I'll be thy second.
                                  (III.iii.103-04)
```

The final daemonic power exhibited by Ariel is
his control over sleep and love. Apuleius attributes
these powers to his exalted species of daemon.[7]
Ariel exercises his control over sleep by causing it
in the sailors of the King's ship (I.ii.230-32) and
in certain members of the court party upon their
arrival on shore (II.i.189-200). Ariel's power to
induce love is illustrated by Prospero's attribution
to Ariel of the love of Miranda and Ferdinand
(I.ii.420-21, 443, 493-94).

[1] Apuleius, p. 360.

[2] Burton, p. 170.

[3] Burton, p. 159.

[4] Aquinas, 1a.53.2; Burton, p. 159; Heywood, p. 261.

[5] Apuleius, p. 357; Iamblichus, p. 155.

[6] Apuleius, p. 357; Randall Hutchins, *Of Specters* (ca. 1593), trans. Virgil B. Heltzel and Clyde Murely, *HLQ*, 11 (1947–48), 421; Burton, p. 166; Heywood, p. 505.

[7] Apuleius, p. 364.

List of Works Cited

Renaissance Poetic Theory and Intellectual Thought
(Including Classical and Medieval Sources)

Agrippa, Cornelius. De occulta philosophia libri tres. Coloniae, 1533. As translated in Charles G. Nauert. Agrippa and the Crisis of Renaissance Thought. Illinois Studies in the Social Sciences. Urbana: University of Illinois Press, 1965, p. 279.

----------. De occulta philosophia libri III. Paris, 1567.

----------. Three Books of Occult Philosophy . . . translated out of the Latin into the English Tongue by J. F. [riske]. London, 1651.

Alvarez, Leo Paul S. de, trans. The Prince. By Niccolo Machiavelli. Irving, Texas: University of Dallas Press, 1980.

Apuleius. The God of Socrates. In The Works of Apuleius. Trans. Hudson Gurney. London: George Ball and Sons, 1889.

Aristotle. Aristotle on the Art of Poetry. Trans. Ingram Bywater. Oxford: Oxford University Press, 1909. Rpt. in Rhetoric and Poetics. New York: Random House, 1954.

----------. Aristotles politiques, or discourses of government. Trans. out of Greek into French by Loys le Roy. Trans. out of French by [I. D.?] London: Adam Islip, 1598.

----------. Metaphysica. Trans. W. D. Ross. Vol. VIII of The Works of Aristotle. Ed. J. A. Smith and W. D. Ross. Oxford: Oxford University Press, 1908.

----------. Rhetorica. Trans. W. Rhys Roberts. In Rhetorica, Rhetorica ad Alexandrum, Poetica. Vol. XI of The Works of Aristotle. Ed. J. A. Smith and W. D. Ross. Oxford: Oxford University Press, 1924. Rpt. in Rhetoric and Poetics. New York: Random House, 1954.

Bacon Francis. The Advancement of Learning. In
Selected Writings of Francis Bacon. Ed. Hugh G.
Dick. New York: Modern Library, 1955.

Bible. Coverdale Bible.

Bible. 1557 Geneva New Testament.

Bible. Tyndale Bible.

Bodin, Jean. La Demonomanie. Paris, 1598.

----------. The six bookes of a commonweale (1606).
Ed. Kenneth Douglas McRae. Cambridge,
Massachusetts: Harvard University Press, 1962.

Boethius. The Consolation of Philosophy. Trans.
Richard Green. Indianapolis: Bobbs-Merrill,
1962.

Burton, Robert. An Anatomy of Melancholy. Ed. Floyd
Dell and Paul Jordan-Smith. New York: Tudor
Publishing Company, 1938.

Campbell, Lily Bess. Shakespeare's Histories: Mirrors
of Elizabethan Policy. San Marino, California:
Huntington Library, 1958.

Castiglione, Baldassare. The Book of the Courtier.
Trans. Thomas Hoby (1561). London: J. M. Dent;
New York: E. P. Dutton, 1928.

Cicero. Classification of Oratory. Ed. Harris
Rackham. Cambridge: Harvard University Press;
London: W. Heinemann, 1942.

Cunningham, J. V. Woe or Wonder. Denver: University
of Denver Press, 1951.

Davies, Sir John. Nosce Teipsum. In An English
Garner. Ed. Edward Arber. Vol. V. Birmingham:
E. Arber, 1877-1896.

Elyot, Sir Thomas. The Boke Named the Governour. Ed.
H. H. S. Croft. 2 vols. London: C. Kegan Paul,
1880.

Ficino, Marsilio. *Marsilio Ficino's Commentary on Plato's Symposium*. Trans. Sears Reynolds Jayne. University of Missouri Studies, 19. Columbia: University of Missouri Press, 1944.

Fraser, Russell. *The War Against Poetry*. Princeton: Princeton University Press, 1970.

Gentillet, Innocent. *A discourse upon the meanes of wel governing against N. Macchiavell*. Trans. S. Patericke. London: Adam Islip, 1602.

Gerber, A. *Niccolò Machiavelli, Die Handschriften, Ausgaben und Übersetzurgen Seiner Werke*. Gotha, 1913. As cited in Felix Raab, *The English Face of Machiavelli*. London: Routledge and Kegan Paul; Toronto: University of Toronto Press, 1964.

Gilbert, Alan H. *Machiavelli's "Prince" and Its Forerunners: "The Prince" as a Typical Book "de Regimine Principium."* New York: Barnes and Noble, 1938, rep. 1968.

Gosson, Stephen. *The School of Abuse* (1579). In *Shakespeare Society Publications*. Vol. XV. Nendelin, Liechtenstein: Kraus Reprint Ltd., 1966.

Greenlaw, Edwin A. "The Influence of Machiavelli on Spenser." *MP*, 7 (1909-10), 187-202.

Greville, Sir Fulke. *A Treatise of Humane Learning*. In *Poems and Dramas of Fulke Greville*. Ed. Geoffrey Bullough. Vol. I. New York: Oxford University Press, 1945.

Guarini, Giambattista. *The Compendium of Tragicomic Poetry* (1599). Trans. Alan H. Gilbert. In *Literary Criticism: Plato to Dryden*. Ed. Alan Gilbert. Detroit: Wayne State University Press, 1962, pp. 505-33.

Hanke, Lewis. *Aristotle and the American Indians*. Bloomington and London: Indiana University Press, 1955.

Hardison, O. B. "Three Types of Renaissance Catharsis," *Renaissance Drama*, n. s. 2. (1969), 3-22.

Harvey, Gabriel. Letter-Book of Gabriel Harvey (1573-1580). Ed. Edward John Long Scott. London and New York: Johnson Reprint Corporation, 1965.

Herrick, Marvin T. "Some Neglected Sources of 'Admiratio.'" MLN, 62 (1947), 222-26.

Heywood, Thomas. The Hierarchie of the blessed Angels. London, 1935. Facsimile edition 530 of The English Experience. Amsterdam: Theatrum Orbis Terrarun; New York: Da Capo Press, 1973.

Hutchins, Randall. Of Spectres (ca. 1593). Trans. Virgil B. Heltzel and Clyde Murely. HLQ, 11 (1947-48), 407-29.

Iamblichus. The Mysteries of the Egyptians, Chaldeans, and Assyrians. Trans. Thomas Taylor. London, 1821.

James I. Demonologie. London, 1597; rpt. and ed. G. B. Harrison. London: Bodley Head Quartos, 1924.

Lewis, C. S. The Discarded Image. Cambridge: Cambridge University Press, 1971.

Machiavelli, Niccolo. Machiavelli's Prince: An Elizabethan Translation. Ed. Hardin Craig. Chapel Hill: University of North Carolina Press, 1944.

Macrobius. Commentary on the Dream of Scipio. Trans. William Harris Stahl. New York: Columbia University Press, 1952.

Mansfield, Harvey. Machiavelli's New Modes and Orders. Ithaca and London: Cornell University Press, 1979.

Mazzoni, Jacopo. "On the Defense of the Comedy." In Literary Criticism: Plato to Dryden. Ed. Alan H. Gilbert. Detroit: Wayne State University Press, 1962, pp. 359-403.

Meyer, Edward. Machiavelli and the Elizabethan Drama. New York: Burt Franklin, 1964.

Minturno, Antonio.   L'Arte Poetica.   In Literary
     Criticism: Plato to Dryden.   Ed. Allen H.
     Gilbert.   Detroit: Wayne State University Press,
     1962, pp. 275-303.

----------.   L'arte poetica.   Napoli, 1725, p. A₃V.
     As quoted in Baxter Hathaway.   The Age of
     Criticism: The Late Renaissance in Italy.
     Ithaca, New York: Cornell University Press,
     1962, p. 435.

Montaigne, Michel de.   The Essayes of Montaigne.
     Trans. John Florio. New York: Modern Library,
     1933.

Orsini, Napoleone.   "Elizabethan Manuscript Trans-
     lations of Machiavelli's Prince." Journal of the
     Warburg Institute, 1 (1937), 166-69.

----------.   Studi sul Rinascimiento Italiano in
     Inghilterra. Florence: G. C. Sansoni, 1937.

Northbrooke, John.   A Treatise Against Dicing, Danc-
     ing, Plays, and Interludes (1577).   In
     Shakespeare Society Publications.   Vol. XV.
     Nendelin, Liechtenstein: Kraus Reprint Ltd.,
     1966.

Pettet, E. C.   "Shakespeare's Conception of Poetry."
     Essays and Studies, n. s. 3 (1950), 29-46.

Plato.   Ion.   In Phaedrus, Ion, Gorgias, and
     Symposium.   Trans. Lane Cooper.   Ithaca, New
     York: Cornell University Press, 1955.   Rpt. in
     The Collected Dialogues of Plato, Ed. Edith
     Hamilton and Huntington Cairns.   Bollingen
     Series, 71. New York: Random House, 1961, pp.
     215-28.

----------.   Phaedo.   Trans. Hugh Tredennick.   In The
     Collected Dialogues of Plato.   Ed. Edith Hamilton
     and Huntington Cairns.   Princeton: Princeton
     University Press, 1961, pp. 40-98.

----------.   Phaedrus.   Trans. W. C. Helmbold and
     W. G. Rabinowitz. Indianapolis: Bobbs-Merrill,
     1975.

----------. _Plato's Symposium, or the Drinking Party_. Trans. Michael Joyce. New York: E. P. Dutton; London: J. M. Dent, 1935. Rpt. in _The Collected Dialogues of Plato_. Ed. Edith Hamilton and Huntington Cairns. Bollingen Series, 71. New York: Random House, 1961, pp. 526-74.

----------. _The Republic of Plato_. Trans. Allan Bloom. New York: Basic Books, 1968.

----------. _Timaeus_. Trans. Benjamin Jowett. In _Plato: The Collected Dialogues_. Ed. Edith Hamilton and Huntington Cairns. Princeton: Princeton University Press, 1961, pp. 1151-1211.

Rainolds, John. _Oratio in laudem artis poeticae_ (1572). Ed. William Ringer. Trans. W. Allen. Princeton: Princeton University Press, 1940.

Ribner, Irving. "Machiavelli and Sidney's _Discourse to the Queenes Majesty_." _Italica_, 26 (1949), 177-87.

----------. "Machiavelli and Sidney: The _Arcadia_ of 1590." _SP_, 46 (1950), 152-72.

----------. "Sidney's 'Arcadia' and the Machiavelli Legend." _Italica_, 27 (1950), 225-35.

Rossky, William. "Imagination in the English Renaissance: Psychology and Poetic." _Studies in the Renaissance_, 5 (1958), 49-73.

Saint Augustine. _The City of God_. Trans. Henry Bettensen. Baltimore and Middlesex: Penguin Books, 1972.

Saint Albert the Great. _Opera Omnia_. Ed. Augustus Borgnet. Vol. VI. Paris, 1890.

Saint Thomas Aquinas. _Summa Theologiae_. 60 vols. New York: McGraw-Hill; London: Eyne and Spottiswoode, 1964-1976.

Sandys, George. _Ovids Metamorphosis Englished, Mythologized and Represented in Figures_ (London, 1632); rpt. and ed. Karl K. Hulley and Stanley T. Vandersall. Lincoln: University of Nebraska Press, 1970.

Seznec, Jean. <u>The</u> <u>Survival</u> <u>of</u> <u>the</u> <u>Pagan</u> <u>Gods</u>. New York: Bollingen Foundation, 1953.

Sidney, Sir Philip. <u>An</u> <u>Apology</u> <u>for</u> <u>Poetry</u>. Ed. Geoffrey Shepherd. New York: Barnes and Noble; Manchester: Manchester University Press, 1973.

Smith, G. Gregory. <u>Elizabethan</u> <u>Critical</u> <u>Essays</u>. 2 vols. London: Oxford University Press, 1937.

Spenser, Edward. <u>An</u> <u>Hymne</u> <u>of</u> <u>Heavenly</u> <u>Beauty</u>.

Strauss, Leo. <u>Thoughts</u> <u>on</u> <u>Machiavelli</u>. Seattle and London: University of Washington Press, 1969.

Tasso, Torquato. <u>Discources</u> <u>on</u> <u>the</u> <u>Heroic</u> <u>Poem</u>. In <u>Literary</u> <u>Criticism</u>: <u>Plato</u> <u>to</u> <u>Dryden</u>. Ed. Alan H. Gilbert. Detroit: Wayne State University Press, 1962, pp. 466-503.

Vives, Juan Luis. <u>Vives</u> <u>on</u> <u>Education</u>. Trans. Foster Watson. Cambridge: Cambridge University Press, 1931.

Weinberg, Bernard. <u>A</u> <u>History</u> <u>of</u> <u>Literary</u> <u>Criticism</u> <u>in</u> <u>the</u> <u>Italian</u> <u>Renaissance</u>. 2 vols. Chicago: University of Chicago Press, 1961.

West, Robert Hunter. <u>The</u> <u>Invisible</u> <u>World</u>. Athens: University of Georgia Press, 1939.

Whitaker, Virgil K. <u>Shakespeare's</u> <u>Use</u> <u>of</u> <u>Learning</u>. San Marino, California: Huntington Library, 1953.

Willey, Basil. <u>The</u> <u>Seventeenth</u> <u>Century</u> <u>Background</u>. Garden City, New York: Doubleday, 1953.

Wills, Richard. <u>De</u> <u>Re</u> <u>Poetica</u>. Ed. A. D. S. Fowler. Oxford: Luttrell Society Reprints, 1958.

Wilson, J. Dover. "The Puritan Attack Upon the Stage." <u>The</u> <u>Drama</u> <u>to</u> <u>1642</u>. Vol. VI of <u>The</u> <u>Cambridge</u> <u>History</u> <u>of</u> <u>English</u> <u>Drama</u>. New York: Macmillan; Cambridge: Cambridge University Press, 1933, pp. 421-61.

Post-Renaissance Poetic Theory and
Intellectual Thought

Barthes, Roland. <u>Mythologies</u>, Trans. Annette Lavers.
New York: Hill and Wang, 1972.

----------. <u>On</u> <u>Racine</u>, Trans. Richard Howard. New
York: Hill and Wang, 1964.

Bate, Walter Jackson. <u>From</u> <u>Classic</u> <u>to</u> <u>Romantic</u>. New
York: Harper, 1946.

Charlton, H. B. <u>Shakespearian</u> <u>Comedy</u>. New York:
Macmillan, 1940.

Coghill, Nevill. "The Basis of Shakespearian Comedy."
<u>Essays</u> <u>and</u> <u>Studies</u>, n. s. 3 (1950), 2-28.

Coleridge, Samuel Taylor. <u>Shakespearean</u> <u>Criticism</u>.
Ed. T. M. Raysor. New York: E. P. Dutton;
London: J. M. Dent and Sons, 1960. Rpt. in
<u>English</u> <u>Romantic</u> <u>Writers</u>. Ed. David Perkins.
New York: Harcourt, Brace and World, 1967, pp.
496-502.

Crane, Milton.   "Shakespeare's Comedies and the
Critics." <u>SQ</u>, 15 (1964), 67-73.

Derrida, Jacques.   "Structure, Sign and Play in the
Discourse of the Human Sciences." In <u>Writing</u> <u>and</u>
<u>Difference</u>.   Trans.   Alan   Bass,   Chicago:
University of Chicago Press, 1978, pp. 278-93.

Donato, Eugenio. "On Structuralism and Literature."
<u>MLN</u>, 82 (1967), 549-74.

Foucault, Michel.   "Nietzsche, Genealogy, History."
In <u>Language</u>, <u>Counter-Memory</u>, <u>Practice</u>: <u>Selected</u>
<u>Essays</u> <u>and</u> <u>Interviews</u>. Trans. Donald F. Bouchard
and Sherry Simon. Ithaca: Cornell University
Press, 1977.

----------. <u>La</u> <u>Volonté</u> <u>de</u> <u>savoir</u>, Paris: Gallimard,
1976.

Gordon, George. <u>Shakespearian</u> <u>Comedy</u>.   London:
Oxford University Press, 1944.

Harari, Josué V. "Critical Factions / Critical Fictions." In Textual Strategies: Perspectives in Post-Structuralist Criticism. Ed. Josué V. Harari. Ithaca: Cornell University Press, 1979, pp. 17-60.

Hirsch, E. D., Jr. Aims of Interpretation. Chicago and London: University of Chicago Press, 1976.

----------. Validity in Interpretation. New Haven and London: Yale University Press, 1967.

Kant, Immanuel. Analytic of the Beautiful from the Critique of Pure Judgment. Trans. Walter Cerf. New York: Bobbs-Merrill, 1963.

Knight, G. Wilson. The Crown of Life. New York: Barnes and Noble, 1966.

----------. The Imperial Theme. London: Oxford University Press, 1931.

----------. The Wheel of Fire. London: Oxford University Press, 1930.

Lentricchia, Frank. After the New Criticism. Chicago: University of Chicago Press, 1980.

Miller, J. Hillis. Charles Dickens and George Cruikshank. Los Angeles: William Andrews Clark Memorial Library, University of California, 1971.

Said, Edward. The World, the Text, and the Critic. Cambridge: Harvard University Press, 1983.

Thorndike, Ashley H. English Comedy. New York: Macmillan, 1929.

A Midsummer Night's Dream

Allen, John A. "Bottom and Titania." SQ, 18 (1967), 107-17.

Barber, C. L. Shakespeare's Festive Comedy. Princeton: Princeon University Press, 1959.

Brown, John Russell. "The Interpretation of Shakespeare's Comedies: 1900-1953." Shakespeare Survey, 8 (1955), 1-13.

Briggs, Katherine M. *The Anatomy of Puck*. London:
Routledge and Kegan Paul, 1959.

Bullough, Geoffrey. *Narrative and Dramatic Sources
of Shakespeare*. Vol. I. London: Routledge and
Kegan Paul; New York: Columbia University Press,
1957.

Burgess, William. *The Bible in Shakespeare*. Chicago:
Winono Publishing Company, 1903.

Calderwood, James L. "*A Midsummer Night's Dream*: The
Illusion of Drama." *MLQ*, 26 (1965), 506-22.

Chambers, E. K. "The Occasion of 'A Midsummer Night's
Dream.'" In *A Book of Homage to Shakespeare*.
Ed. Israel Gollanez. Oxford: Oxford University
Press, 1916.

Dent, R. W. "Imagination in *A Midsummer Night's
Dream*." *SQ*, 15 (1969), 115-29.

Doran, Madeline. "*A Midsummer Night's Dream*: A Metamorphosis." *Rice Institute Pamphlet*, 46 (1960),
113-35.

Dowden, Edward. *Shakespeare: A Critical Study of His
Mind and Art*. New York: Harper, 1902.

Draper, John W. "The Queen Makes a Match and
Shakespeare a Comedy." *Yearbook of English
Studies*, 2 (1972), 61-67.

Fender, Stephen. *Shakespeare: A Midsummer Night's
Dream*. London: Edward Arnold, 1968.

Furnivall, Frederick James. *Leopold Shakespeare
Introduction* (1877). As quoted in *The Tempest*.
Ed. Horace Howard Furness. New York: Dover
Publications, 1964.

Girard, René. "Myth and Ritual in Shakespeare: *A
Midsummer Night's Dream*." In *Textual Strategies*.
Ed. Josué V. Harari. Ithaca: Cornell University
Press, 1979, pp. 189-212.

Hassel, R. Chris. *Faith and Folly*. Athens, Georgia:
University of Georgia Press, 1980.

Homan, Sidney R. "The Single World of *A Midsummer Night's Dream*." *Bucknell Review*, 17 (1969), 72-84.

Hunter, G. K. *Shakespeare: The Late Comedies*. London: Longmans, Green and Company, 1962.

Kermode, Frank. "The Mature Comedies." In *Early Shakespeare*. Ed. John Russell Brown and Bernard Harris. New York: St. Martin's, 1961, pp. 210-27.

Olson, Paul. "*A Midsummer Night's Dream* and the Meaning of Court Marriage." *ELH*, 24 (1957), 97-119.

Pearson, D'Orsay. "'Unkinde' Theseus: A Study in Renaissance Mythography." *English Literary Renaissance*, 4 (1974), 276-98.

Quiller-Couch, Sir Arthur, and J. Dover Wilson, ed. *A Midsummer Night's Dream*. Cambridge: Cambridge University Press, 1924.

Rougement, Denis de. *Love in the Western World*. Trans. Montgomery Belgion. Greenwich, Connecticut: Fawcett, 1966.

Schanzer, Ernest. "The Central Theme of *A Midsummer Night's Dream*." *UTQ*, 20 (1951), 233-38.

Shakespeare, William. *A Midsummer Night's Dream*. Ed. Wolfgang Clemen. New York: New American Library, 1963.

Siegel, Paul N. "*A Midsummer Night's Dream* and the Wedding Guests." *SQ*, 4 (1953), 139-44.

Welsford, Enid. *The Court Masque*. Cambridge: Cambridge University Press; New York: Macmillan, 1927.

Vyvyan, John. *Shakespeare and Platonic Beauty*. New York: Barnes and Noble, 1961.

Young, David P. *Something of Great Constancy*. New Haven and London: Yale Univesity Press, 1966.

The Tempest

Berger, Harry. "Miraculous Harp: A Reading of Shakespeare's Tempest." Shakespeare Studies, 5 (1969-1970), 253-83.

Brower, Reuben Arthur. The Fields of Light. New York: Oxford University Press, 1951.

Bullough, Geoffrey. Narrative and Dramatic Sources of Shakespeare. Vol. VIII. London: Routledge and Kegan Paul; New York: Columbia University Press, 1975.

Cantor, Paul. "Prospero's Republic: The Politics of Shakespeare's The Tempest." In Shakespeare as a Political Thinker. Ed. John Alvis and Thomas G. West. Durham: Carolina Academic Press, 1981, pp. 239-55.

----------. "Shakespeare's The Tempest: The Wise Man as Hero." SQ, 31 (1980), 64-75.

Cawley, R. R. "Shakespeare's Use of the Voyagers in The Tempest." PMLA, 41 (1926), 688-726.

Cope, Jackson. The Theatre and the Dream. Baltimore: Johns Hopkins University Press, 1973.

Coursen, Herbert R., Jr. Christian Ritual and the World of Shakespeare's Tragedies. Lewisburg: Bucknell University Press, 1976.

Curry, Walter Clyde. Shakespeare's Philosophical Patterns. Baton Rouge: Louisiana State University Press, 1937.

Dobrée, Bonamy. "The Tempest." Essays and Studies, n. s. 5 (1959), 13-25.

Edwards, Philip. "Shakespeare's Romances: 1900-1957." Shakespeare Survey, 11 (1958), 1-18.

Egan, Robert. "This Rough Magic: Perspectives on Art and Morality in The Tempest." SQ, 23 (1972), 171-82.

Ehrlich, Bruce. "Shakespeare's Colonial Metaphor: On the Social Function of Theatre in The Tempest." Science and Society, 41 (1977), 43-65.

Felperin, Howard. *Shakespearean Romance*. Princeton: Princeton University Press, 1972.

Frye, Northrop. "Introduction." *The Tempest*. Baltimore: Penguin Books, 1959, pp. 15-26. Rpt. in *Twentieth Century Interpretations of The Tempest*. Ed. Hallett Smith. Englewood Cliffs, New Jersey: Prentice-Hall, 1969, pp. 61-67.

Hankins, John E. "Caliban and the Bestial Man." *PMLA*, 72 (1947), 793-801.

Henze, Richard. "The Rejection of a Vanity." *SQ*, 23 (1972), 420-34.

Hodgen, Margaret. "Montaigne and Shakespeare Again." *HLQ*, 16 (1952-53), 23-42.

Hoeniger, F. D. "Prospero's Storm and Miracle." *SQ*, 7 (1956), 33-38.

James, D. G. *The Dream of Prospero*. Oxford: Oxford University Press, 1967.

Johnson, W. Stacy. "The Genesis of Ariel." *SQ*, 2 (1951), 205-10.

Kermode, Frank, ed. *The Tempest*. London: Methuen, 1958.

Kernan, Alvin. *The Playwright as Magician*. New Haven and London: Yale University Press, 1979.

Kirsch, Arthur. *Jacobean Dramatic Perspectives*. Charlottesville: University of Virginia Press, 1972.

Knight, G. Wilson. *The Shakespearian Tempest*. London: Oxford University Press, 1932.

Leininger, Lorie Jerrell. "Cracking the Code of *The Tempest*." In *Shakespeare: Contemporary Critical Approaches*. Ed. Harry R. Garvin. Lewisburg: Bucknell University Press, 1980, pp. 121-31.

Luce, Morton, ed. *The Tempest*. Indianapolis: Bowen-Merrill, 1899.

McFarland, Thomas. _Shakespeare's Pastoral Poetry_. Chapel Hill: University of North Carolina Press, 1972.

Mannoni, O. _Prospero and Caliban: The Psychology of Colonialization_. Trans. Pamela Powesland. New York: Frederick A. Praeger, 1956.

Mason, Philip. _Prospero's Magic: Some Thoughts on Class and Race_. London: Oxford University Press, 1962.

Merrill, Robert. "The Generic Approach in Recent Criticism of Shakespeare's Comedies and Romances: A Review Essay." _Texas Studies in Language and Literature_, 20 (1978), 474-87.

Mowat, Barbara. _The Dramaturgy of Shakespeare's Romances_. Athens, Georgia: University of Georgia Press, 1976.

Orgel, Stephen K. "New Uses of Adversity: Tragic Experience in _The Tempest_." In _In Defense of Reading_, ed. Reuban A. Brower. New York: E. P. Dutton, 1962, pp. 110-32.

Pearson, D'Orsay. "'Unless I Be Relieved by Prayer': _The Tempest_ in Perspective." _Shakespeare Studies_, 7 (1974), 253-82.

Phillips, James E. "_The Tempest_ and the Renaissance Idea of Man." _SQ_, 15 (1964), 147-59.

Reed, Robert R. "The Probable Origin of Ariel." _SQ_, 11 (1960), 61-65.

Shakespeare, William. _The Tempest_. Ed. Robert Langbaum. New York: New American Library; London: New English Library, 1964.

Sharp, Sister Corona. "Caliban." _Shakespeare Studies_, 14 (1981), 267-83.

Smith, James. _Shakespearian and Other Essays_. London: Cambridge University Press, 1974.

Spencer, Theodore. _Shakespeare and the Nature of Man_. New York: Macmillan, 1942.

Strachey, Lytton. "Shakespeare's Final Period."
    Independent Review, 3 (1904). Rpt. in _Literary
    Essays_. New York: Harcourt, Brace and Company,
    1949.

West, Robert Hunter. _Shakespeare and the Outer
    Mystery_. Lexington, Kentucky: University of
    Kentucky Press, 1968.

Wilson, J. Dover. _The Meaning of the Tempest_. New-
    castle Upon Tyne: The Literary and Philosophical
    Society of Newcastle Upon Tyne, 1936.

Zimbardo, Rose A. "Form and Disorder in _The Tempest_."
    _SQ_, 14 (1963), 49-56.

Other Shakespearian Plays

Baldwin, T. W. _Shakespeare's Five-Act Structure_.
    Urbana: University of Illinois Press, 1947.

Mack, Maynard. "The World of Hamlet," _Hamlet_, ed.
    Edward Hubler. New York: New American Library,
    1957, pp. 234-56--reprinted from _Yale Review_, 41
    (1952), 502-23.

----------. "Engagement and Detachment in
    Shakespeare's Plays," _Essays on Shakespeare and
    Elizabethan Drama_. Columbia: University of
    Missouri Press, 1962, pp. 275-96.

Myers, Henry Alonzo. _Tragedy: A View of Life_.
    Ithaca, New York: Cornell University Press, 1956.

Shakespeare, William. _Complete Signet Classic
    Shakespeare_. Ed. Sylvan Barnet. New York, 1972.

Spevack, Marvin. _The Harvard Concordance to
    Shakespeare_. Cambridge: Harvard University
    Press, 1973.

music, 102, 112-13, 114, 117, 135, 158, 161, 167, 187
myth, 10-11, 15-16
Nash, Thomas, 3
natural slave, 136-37, 142-43, 146 n. 32, 185
nature
   dissorder in, 58
   harmony with humans, 116-17, 130-31, 149, 161-62, 176
   hostility of, 129-31, 176
   Machiavelli on, 129-31
   man in state of, 133-37, 141-42, 202
   support for virtue; 185; see also nature, harmony with humans; 188
   Theseus as ordering, 49
   Titania and Oberon order, 53, 58
   versus city, 36-37
NeoPlatonism, 1, 103-09, 130, 168, 178, 219-20
Newton, Sir Issac, 7
Northbrooke, John, 3, 34
numerology, 111, 113
De occulta philosophia libri tres, 219
Offices, 34
Olson, Paul, 10, 55
Oratio in laudem artis poeticae, 3
Orgel, Stephen, 169
Orsini, Napoleon, 125

Ovid, or Publius Ovidius Naso, 55, 197
Il Pastor Fido, 171
Pearson, D'Orsay, 66
Pericles, 101, 143
Peter, 169
Pettet, E. C., 13
Phaedo, 210
Phaedrus, 72-74, 89, 159, 161
Phillips, James E., 1
philosopher
   as free, 143
   as king, 110-17, 143, 149-75, 183-84, 190-95
   as poet; 99; cf. philosopher, poet as
   Falstaff as, 210-11
   insufficient attention to temporal; 176-77, see also philosopher, as king
   meditates upon death, 167-68, 194-95
   of Plato's Republic, 110
   poet as; 97-118; 125; 149-75; 202-04; cf. philosopher, as poet
   Shakespeare's attitude towards, 215
   studies state of nature, 202
Piaget, Jean, 20

ABOUT THE AUTHOR

Diana Akers Rhoads lives with her husband Steven and her three sons Christopher, Nicholas and John in Charlottesville, Virginia. She is currently teaching at Hampden-Sydney College.